Narratives of the Great War in Africa

Narratives of the Great War in Africa

Personal Experiences of Two Soldiers in the East African & South West African Campaigns of the First World War

A Doctor's Diary in Damaraland

H. F. B. Walker

The Story of a Lion Hunt With Some of the Hunter's Military Adventures During the War

Arnold Wienholt

Narratives of the Great War in Africa
Personal Experiences of Two Soldiers in the East African & South West African
Campaigns of the First World War
A Doctor's Diary in Damaraland
by H. F. B. Walker
and
The Story of a Lion Hunt With Some of the Hunter's
Military Adventures During the War
by Arnold Wienholt

First published under the titles
A Doctor's Diary in Damaraland
and
The Story of a Lion Hunt With Some of the Hunter's
Military Adventures During the War

FIRST EDITION

Leonaur is an imprint
of Oakpast Ltd

Copyright in this form © 2013 Oakpast Ltd

ISBN: 978-1-78282-176-2 (hardcover)
ISBN: 978-1-78282-177-9 (softcover)

http://www.leonaur.com

Publisher's Notes
The views expressed in this book are not necessarily
those of the publisher.

Contents

A Doctor's Diary in Damaraland 7

The Story of a Lion Hunt With Some of the Hunter's
Military Adventures During the War 145

A Doctor's Diary in Damaraland

WHAT THE NATAL CARBINEERS LOOK LIKE AT GIBEON,
SENTRY OUTSIDE THE HOSPITAL.

Contents

Cape Town	11
To Walfisch Bay	17
Swakupmund	26
The Trek	46
Otjimbingwe	59
The Trek from Otjimbingwe to Windhuk	78
Windhuk	92
To Otjihangwe	113
Windhuk to Luderitzbucht	123
Luderitzbucht	138

CHAPTER 1

Cape Town

Like thousands of loyal South Africans, I offered my services to the government when the rebellion broke out, but for several months I heard nothing. During the last week in January, 1915, I received a wire from the Director of Medical Services, saying that, if I were still willing to serve, I must report in Cape Town to the Senior Medical Officer not later than February 1. This was rather short notice, seeing that three out of the six days would be taken up in getting to Cape Town. However, feeling that I must be required to fill some important gap in General Botha's armies, I "mobilised" within the time specified, and arrived in Cape Town the last night of January.

February 1.—Nine a.m. seems to me a reasonable hour in war-time to begin the day's work, so I approach the castle at that hour to report myself. A very new-looking soldier in very new-looking khaki stands at the gate. He salutes like a clockwork doll. Being still a civilian and inexperienced in taking salutes, I feel rather flattered thereby, until I reflect that perhaps he is only practising. At last he relaxes. Sentry-like, he can give no information, but he can call the sergeant, and he leaves his post to summon this dignitary. I am directed across the courtyard to the medical quarters, where a sick-parade is going on. A lot of young soldiers in various degrees of undress are waiting outside the doctor's door. They all look bright and well. A sudden silence falls upon them as a vision in khaki and red passes quickly and enters the door, tripping over its spurs as it does so.

A moment's interval, and a corporal appears at the door and calls "Private Smith!": Private Smith's face instantly takes on that look of settled suffering so characteristic of *habitués* of a sick-parade, and he enters the doctor's room to receive a pill or potion, looking the picture of misery. At the second or third attempt I succeed in attracting the corporal's attention. The S.M.O. does not arrive before ten o'clock.

A little after this hour I return, and am shown into the great man's office. A lieutenant-colonel and several majors, all humble practitioners in civil life, seem to have nothing to do or are leisurely driving a pen. The S.M.O. himself is at the telephone. Some important business transacted, he turns to me. "Yes, I think the D.M.S. wrote to me about you;" and he looks through some papers. "No, there is no mention as to the disposal of an officer of your name; but I will send you over to the A.D.M.S. of the Northern Force, and if he has nothing for you to do, I will try to find you something at Wynberg."

Feeling hurt, slighted, belittled, insignificant, I slink off to the A.D.M.S., who officiates in another building. As I enter his office, a red Scotchman emerges, brandishing his income-tax returns. "Look yu herre," he was saying—"look yu herre! See what I've given up to be slighted like this!": Inside, a military-looking old major with a very raucous voice is explaining to the A.D.M.S. that he, and he alone, is fitted for a certain billet, and that billet he means to have.

The A.D.M.S. turns to me (we had met in civil life). "Hullo! you here? Come to help push the cart? What would you like to do?"

I try to stammer out that I am willing to serve in any capacity. He seemed surprised, and said:

"Your middle-aged practitioner is simply impossible. They all want to be Colonels or Majors, and are huffed at the slightest thing."

Then he told me that, owing to illness of an officer, there was a vacancy in the —— M.B.F.A. I accepted with alacrity. Anything to avoid playing at soldiers at the base, where I hear medical officers are falling over each other. But I left the office with misgivings. Was it possible that I had made sacrifices—perhaps comparable to those of the red Scotchman—to take part in Gilbertian comedy?

The medical training camp is at Wynberg on a sandy flat known as Young's Fields, an ideal place for a camp in the summer, free from flies and dust. Several other Mounted Brigade Field Ambulances are in training here. Today happens to be payday. Each man receives a sovereign for the month, non-coms a little more. The rest of the pay, £3 10s. or so, is allotted to wife or mother, and not touched by the men. A pound a week certain and no husband must be a godsend to many a poor woman.

With little enough to do, a nice clean tent, a personal servant, a good horse, and the whole Cape Peninsula at my disposal, the first stage of the campaign promises to be pleasant enough.

February 10.—Our medical service is being organized on practically the same lines as that of the Imperial Army. Each brigade of troops, numbering in the case of the mounted brigades between 2,000 and 3,000 men, is to have its own medical personnel, equipment, and ambulance. In the first place there are regimental medical officers, one to each 500 men. The duties of this officer, assisted by trained orderlies, are the health and sanitation of the troops. In case of fighting he is to establish a dressing-station or first-aid post in rear of the firing line, and then to hand over the collection and care of the wounded to the Mounted Brigade Field Ambulance. To assist in the collection of wounded before the ambulance can take over, each fighting unit is to have a few men known as "regimental stretcher-bearers."

The field ambulance is organized on the following plan. To begin with, it is really two complete ambulances, each capable of acting independently. It is cut up in this way to correspond with the brigade, which consists of two wings—"right" and "left" they are called, and are really distinct and complete fighting units. Each section of an ambulance is therefore attached to a wing of the brigade, and follows it into action. A section of the ambulance has two subdivisions. One, called the "bearer division," goes out to collect wounded and render first aid, taking over the dressing-stations from the regimental medical officers.

The other subdivision remains behind, and is equipped to form a field hospital. If there are more wounded than can be accommodated in the ambulance waggons, or if emergency operations have to be performed, the tent subdivision pitches its tents and establishes a field hospital. A bearer division is under the charge of a medical officer, and consists of mounted orderlies and stretcher-bearers, about fifteen men in all. It has three ambulance waggons and a motor ambulance. The tent subdivision has also a medical officer and the same number of men trained as nurses.

Now, it is not in the plan that a field hospital remain in charge of wounded for many hours, because it must follow the movements of the troops to which it is attached. It must therefore be evacuated at once. In the plan as we have it there is a missing link here, for we have no transport, no personnel, to convey wounded from the field hospital to the base hospital, and we can see it sticking out that our field ambulances will have to do this duty, and we shall thus become detached from, and out of communication with, our brigades. Another weak point, too, is the fact that the officer in command of the whole medical service to a brigade is not on the staff of the colonel commanding the brigade, but is in charge of one of the tent subdivisions of the ambulance far in the rear, and out of touch with the movements of the troops.

Further, we have no signallers, unless a couple of men carrying flags come under this category, who, of course, cannot be other than useless under the conditions in which we are likely to act. If movements are at all rapid, there can be no doubt that the ambulances will get left behind, get lost, and not be there when wanted. And, to make matters worse, it is not to be expected that irregular forces, like the Burghers, badly staffed, will always remember to give the ambulances timely warning of their intentions.

February 12.—It will be remembered that the rebellion last year delayed the preparations for the invasion of German West. But now, this being over, and General Botha having taken command, preparations for the campaign are being hurried forward. Four distinct columns are to operate against the country. General Mackenzie has his base at Luderitzbucht, the southern of the two German ports. He is held up at Aus, on the edge of the desert, and further advance towards Keetmanshoop is not practicable at present from the Luderitzbucht side. This army is known as the Central Force. Along the drifts of the Orange River from Upington towards the west is a diffuse force under Colonel Van der Venter, known as the Southern Force.

Their objective is also Keetmanshoop. The Eastern Force, under Colonel Berrangé, is concentrating at Vryburg. They have to cross the desert through Kuruman to Rietfontein to reach the German border, 300 miles of sand. Keetmanshoop is also their goal, so that these three forces may be said to mutually support each other. If the Germans concentrate against any one of these forces, then their flank and rear will be menaced by the other two.

What, then, is the significance of a small force of infantry collected at Swakupmund, the Germans' other port. They are the nucleus of General Botha's Northern Force. There are collecting at Kimberley, Potchefstroom, and I think Bloemfontein, four large brigades of Mounted Burghers, a total of close on 12,000 men. These are to be shipped to Swakupmund, or rather to Walfisch, quite near, when ready. Colonel Britz commands the 1st Brigade, Colonel Alberts the 2nd,

Colonel Myburg the 3rd, and Colonel Marnie Botha the 5th Brigades, who are Free Staters and all volunteers. The 4th Brigade belongs to the Southern Force under Colonel Van der Venter.

Now, mounted men mean movement, and we foresee a rush from Swakupmund to Karibib, Okahandya, and Windhuk, which, if it can be done suddenly and unexpectedly, may result in General Botha's catching the Germans between the Northern Force on the one side and the Central, Southern, and Eastern Forces on the other. As far as one can gather, the Northern Force will be about 20,000 strong, the other three together amounting to a like number.

February 14.—A good deal of time is taken up in lecturing to the men on first aid, hygiene, and so on. Some of our men are very expert, having had long experience in bandaging and ambulance work. The stretcher drill is also very good, and you can teach them nothing in the way of lifting and carrying wounded. In the —— we have ten or twelve Germans. They come from a German colony in the neighbourhood of King William's Town. They will no doubt be very useful as interpreters, and as far as one can judge their sympathies are with their adopted country.

February 16.—A little to the east of our lines a large camp is being erected for the Burghers. Kitchens, shower-baths, and sanitary accommodation, are being built of wood and iron on a very lavish and extensive scale. Horse-lines are being made by pegging long thick ropes to the ground at intervals. We calculated that this one camp was prepared to receive 4,000 men and a like number of horses.

February 18.—The 3rd Mounted Brigade have arrived in camp here. Their tents, horses, and transport, seem to fill the whole plain. They are men chiefly from Northern and Eastern Transvaal and Northern Natal. There are a good many men of British descent among them, but these are mostly Africanderised and regard the Taal as their mother-tongue. They are of all ages—some mere lads, others are grandfathers no doubt; but on the whole they are a likely-looking lot of men well above average size, and inured to camp life and hardship. The oldest among them fought at Majuba, and most of them remember the Tugela. One boyish-looking *burgher* told me he was at Spion Kop, aged eleven. Being so young, he was left behind with the horses. A shell burst near and killed the horse he was on, and several others. Consequently he says he is rather nervous about the big guns, but is not afraid of rifle-fire.

They are dressed in khaki shirts and breeches, leggings, a soft felt hat with *pugaree*. A feather or a piece of coloured cloth on the hat alone distinguishes the commandoes. There is nothing uniform about them, for the government have bought up all the makes and shades of shirts, breeches, leggings, and hats, that they could lay their hands on. Many of the men wear a coloured handkerchief about the neck, which, with the shirt collar loose, is useful and comfortable, if not very military-looking. *Bandoliers* are carried over each shoulder, and under the opposite arm. They hold 120 cartridges, but the latter are not arranged in clips. The rifle, for which they have a cover, is carried in a bucket attached to the saddle. They have no bayonets. An overcoat, a large water-bottle, a mess-tin, a haversack, and one blanket, constitute their equipment. Each man has brought his own horse and saddle. Consequently, the horses, if useful, are a very miscellaneous lot as regards colour and size.

Most of the officers, however, look very Anglicised in khaki drill tunics and breeches, irreproachable leggings, boots, and spurs, with helmet and Sam Browne belt complete. They are thus easily distinguished from their men, which is not a very wise arrangement for men going on active service.

February 27.—The governor-general reviewed Myburg's brigade this afternoon. We were drawn up in squadrons. The whole thing was very impressive, and the march-past, which had been rehearsed in the morning, was very well done. The fine marching of the ambulance men and their military appearance seemed to receive special recognition.

March 4.—The powers that be have at the eleventh hour ordered a medical examination of the *burghers*. For the last two days several of us have been engaged in this work. As we had no instructions to go upon, we just threw out a few who on account of defect or decrepitude were obviously unfitted to undertake the rigours of a desert campaign. On the whole these men from the Northern Transvaal are a well-set-up lot. We passed several tough old boys well into the sixties.

Just before starting this work, somebody told us the yarn that a man with a wooden leg had been accepted somewhere or other; but, although we did them at the rate of something like a hundred an hour, I don't think a man with this defect escaped us.

CHAPTER 2

To Walfisch Bay

March 9.—Punctually at noon the —— M.B.F.A. arrived at the docks. Three or four troopships were filling up with the 3rd Mounted Brigade and their effects. Our ship is one captured on the west coast early in the war. She is very high in the water, and has main, upper, promenade, and hurricane decks, and a bridge. She looks as if she would topple over the moment she is released from the quay. There is plenty of accommodation for the officers, but the men are crowded together in every available part of the ship.

The holds are crowded with rough plank bunks as close as they can get them, strange housing for the *burghers*, who are accustomed to the illimitable *veldt*. It is very peculiar to see a German ship crowded with Dutch Africanders going to fight the battles of the British Empire against the Germans themselves, and no doubt one that would evoke characteristic utterances from the *Kaiser*, could he be privileged to see it. By three o'clock everybody seemed to have got on board somehow, and the other transports departed, a Clan liner so crowded with our horses that they could not swing their tails, and another ship with the right wing of the brigade. Kind women had dispensed tea and coffee all round; Smuts, Merriman, and other visitors, had gone on shore, and we seemed ready to start. A cold mist came up, and the friends and visitors melted away. Somebody said we were waiting for some parts belonging to an aeroplane. At 7 p.m. our ship left the docks, steamed into the bay, and anchored in a fog.

March 10.—A good many men were rather wild last night as the effect of excitement. It appears that we are delayed owing to a shortage of stokers, who are expected at any moment. We hear it is quite a problem to find crews for these transports, the demand all over the world being very great for men with nautical knowledge. After breakfast we noticed a steam-launch approaching, and everybody thought it must be the stokers. However, when it got nearer we saw only a policeman and a woman who was standing upon the stern gesticulating wildly, to her imminent peril. Naturally, I thought she was on the tracks of an erring husband, but it turned out she was after a little boy scout who thought he would like to go to the war. He, when he found the game was up, quietly slipped down a rope into the launch, and took his seat beside his mother in a most complacent manner. She, too, as soon as she had got him, quieted down and took no further notice of him. I had seen the youngster knocking about the ship with a soldier. He had a shallow, shifty pale blue eye which suggested a doubtful career.

At 3 p.m. we left the bay, one or two very unprofessional-looking stokers having arrived, and several men from among the troops having also volunteered for the work.

March 11.—We are now well at sea, and many of our noisy landsmen are suffering from a reaction. The captain and the P.M.O., however, are doing their best, and fatigues are being established, in units where discipline prevails, to clean up the ship.

In the evening we had an *impromptu* concert, of which an electrically driven pianola was the basis. A sergeant who in private life is a circus clown held the boards most of the evening with some rather risky recitations.

March 12.—It is cold this morning, and a thick mist hangs over the sea. The buzzer is going off every minute as a warning to other ships. At 8 a.m. we were 410 knots from Cape Town—that is, we are averaging 10 knots an hour. When I went to have a look at the log, there were two *burghers* leaning over the stern and arguing as to how the ship maintained her course in the dark or in a fog out of sight of land. The one man thought that the slender rope towing astern kept the ship in her course. The other looked at this for a while, and then, noticing on the smooth ocean the track of the ship, said: "*Kijk hier, on kerel! Daar's die pad*" (Look there, my boy! There's the path).

March 13.—We are off Walfisch Bay now. Another fog is on. Indeed, they say there is always fog on this coast at this season of the year. In consequence of the fog we are going very slowly, and sounding every few minutes. About noon it lifted, and we caught a glimpse of a low sandy bank, and on the farther side of it smooth water where a few ships were anchored.

Walfisch Bay opens toward the north. It is protected from the Atlantic on the west by a long sandy bank four or five miles long, which runs out to Pelican Point, where there is a lighthouse. At the southern extremity of the bay is Walfisch itself, very inconspicuous, a few tents and small buildings marking the spot. Two or three miles north is a collection of eight or nine reddish buildings, which we are told is a whaling-station rented by a Norwegian firm; but when the war broke out the fishermen fled off to Norway or some equally safe place, leaving everything behind. Eastward is the mainland, a low and arid coast rising here and there into rounded sand-hills. Along the coast close to the shore we can see a train steaming north to Swakupmund. Five or six steamers are anchored in the bay.

A portion of our men went ashore this afternoon. Quite a lot of tugs and lighters seem to be available.

March 14.—Yesterday, talking to an officer who seemed very retiring and quiet, I made somewhat of a *faux pas*. I noticed he wore a black badge on his collar, with a leaf in gold thread. To lead the conversation into what I hoped would be an interesting channel, I said: "I see you belong to the aviation corps." He replied that he did not, and looked at me very hard. At lunch I pointed him out to a friend, saying I thought he was an aviator. "That, my dear fellow," I was told, "is the chaplain to the left wing!"

This morning we disembarked. After an early breakfast all the officers came ashore in a tug—the *Stork*, of East London, by the way. Our *burgher* friends were in the best of spirits, relieved, I think, to see *terra firma* again, however bleak it might appear. They sat there in the tug spinning yarns as only Dutchmen can. We were dumped down on the sand, this hot Sunday morning, without food or orders, and with nothing but our blankets.

Apart from man's handiwork, which is very scanty, there is nothing but sand and water to be seen at Walfisch. To the south and west are sand-flats and lagoons. To the east and north there are sand-hills, rising, in some places, in tiers to hills of considerable height. The surface of the ground looks as smooth as it would if covered by a heavy fall of snow, only instead of the snow you have loose yellowish-grey sand. Spoors, too, resemble those made in the snow, and the tracks of waggons can be seen over the sand-hills for miles and miles. Mirage distorts everything, buildings, hills, and especially men and horses, looking much taller than they are. Horses, particularly, often look very grotesque in the distance, with an ordinary sized body on very spindly legs about 10 feet long.

Buildings there are none, unless one included a few wood and iron shanties in that category. One of these places, distinguished only by a small belfry, does duty as a church for Anglicans, Romans, Wesleyans, and Dutch Reformed. There are one or two stores, and another place calls itself an hotel. All are in a shocking state of repair, iron rusting, wood rotting, and what little paint they may have had at one time now desquamating freely. When one thinks of our poor friends and neighbours with their fine town of Swakupmund on the open Atlantic, where with luck they can land every third day or so, it does seem as if Britannia had been playing dog in the manger with this splendid harbour, where only two or three ships a year call under normal circumstances.

The white population is said to have been thirty-nine at one time, but I think this must be an exaggeration. One man, a store-keeper named Green, has done very well here trading in the Hinterland with Hottentots. He is quite a patriot, and in season and out of season he has emphasized the importance and splendid position of Walfisch, which is the only decent harbour on the whole coast.

Of course, it is all hubbub here now, for it is the one and only base for the whole Northern Force. Twenty-one thousand men and as many horses and mules have to be fed. This means that 500 tons of food, etc., have to be landed daily if a reserve is to be built up. Besides food, even water has to be brought from Cape Town in ships, to say nothing of locomotives, rails, sleepers, waggons, and a thousand and one things necessary to maintain an army in the field. Although Walfisch affords such good anchorage, the surrounding shore is so low that only little bits of sand-bank here and there are not covered by the sea at high-tide. In order to provide space for camps and storage of material, it has been necessary to build an extensive sea-wall to keep the water off the flats. Piles have been driven into the sand, to which boards are fastened to the height of 4 or 5 feet, and the whole is backed by piling up sand behind. Dykes, too, are cut in all directions to drain off the water. So far these arrangements have not been very satisfactory, and here and there there are large stagnant lakes of sea-water, in which our war-material soaks continuously, or periodically.

The camps, too, are below the level of high-tide, and are consequently very damp. We have been given a spot for ours which was previously occupied by horses, and is much contaminated; so that, where a tent is erected over this warm, wet, manure-sodden sand, the effluvium in that tent is not very pleasant. The flies, too, are numerous as the sea-sand, and are very energetic and voracious. The days are hot and windy, the nights are cold and damp. The water is bad, and there is not much of it. For the animals it is mixed with a certain percentage of salt water. Our food is contaminated with dust, dirt, and flies, so that altogether Walfisch cannot be described as a salubrious spot just now.

There is great difficulty in getting the material ashore, owing to very inadequate pier accommodation. The smaller things, such as boxes of food and perishables, are landed at a small jetty in tugs and barges, and stored on a little ridge of sand which is, fortunately, a little drier. The animals and heavy material are brought from the ships on rafts. A tug tows the rafts inshore as far as it can, then about fifty or sixty natives pull the rafts in until they ground. Through the shallow water the smaller things are carried, and the larger, such as rails, are towed through the water by means of a rope attached to a winch on the shore. About 3,000 natives are engaged in this work at two shillings a day and their rations. Gangs are working night and day, Sundays included, and their sonorous chanting as they pull on the ropes never ceases.

A very conspicuous structure in Walfisch is the condenser, a row of boilers and four tall iron chimneys. It comes from America, and the man in charge says it is supposed to supply 80,000 gallons a day but is only doing half this amount. Similar plants elsewhere are also doing very badly. This condensed water is most insipid. The water is conveyed to the various camps in a large barrel *à la* garden roller, much being lost in transit and also when attempts are made to get it out of the barrel.

The camp is so malodorous and damp that the O.C. and I decided to take up our quarters for the night in some empty railway trucks standing near. We have chosen one with high sides and a little straw in it, which, besides being dry, affords some shelter from the cold, damp sea-breeze which comes up after sunset.

March 15.—This morning I explored the sand-flats towards the south-west; they extend for many miles, and every now and then there is a lagoon. Evidently the sea is gradually receding here, and sand-hills can be seen in the making from the earliest stages. The wind and tide collect a little *débris* in one place. This debris consists of dry seaweed, dead birds, etc. A little sand is washed up around this nucleus. Every wind and tide adds to this little mound, which by-and-by becomes quite big. After a while a little coarse vegetation appears, and the growth and permanence of this embryo sand-hill is assured. These various stages in the growth of a sand-hill are so obvious on the flats here that there can be no doubt as to how they are formed.

Above the level of the water and among the sand-hills two species of beetles are to be found in great numbers. One is a greenish-bronze colour, and is about half an inch long. It runs in a quick, jerky way, and finally escapes by flying. The other is black and rather smaller. It is very timid, and runs with incredible quickness when approached, swaying from side to side as an ostrich does. These beetles are very conspicuous objects on the dunes, especially the black one, and they exhibit wonderful nimbleness and agility in negotiating the little irregularities in the sand.

Two kinds of birds were noticeable—a small wader and a pale salmon-coloured flamingo. The latter is a very beautiful bird about 3 feet high, and frequents the lagoons in small flocks of twenty or thirty.

Out on these flats there are ten or twelve blockhouses protecting the camp. These blockhouses are small round huts constructed of sandbags and surrounded by wire entanglements, and in the intervening spaces between them there is a wire fence. They are joined up by telephone to each other and to headquarters. The Durban Light Infantry are the garrison at present, and they have outposts on the neighbouring hills, with maxims; there is also a high-angle gun to ward off attacks of aircraft. If the Germans attacked and held Walfisch now for a week, the Northern Force in the neighbourhood of Swakupmund would be in a very precarious position; for it is living from hand to mouth, and has no reserve provisions for man or animal. The croakers in the transport and commissariat departments say that the arrival of the troops at Walfisch was premature, and that they should have been allowed six weeks or so to establish depots.

March 16.—During the night I heard considerable disturbance and the sound of moving water. Looking out of my truck as soon as it was light, I saw that a considerable portion of the camp was under water. During the night the tide had broken in, and the truck we were in had become an island. We hastily waded out to arrange platforms out of sleepers to protect our goods. Several units were less fortunate than our men. Their tents were flooded out, and their belongings were floating about. Men were to be seen on every side digging feverishly and throwing up banks to keep out the water, in most cases rather unsuccessfully, for the Atlantic laughed at their efforts. This inroad of water will make Walfisch a worse camp than ever; and the sooner the brigade, which is now all here, is moved on to Swakupmund, the better.

March 17.—General Botha was here today. He came down from Swakupmund on a motor trolley. We hear his reason for coming was to buck the quartermaster-general's department up a bit, in which case a move may be expected very shortly.

March 18.—Early this morning a messenger came over from Swakupmund. We asked him what sort of place it was. "Oh, fine place! Everybody lives in 'ouses and 'as 'lectric light." A contrast to Walfisch in two respects, at any rate.

A gale is raging today, and in all directions tents are flapping about in clouds of dust, for it is quite impossible to make the pegs hold in the loose sand, and men are spending all their time vainly endeavouring to hammer them in. The arrival of a few prisoners was the only diversion we had this day. Eight coloured men and three Bantus had surrendered voluntarily about forty miles to the southeast.

The former were dressed in khaki, very neat in appearance, and clean-looking, active, intelligent fellows. They had with them a very heavy two-wheeled cart drawn by ten oxen in good condition. They were armed with Mausers, but are reported to have said that they would not fight against us, however much ammunition they were given, and that there were many more of the same opinion. This is good news, for we have heard frequently that the Germans have armed the Bastards, and that in guerrilla warfare they are very formidable, being excellent shots and knowing the country so well.

Our transport has arrived: 168 white mules, twelve spans of twelve each for the ambulance waggons and general service waggons, and four spans of six each for the water-carts and Scotch carts. Besides we have two motor ambulances, both having a Hupmobile chassis.

March 19.—Today the —— M.B.F.A. was ordered to move on to Swakupmund. The transport and the mounted men went by road, or rather along the seashore, for there is no road. The rest of the brigade went by train. Preferring to ride, I accompanied the mounted men. For the first six miles or so the shore is quite sandy and easy-going.

Here the water in the bay is very smooth. Afterwards the shore becomes more rocky, and, being no longer under the shelter of Pelican Point, the full majesty of the Atlantic can be observed, great billows rolling in and breaking on the rocks. The authorities have erected many beacons along the shore, and every thousand yards or so near the railway there is a blockhouse.

The line is laid along the shore practically the whole way, and in some places it is built upon sand-bags. Consequently, at many spots it is at the mercy of a tide a little higher than the average, and almost every day at some point or other it is washed away. The line cannot be laid farther inland, for there is only a narrow strip of firm ground between the sea and the shifting sand-hills, which extend all the way from Walfisch to Swakupmund. For the present the D.E.O.R.[1] guard the line.

Life in the blockhouses is terribly dull, they say, as there is nothing to do except to bathe and fish and wait for the train which brings water and food. The men look very well, and are tanned the colour of the aborigines, spending the bulk of their time in shirts and knickers, and often not even in these. At one blockhouse I saw two young soldiers engaged in a violent altercation over a young penguin. The man who was holding it wouldn't let it go, because he was certain it would fly away; whereas the other man was game to bet him anything that it couldn't.

We reached Swakupmund a little after noon. It is said to be twenty-two miles from Walfisch along the coast, and a very heavy twenty-two miles it is. Waggons generally take more than one day to do it, partly because of the heavy going, partly because of the tides and travelling at night being prohibited.

To suddenly come upon a city in the howling wilderness causes rather a strange sensation, and is the sort of thing one only expects in a fairy tale. Without any warning, when rounding a little bend, there suddenly sprang into view a conglomeration of unnatural-looking buildings standing on a sand-hill some 30 or 40 feet above the sea. It seemed to be a city of towers and turrets—white towers, pink towers, blue towers, little towers, big towers, church towers, and lighthouse towers. A few soldiers plough their way through the sandy streets; otherwise it is a city of the dead. There is not a civilian, a tame animal or bird, in the place.

Windows are boarded up, and the blinds are down. Only a few

---

1. Duke of Edinburgh's Own Rifles, a Cape Town regiment.

buildings are occupied by various headquarters. The inhabitants left in a hurry at the beginning of the war, taking much of their belongings with them, and destroying water-tanks, surf-boats, cranes, and other useful things before they left. From August until about Christmas the place was empty; then a small force of Union troops occupied it.

CHAPTER 3

Swakupmund

Nothing but sheer necessity would ever make anybody build a town in such a god-forsaken spot as this. As the name implies, the place is situated at the mouth of the Swakup. It is on the north bank, the south bank being British territory. Recently this river had been in flood, and had washed away the railway, which crosses it on trestles. This is a very unusual occurrence, for this river had been dry for fifteen years. Nevertheless, although the river is practically always dry, it is the only reliable source of water all through the desert in this region. At Swakupmund a plentiful supply is obtained from the riverbed by pumping, but it is very "brak" and nauseous. It also contains a large percentage of Epsom salts. It is really horrible water to drink, and strong coffee is the only thing which covers the taste of it. Tea made from it is vile and "mineral" waters are not much better. I suppose the Germans made beer from it, for there are several breweries in the place.

There is not the slightest shelter for vessels here, and even the anchorage is not good. An attempt on a large scale has been made to build a harbour by making an enclosure with walls, but it has been a costly failure; for it silted up immediately, and has been abandoned. There is a large wooden pier about 300 yards long, and close to it is a fine iron one in process of construction. The Germans made some attempts to destroy these piers, but a few rounds from a British cruiser drove the would-be dynamiters away. But at the best landing at Swakupmund is a doubtful business, for the sea is always rough, and it often happened that passengers could not disembark for several days, and that merchandise was lost. The Woermann Linie had ten or a dozen lighters specially constructed for this coast, but they blew the bottoms out of them before evacuating the place, rendering them utterly useless and beyond repair.

It is difficult to give an impression of this town. It is very un-English, big, and pretentious. I should say it is the whitest and largest of white elephants extant. The German spirit in it seems to say to us:

> You British have taken all the titbits of the earth; but for all that, and in spite of you, we will have colonies, even if we have to make them out of nothing.

I am sure the *Kaiser* said to his colony manufacturer:

> Build me a port and harbour in Sud-west Afrika. Make it complete with customs, barracks, and railways. Make a town for 5,000 of my people. Take these 50,000,000 *marks*. Apply to the Imperial Chancellor when you require more.

Result: Imperial Swakupmund.

There is plenty of room here for such schemes, with the endless desert to fall back upon when the sandbank is filled with fine buildings, wide streets, squares, promenades, and monuments of Imperial achievements in the Hinterland. What high pressure in the Teutonic boiler, what energy craving for outlet, with the British fleet and British repressive policy sitting on the safety-valve! Little wonder that something has had to burst somewhere! The streets are arranged at right angles, and are very wide; but they are useless for traffic, consisting of the deepest and loosest sand imaginable.

The Germans must have quickly realised this, for in all the principal streets they have constructed side-walks of wood, raised well above the sand, and are said to have brushed them every day. Now the sand, since they are neglected, is rapidly covering them. There are miles and miles of this paving, and the *burghers* are finding it very good firewood. Down the middle of each street runs a two-foot gauge railway laid on metal sleepers, on which all the wheeled traffic must have moved; for there is no evidence that there were any waggons or carts, and the most powerful motor in the world would not be able to move a yard in this sand.

There is a great sameness and tameness about the streets, and with the exception of Post Street, which is at the north end of the town, running down to the sea, they do not merit description. At the top of Post Street stands the fine new Lutheran Church, and it contains one or two other fine buildings, notably the new school, the Antonius Hospital, the post-office, and the public buildings. Near the sea is a little promenade leading round to the lighthouse, and just above this is a diminutive ornamental garden, where, as the result of much labour, a few sickly shrubs maintain a precarious existence. In this garden is the only really nice thing in Swakupmund, a monument erected to the marines who fell in the Herero War. On a great rough block of granite are two figures in bronze, weathered to a bluish colour. A marine, hatless, and with a bandage round his head, stands with fixed bayonet awaiting death, and protecting to the last a helpless comrade at his feet. The inscription on the table below reads as follows:

> *Mit Gott für Kaiser und Reich, kampften Angehörige des Marine Expeditionkorps in folgenden Gefechten* . . .[1]

The names of the battles are given, also the names of the fallen, numbering ninety-five.

Before taking a photograph of a large and impressive-looking building, I asked a soldier standing near what building it was. "The D.L.I.,[2] sir."

"Yes; but before we came here what was it?"

"I don't know, sir. It is the headquarters of the D.L.I."

It turned out to be the railway-station. So much for the curiosity of the man in the ranks.

The camp of the Transvaal Irish is really a quaint sight. It occupies a hollow space in the middle of the town. As the men had no tents, they have used all sorts of material taken from the stores. A hut is made as follows: A framework of wood, cubical in shape, and about 7 feet high, is covered with any material which comes to hand, rolls of cretonne, print suiting, etc. This material is just nailed to the roof, and the ends hang down at the sides and back like curtains. The huts are crammed with furniture. I saw a large double bed in one, and a whole bedroom suite. Most have chairs, tables, looking-glasses, and often large clocks. The huts are all different colours, white, pink, green, and blue, predominating. It looks more like an Oriental bazaar than the quarters of His Majesty's soldiers.

March 20.—There are three lines of advance from Swakupmund into the interior. The one to the north is along the Otavi railway, through Ebony and Usakos. In the middle there is the old railway through Jackalswater to Karibib. The third line is along the Swakup

---

1. "With God for *Kaiser* and Empire, Members of the Marine Expeditionary Corps fought in the following fights . . ."
2. The Durban Light Infantry.

River. North and south of these lines the country is impassable for large numbers of troops, as there are neither roads nor water. And not only is the country waterless desert, but in many places there are mountains so steep, rough, and intricate, that any idea of finding a way through is out of the question.

Of these three routes, the one along the Swakup must be chosen for a rapid advance; for there is a more or less defined road, sometimes in the river-bed, but more often a few miles to one side of it. All along the river there are water-holes; and even a few miles from here, in the bed of the river, there is a certain amount of grazing for animals. If advances along the railways are attempted, the Germans will, of course, render them impracticable as such; and any advance along them must be slow, and the positions consolidated at every step. Both these railways are only two-foot gauge, and the northern is the one more generally used. At present we are pushing on a wide-gauge railway along the upper line, and our outposts are now as far as Rossing.

Until a few days ago the Germans have been coming down to the very gates of Swakupmund almost every day, and there have been frequent little engagements. No attempt has been made to drive them back hitherto, and everything points to the conclusion that the general wishes to entice them down here as much as possible. It seems, however, that they are aware that we have a considerable force here now, for they are consolidating and fortifying a position at Jackalswater. Three days ago Botha with two mounted brigades (the first and second) left Swakupmund by the river route to attack this position. The 3rd Brigade (ours) has been advanced from Walfisch, and the 5th is expected any time. We have heard that these two brigades are intended for the rush upon Windhuk, and, although it is only rumour, we already feel that we are destined for something great.

The two infantry brigades are holding the line from Walfisch to Rossing, also the water-holes Nonidas, Goanikoutis, and Heiguinchab, along the Swakup. The I.L.H. are at Nonidas patrolling the line up towards Rossing, and along the Khan River. This river on the map looks a promising line of advance; but in reality it has no military value, for the country on either side is impassable, and advancing up the sandy river-bed with high vertical banks would be courting disaster.

March 21.—Today we went to church parade in a desolate sandy square in front of the Hotel Germania. About 800 men were drawn up on three sides of a square, harmonium and parson in the centre. It was an Anglican service attended only by the English-speaking men, for the *burghers* have their own ministers and services. It was very impressive when a prayer for "our brethren now engaged in battle" was given out, especially as it was the first intimation we had that fighting was in progress. During the day various rumours of the fighting came through, stories of rapid advance and prisoners taken.

March 22.—Today I was sent out with two motor ambulances and four ambulance waggons to bring in wounded from Nonidas, about ten miles east from Swakupmund, along the river. Fighting had been in progress during the two previous days in the neighbourhood of Riet, sixty miles farther on. The message said there were sixteen wounded men, and that they were expected at Nonidas about noon.

For two miles out of Swakupmund there is a high plateau where the sand is too heavy for motors, so they have to be towed out to a spot called Martin Luther, which consists of two derelict traction-engines, two tents, and a few extemporized shelters occupied by motor cyclists engaged as despatch riders between here and the front. From thence the road is well defined and quite hard, a thin layer of coarse flinty gravel or broken-up limestone overlying the rocks. To the south are the sand-dunes of Walfisch, to the north undulating hills, and away to the east there is a high mountain range, the Ha-Noas Berg. There is not a sign of vegetation except along the river-bed, to which the road runs roughly parallel. Nonidas is the spot where the road crosses over to the south bank of the river, and there is plenty of water, much superior to that of Swakupmund. The epicures are known to ride out to this camp to get a decent cup of tea, and anybody in Swakupmund who says he has a little "Nonidas water" is generally much sought after.

As we arrived we saw everybody running away to the left, towards a cloud of dust. Someone said it was German prisoners, and I hurried up to have a look. A detachment of the Rand Rifles was escorting 200 German prisoners to rail-head. Big burly fellows they were, marching slowly in rank, with their heads down, looking very dejected, dusty, and tired. They wear a long slouched hat of grey turned up on the right with a black rosette (centre red), stamped out of tin. Their khaki cord tunics and breeches are very nice, neat, and of good material; but the top-boots they wear give them a rather clumsy appearance—at any rate when they are marching on foot.

We moved over the river to where the Motor Transport Corps

had a depot, and outspanned our waggons on a gentle rise. After a while sixteen wounded arrived in charge of a sergeant. It was a most exhausted-looking procession that came in. The sergeant, his men, and the drivers of the four waggons were besmeared with a paste of dust and sweat. The waggons—of the type known as "general service," rather lighter than the ordinary farm waggon, and without tents—came on at a crawl, only a mule pulling here and there in spite of the liberal use of the whip. With every jolt of the wheels somebody groaned. For two days and nights the wounded had been exposed to the heat, cold, wind, and dust, with little water and less food, previous to which they had had forty-eight hours of *trekking* under most trying conditions, and the excitement of a fight thrown in.

We lifted them out of the waggons and arranged a bandage here and there. Only one or two of the wounds were very severe, but several of the men were in high fever due to the wounds going wrong. Two of the worst cases had died on the way in. They were all very hungry and thirsty, and were very grateful for the tea and bread we were able to give them. One was bound to admit that with the first strain, not a very great one at that, the medical transport had broken down; or rather, I should say, it was brought home to us that we were without adequate transport for dealing with wounded in warfare of this nature. The sergeant told me that a much larger number of wounded might be expected down soon. So we got this lot off to Swakupmund as quickly as possible, and instructed the waggons and motors to come out again immediately.

I gleaned a little disjointed information about the fight. The *burghers* seem to have been most gallant at one point, and made a frontal attack without the aid of artillery; one of the commandoes was on the point of surrendering, but Britz and the guns had saved them. Subsequently the German rear-guard of 200 had been captured.

Save in the river-bed, where there is a little grass and scrub, there is nothing to see at Nonidas except an ocean of sand and rock; and soon after it is up the sun beats down in a merciless stinging way, so that all thoughts other than finding shelter from it are driven from the mind. At noon even the very flies, which abound, seem scorched.

The officer in charge of the motor transport kindly offered me the hospitality of his tent and mess. And here I waited all day for wounded who did not come. Just as we were sitting down to supper, a company of the Rand Rifles turned up. They had been marching all day with prisoners, and were now on their way back to a water-hole, twenty miles farther on, where they were stationed. They hoped to get motor lorries here to convey them to their destination, but none were starting until the morning. Their captain, an old sport, called for volunteers to footslog it. One grizzled warrior only stepped out of the ranks. However, after they had had a little refreshment and rest, eighteen were found willing to proceed. Their officers behaved with childish glee when they saw the little loaf of bread I produced, for they had not tasted any for three weeks. After supper the captain started off with the stalwart eighteen. I remember he said it was his birthday, so I gave him two tablets of "Oxo" to commemorate the event and cheer him through the long night-march before him.

It was a hot, stuffy night, and, although we were half a mile from the river-bed, mosquitoes were very bad. I had visions of malaria, which occurs in these parts a little, but when I had satisfied myself that they were the harmless Culex I went off to sleep.

March 23.—Our ambulance spent the day hanging about at Nonidas waiting for wounded, of whom we saw not a trace. I learnt a few details about transport and its difficulties from an officer in charge of eleven motor lorries, and whose base is here. These motor lorries are most serviceable, but, unfortunately, the condition of the roads limits their sphere of utility greatly. For although the general surface of the roads in these parts is hard if rough, and practicable for motors, sandy stretches or wide *sluits* occur every now and then, through which they are not able to go. Along this route, for instance, to get supplies up to the advanced base at Husab, the following procedure has to be gone through. Our new wide-gauge railway brings them to rail-head three miles from here; from rail-head to this depot mule waggons are employed, because it is too sandy for the motors across the bed of the Swakup. From here to a point called "42 Kilo" the lorries are able to work, but there another patch of sand intervenes, and mule transport is again requisitioned to complete the journey.

At the present time these eleven lorries are transporting everything for a force of 7,000 men over a distance of eighteen miles, and it means 500,000 pounds weight of stuff every week. As the lorries carry 6,000 pounds, each lorry has to make the journey eight or nine times a week. Some of the stronger ones are doing it twice a day. To drive a motor lorry eighty miles through a blazing desert in one day is a feat much greater than it may appear, but to continue to do so day after day and week after week, as these drivers are doing, without complaining, without kudos or reward, is a great test. While we were talking this over, one of the drivers came into the tent. He was filthy beyond description with grease, sand, and sweat, and his modest request was that he might be allowed to have tomorrow off to "clean himself up a bit," as he had had no opportunity to do so for a fortnight!

March 24.—The sick and wounded whom we were waiting for turned up at dawn, about sixty in all, including twenty of the enemy. Although they had been hit on the 20th or 21st, and had undergone considerable privation, none of the wounded, with the exception of one German, were doing very badly. More than anything else they were suffering from hunger and thirst, and they put away tea and bread as fast as we could supply them. The prisoners were subdued and obedient. From them and from our men we learnt a little of the doings of the last few days. The Germans said that most of their troops had gone down to Aus to meet Mackenzie. The Germans held a very strong position along a ridge which they had fortified, and had guns in position.

Two of our commandoes failed to carry out flanking movements, and Botha ordered a frontal attack partly because provisions and water were low and he could not delay. Albert's men were in a tight corner until relieved by artillery and Britz's advance. One battery of Germans was entirely destroyed—men, mules, and guns—by our artillery. In another place about a hundred of our horses were killed by maxim fire. They had been left in a *kloof* while the *burghers* lined a neighbouring *kopje*. The Germans stalked them with a machine gun, stampeding the horses of a whole commando, and killing about a third of them. After their horses had gone, the Germans expected the men on the *kopje* would surrender; but they continued to hold the ridge until relieved.

Sunday and Monday our men followed up, occupying Jackalswater and Salem, the Germans offering little resistance, and retiring north after burning a lot of stores. Further advance for the present is not possible, owing to our long communications and the difficulty of getting up supplies. Infantry have been sent up to hold the positions won, and the tired *burghers* are travelling back to Nonidas and Swakupmund. The Germans admit that they were very much surprised. They say they never expected such fighting, the *burghers* riding at them in all directions, lying upon their horses' necks. Our losses were thirteen killed, thirty-eight wounded, and forty-three missing, mostly from Albert's brigade.

I asked a German prisoner, "What about Maritz?"

"Yes, he is at Windhuk."

"You have not shot him, then?"

"No; we are leaving that for you."

A Dutchman among the prisoners said to one of his compatriots: "My wife and children are at Karibib. When you go there, you must look after them. But keep to the ridges; the road and river are mined the whole way."

March 25.—At a dinner of *medicoes* tonight we discussed the periodic descent of soles and other fish in a stupefied condition to Walfisch Bay. Every year just at Christmas a very large number of fish, chiefly soles, are found floating in the bay, dead or dying. There is no doubt that this windfall of fish happened this year, for a well-known surgeon in Cape Town told me that when he went down to bathe one morning they were so plentiful that he filled his pyjamas with them, though he did not relate how he got back to camp. It is difficult to explain this phenomenon. People talk glibly of "volcanic action" and "sulphurous smell." But such agencies might be expected to operate at other times besides Christmas. It is much more probable that the fish are stupefied by gases resulting from vegetable decomposition; for, walking about in the lagoons here, one noticed in some places that bubbles in great quantity were escaping to the surface, and that the dirty black mud had distinctly the odour of sewage.

March 26.—Our camp is really becoming very unpleasant and insanitary. The men are much too crowded. This, combined with the dust, number of horses and mules, want of cleanliness on the part of the Burghers, and the prevalence of flies, is a grave menace to the health of the troops. Almost everybody who comes to Swakupmund suffers more or less from dysentery for a while, due partly to the laxative properties of the water. But there is a good deal more in it than that, and there seems to be little doubt that the men's food is being contaminated by dust and flies; for the illness our men are suffering from is in many cases severe and accompanied by fever in many ways resembling typhoid.

To give some sort of idea of the circumstances under which the men are living, I might describe the camp occupied by the —— M.B.F.A. It is on a small patch of manure-polluted sand. To the north, 20 yards from the tents, is a railway embankment 20 feet high. On the same level, immediately beyond, is a dusty road up and down which horses and vehicles go the whole day long. To the east, 30 yards from the tents, are our horses and mules, 200 in number, as well as the latrines for the brigade. Beyond the horse lines in this direction are camps similar to ours.

To the south, 40 yards away, are washing-places and grease-pits, a road along which 3,000 men and horses are continually moving to and fro. Immediately beyond this is the camp of the 3rd Brigade, and for about eighteen hours out of the twenty-four a strong wind blows from this direction. On the west, within five yards of our kitchens, are the transport lines for the 3rd Brigade, with hundreds of mules and natives. Thus we are surrounded on all sides by things any one of which is sufficient to condemn a camp.

In the town, colonels and majors of the medical and sanitary staff are falling over each other, and, in spite of our protests and entreaties, it seems to be nobody's business; for our camp is not even visited by those whose duty it is to attend to these matters. Nearly a quarter of our men parade sick every day, and, although the illnesses are not severe, the general health and morale will rapidly deteriorate if we stay here the month or so we expect to do. It is not very good for men to sit the greater part of the day and all the night in non-dustproof tents endeavouring to keep the flies off themselves and out of their food.

This evening we had a little diversion in the shape of a fire, a large store in one of the main streets making a fine blaze. The only explanation forthcoming to account for this outbreak was that it belonged to a firm of the name of Hertzog.

March 26.—The *burghers* are a very peculiar army, wanting in discipline in camp, yet full of dash, energy, and endurance, in the field. I doubt whether any other troops would have made the sudden dash on Jackalswater and Riet as they did.

March 27.—I have learnt from a staff officer the real nature of the action at Jackalswater how it succeeded, and where in part it failed. The Germans, about a thousand strong, occupied very good positions at Pforte, Jackalswater, and Riet, at the angles of an equilateral triangle nine or ten miles apart. Jackalswater, at the apex between the other two places, is connected to them by railway, and was their line of retreat. The position at Riet was particularly strong. The German right rested on the Swakup River, their fire enfilading its bed; the left was protected by a very steep mountain, Langer Heinrich, the foothills of which they had occupied and fortified. Between the river and

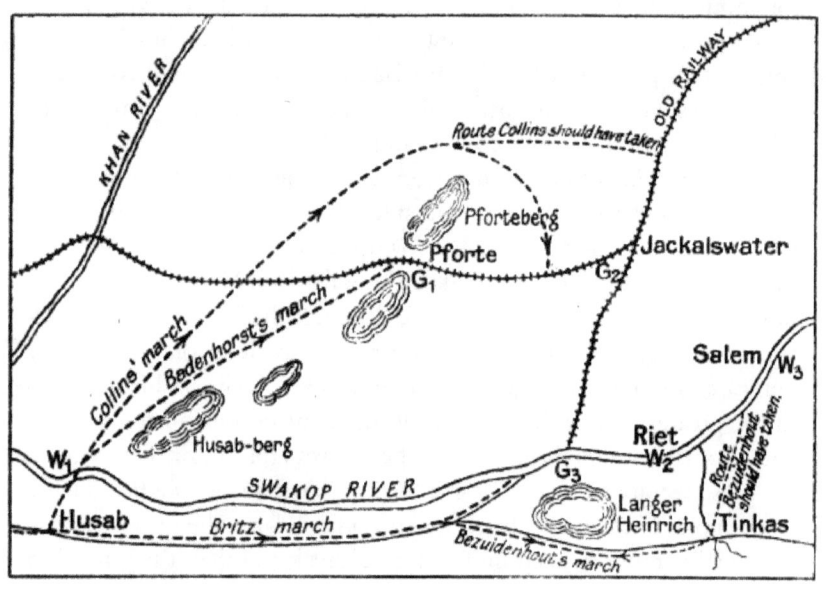

FIGHT AT PFORTE, JACKALSWATER AND RIET.

G_1, Germans at Pforte, captured.
G_2, Germans at Jackalswater, escaped.
G_3, Germans near Riet, escaped.
W_1, Water near Husab.
W_2, Water at Riet, partly destroyed by Germans.
W_3, Water at Salem.

the mountain an open space 800 yards long rendered a frontal attack very difficult. The Germans expected General Botha to attack at one or other of these points. His idea was to attack and outflank all three simultaneously, so that reinforcements could not reach one point from either of the other two. With this object in view, he concentrated the 1st Brigade (Britz's), the 2nd Brigade (Albert's), and the Transvaal Horse Artillery, 6,000 men in all, at Husab, about twenty-five miles from the German positions, on Friday, the 19th. This was done quickly and secretly, the bulk of the men only leaving Swakupmund on the evening of the 18th.

On the night of the 19th the left wing of Albert's brigade (Collins) was sent round the north of the Pforteberg to cut the line above Jackalswater, and also to attack the place at dawn. It meant a night march of some forty or fifty miles through most difficult and puzzling country, and the guide may be pardoned for bringing them on to the line on the wrong side of Jackalswater, between that place and Pforte. Collins attacked Jackalswater, but was, of course, between two German positions. The right wing of Albert's brigade attacked Pforte as instructed, and the Germans, here between the two wings of the brigade, surrendered during the day. Britz's brigade was detailed to attack the position at Riet, and here also the flanking movement was not carried out.

In fact, it was a complete failure, for Bezuidenhout's commando never got round the mountain Langer Heinrich *via* Tinkas at all. It is not clear why this flanking movement was not carried out, because an officer who was there said there was a road, and that his sergeant went along it right down to Salem; but instead of doing so this commando returned to Husab and the river early in the afternoon. In consequence of these flanking movements not being carried out, the Germans at Riet and at Jackalswater were able to escape, which they did during the afternoon.

A German artilleryman taken prisoner in the recent fight paid a glowing tribute to the manner in which his battery was stalked. They were on an eminence, and he had just trained his gun on some horsemen advancing on his right front. "Don't fire there," said his officer. "Shoot at these men in our left rear." While he was turning the gun round they were shot at by riflemen on their right rear, and the officer was slightly wounded.

"What shall I do?" said the gunner.

"Wait a moment," replied the officer. "I will be all right, and will direct your fire." Just as he spoke a shell fell on them, as if from the clouds. It decapitated the wounded officer and killed the mules.

Another and another shell, and the gunner was the only living thing left in the vicinity. "I then crawled under the gun and took out my rifle. The battery never fired a shot," he concluded.

I have had conversations with a number of boys (most of them were little more) who took part in the fight and were wounded. In one bright little ward at the Antonius Hospital are three youths who were severely wounded. They are on the highroad to recovery, and are very cheerful and happy. They do not seem to realize in the slightest what they have gone through or what they have been doing; for they relate their experiences of killing and being killed in a flippant, cheerful manner that is rather terrible. One with the eyes of a cherub, and another child whose downy beard may or may not have experienced the razor, were with Collins in the attack upon Jackalswater. Early in the afternoon they found themselves on a small *kopje* with but little shelter, only 300 yards from some Germans who were sheltering in railway waggons and in one or two small houses.

Said the child: "We could not see the Germans very well, but whenever we saw a little smoke our fellows let rip at it. They had a little black dog which stood in front and wagged his tail, but we did not shoot at it."

"Men kept crawling up behind us," interrupted the cherub, "and firing off their rifles close to our heads, at anything they could see. It made my head ache. Somebody put his rifle very near my ear. 'Don't shoot,' I said; 'there is nothing to aim at.' 'I'll let them have it through the windows, anyhow,' he said; and he put a bullet through each of the four windows of the little house. Just then M—— hit a German, under a truck, in the leg. He got up and limped off to get behind a big stone. We didn't shoot at him while he was going; I don't know why. M—— looked out to see where the man was, and I saw the pith fly out at the back of his helmet. I thought he was shot through the helmet, but he sank down dead without a sound. The German looked out, and I shot him. I know he was dead because he threw up his arms."

"But the worst was," said the child, "when we had to clear. We got on our horses, and bullets were falling all round. My arm was so painful I had to hold it with my other hand, and put the reins in my teeth. Twice my horse stumbled, but we got away. We came to a Scotch cart, and were put in, the cherub and I. We lost our way all Sunday and till

Monday. We had plenty of food, but no water. We tried to eat biscuits, but they came out of our mouths like powder. I shan't forget that drive! But I'm going back if the guv'ner lets me."

March 28.—I took a snap of the house occupied by General Botha, a large place north of the jetty. The general's underclothing was drying in the yard, and his fowls were in the same place, acting up to their great responsibilities, with a cow or two as well standing about. We hear he has to be very careful about food, on account of health; hence the milk and eggs. We were all very depressed a little while ago when we heard of his ill-health. "Who else would be able to keep this heterogeneous crowd up to the scratch?" was in everybody's mind. One hears many tales of his skill, humour, and kindness. There has been a good deal of feeling in certain regiments, caused by their not being employed in the recent fighting—a feeling which was quite unjustifiable, I should say.

The colonel of a certain mounted regiment was taking leave of the general. "Goodbye, sir; I hope you won't forget the regiment next time."

Botha replied: "No, next time Briton and Boer shall bleed in the same field."

March 31.—Today the whole brigade was reviewed on the flat to the east of the town by the commander-in-chief. Thirty squadrons of well-equipped horsemen made a gallant show. Our position was on the extreme left of the line. At 10.30 the general, on a white charger, appeared with a small staff. He passed us, looking well and bronzed, with a "Good-morning, Major!" He then went and stood under the Union Jack, this man of the Tugela, and his friends and old enemies marched past, we with the ambulance coming last. We felt rather idiotic, for our motors stuck in the sand under the General's very nose, where we tried not to see them. Three cheers for the general closed the proceedings. His only advice to the men was to look after their horses. Men with horses in poor condition were a menace to themselves and to him. To our O.C. he simply said: "How are your mules?" Everything now depends on the energy of the transport to form other bases, the fighting units being in grand condition and high spirits. Four mounted brigades, 2,500 to 3,000 men each; two infantry brigades, 2,000 men each; besides a few units like the I.L.H., artillery, etc.—about 16,000 men altogether.

April 2.—During the night we had a very heavy thunderstorm at least, tremendous thunder and lightning with a few points of rain. This is most unusual for Swakupmund. They say you might be here thirty years and never see another. So far we have not had a hot day on the coast. The highest the thermometer has been in my tent is 23° C., and the lowest 15°. The prevailing wind at this time of the year is south-west, and, judging from the direction of the sand-hills, it must be the prevailing one at all times. A typical twenty-four hours here is—Six a.m. a cold mist, almost a drizzle. By 10 a.m. this has gradually cleared away, especially if a light breeze rises from the east. Then until three or four in the afternoon the day is bright and warm. Then a cool sea-breeze begins to blow, bringing up the mist which one can generally see during the day as a thick bank on the western horizon. This mist rarely extends inland more than five or six miles.

I visited the sand-dunes. This particular lot extend from Walfisch to the Swakup. Inland, at varying distances of several miles, they gradually merge into the desert. Imagine a hard gravelly *substratum* covered with a layer of fine sand 20 feet deep. By the action of the continual south-west wind this layer of sand is by degrees blown into irregular banks until the gravelly *substratum* is exposed, forming little intervening plains varying from a few feet up to many hundred yards in extent. The irregular banks are naturally raised like waves in lines running roughly at right angles to the direction of the wind—that is, their long axis is north-east. On the windward side the banks make an angle of 40 degrees with the horizontal, but on the lee side the sand is piled up at the highest angle at which it can stand, and this is, roughly, 60 degrees.

The top edge of the banks is very well defined, and when the wind is strong it blows the sand away from the edge, whirling it about and giving one the idea of a miniature volcano in eruption, the sand always falling down on the lee side. Consequently, each dune must be slowly but surely travelling in a north-easterly direction. The sand on the lee side is smooth and loose, and it is very difficult to climb a dune on this side, both on account of the steepness and also because the sand comes tumbling down when the attempt is made. But on the windward side the surface is hard and firm, horses' hoofs making but little impression. On very close inspection you can generally see the surface sand slowly creeping up this side when it is blowing. The wind also causes the surface to be "ribbed," as is often seen on the seashore as the result of the waves. The wind soon obliterates footprints here, and the stillness and desolation are not to be described. A few bleached bones of seabirds here and there are the only signs of inhabitants, and, as one saw no sign of living birds, I presume they only come here to die in peace and alone.

April 4.—We explored the bed of the Swakup today for several miles from its mouth. At first it is very wide say half a mile or so and there are only a few bushes in it. The river had been down recently, and had deposited a lot of shining mica-mud which had dried and cracked into laminated plates, giving the bed an odd crinkled appearance. Several miles farther up there is grass in the river, and a few pools of water, which, however, is too salt for the horses to drink. Hereabouts the bed of the river is more constricted and has high banks. On the right there is a beautiful reef of white marble scintillating in the bright sun, while the left is composed of loose sandstone.

Higher up is a farm-hotel known as the Egg Farm. It was a resort of pleasure-seeking Swakupmunders, and much in vogue for honeymoons. It is, however, only a third-rate country inn, and it had been practically destroyed, including a fine skittle-alley. We were much interested in the garden. Lilliputian beds planted with cabbages, etc., had been laid out with most elaborate care. Great pains had been taken to irrigate it, tiny concrete canals leading the water on, each bed having a little wooden sluice-gate. Cabbages must have been worth their weight in gold in Swakupmund to warrant such expenditure and labour on them.

April 7.—The *burghers* are becoming restive, sitting among the dust and flies doing nothing, and getting not very good reports concerning farming operations at home. But today the general addressed the assembled brigade in a very masterful and tactful speech, and everybody seemed to go away pleased. Men who came scowling cheered, and went away smiling. Thus a few tactful words smoothed over what might have been a very awkward situation if roughly handled.

April 9.—We hear the Rehoboth Bastard Hottentots are favourably disposed towards us, and have offered help which the general has wisely declined. He has further warned them that German women and children are especially to be respected. Their chief Van Wyk has replied that it will be difficult to restrain his men, as the Germans had herded their women and children and shot them down during "rebellions."

April 10.—I went down to Walfisch by train on a little business.

Very great improvement had taken place, and everything was being done in a much more systematic manner. The railway accommodation had been much increased, and there were new facilities for discharging vessels. A large aviation shed is in course of construction. It is shaped like the letter **E**, and is 90 yards long and 30 yards wide. The officer in charge hoped to be ready to begin operations at the end of the month. They were equipped with the very latest biplanes, but he feared their use would be limited in this difficult country. The bush would hamper observation, and alighting in positions unprepared would be fraught with danger. The absence of roads, too, would make it difficult for their motor-cars to follow up with supplies, and to effect repairs when necessary. Dropping bombs where you wanted to, he said, was most difficult, and greatly a matter of luck.

April 11.—The train was timed to leave Walfisch at 6 a.m. It was pitch black at that time, cold, and raining. We stumbled about among all sorts of obstacles, looking for the train. Finally I ran up against a man carrying a lamp in an aimless sort of way, and asked him where the train for Swakupmund was. He replied rather snappily: "Can't you see I'm the guard and I'm looking for it myself?" At last we found some loaded trucks, and, arguing that these would probably belong to the train, we climbed into one in which there was a motor-car with the tent up. Here we were comfortably out of the wind and rain. It was a strange experience, bumping along the coast in the pale grey dawn seated in a motorcar on a goods-train.

April 17.—While we have been idle the transport and engineers have been busy. The wide-gauge railway is being pushed rapidly up towards Karibib, and the narrow-gauge from Rossing towards Riet nears completion. Lately many men have volunteered for this work, including some medicals who are working like navvies. The *burghers* are also employed unloading lighters and putting the bales of lucerne, etc., into railway trucks, but they prefer to sit on the pier dangling their legs and fishing. Gangs of men are also employed tearing up the narrow-gauge railway in the town to be used on the Riet line. We are short of everything for this light railway, not only rails, but rolling stock, and particularly engines, only having two of the latter, I believe, and no chance of getting more. A Herero and his wife came today. They say all the German women and children have left the farms, and are flocking into the towns, particularly Windhuk. Very few troops are left at Windhuk, and they don't think the Germans will defend it. The

Deutschers are "plenty frightened," "cannot sleep at night," etc. But we put little faith in what they say, because we know very well that a Bantu will always tell you what he thinks you would like to hear.

Our scouts tell us the Germans are concentrating along a front from Karibib to Tsaobis. They know we have over 30,000 men, but they say we are not to be feared, for our men are only "dissipated farmers and swineful fat-bellies. "The *burghers* certainly treated the prisoners with scant ceremony. They were not long, either, in finding out that a German's water-bottle generally contained rum. In fact, there is very little doubt that a lot of the courage of our present enemies is of the variety known as "Dutch."

April 22.—There are several Ovampos working in the camp. They belong to a wild Bantu tribe inhabiting the Portuguese border, and have not been subdued by the Germans. Our authorities are alive to the fact that these men, who have offered their services as drivers, may be German spies, although they profess to have a great hatred for them. These Ovampos have a peculiar custom of extracting the central incisor teeth top and bottom. The lateral incisors are then filed to a point, which gives them a very uncanny and ferocious expression.

Today we have received definite orders to move out from Swakupmund on the 26th. This is very good news, for the place and delay have got on a good many nerves. Sand has blown into the wheels of the army, with resulting friction, and there has been a good deal of petty quarrelling, in which the medical service has figured largely.

April 23.—One of our recreations is to visit the well-kept cemetery and read the inscriptions on the graves. All people seem to die young in Swakupmund. Very many young men in the twenties are lying here, the victims of enteric and malaria. Babies seem to have no chance at all. Most of them die within the first few months from intestinal complaints, I hear. Walking about in this depressing place, I met a very disconsolate-looking *burgher.* I thought perhaps he was looking for the last resting-place of a near and dear friend. I started a sympathetic conversation. He was very depressed, rather wild-looking, and said he could not sleep. He was perfectly certain he would shortly be killed by a mine. He had seen much fighting, but the idea of mines was terrifying to him, and he considered it a very unfair and unsportsmanlike way of fighting.

I tried to cheer him by telling him of our latest idea for saving the men from these explosions—namely, driving a large flock of goats in

German Camel Corps.

front of the advancing troops. He replied he knew about it, and had seen the goats. He thought it might have worked, but the natives had discovered the duties of these animals, and none of them at any price would undertake the work of driving the goats forward. So that the plan would have to be abandoned.

Beyond the European cemetery is what is said to be the native burial-place. Rows and rows of little heaps of sand occupy about a thousand yards of desert. Some of these heaps have rude little crosses of sticks placed on them. It was very puzzling to explain why so many natives were buried near Swakupmund, in a place that was not even enclosed. I decided to ask permission to open one or two of these graves, for it seemed possible that, if I did not find a fine specimen of a bushman skull, I might discover valuables that Swakupmunders had placed underground for safety's sake. Unfortunately, we were moved out of Swakupmund before I could get leave to do this.

Chapter 14

The Trek

April 26.—This morning we left our fetid camp, our destination Husab, 59 kilometres from Swakupmund. The orders we received were to go out to Nonidas, and from there proceed with the artillery and their escort. We could see that a general move was on. The 3rd and 5th Brigades had struck camp at dawn, and were engaged in making great fires to burn their rubbish. Transport and guns were all moving out on the Nonidas road. A feeling of excitement and of great things impending seemed to be reflected from every face. Oh, the relief to breathe fresh air and have something to do! At Nonidas we outspanned to allow the heat of the day to pass, and we were a little disconcerted to see no sign of guns or escort.

News has come through that the Germans are attacking our extreme left, the infantry on the line at a place called Trekkoppi. A glance at the map will show that this is a very strategic move, for if they succeed in pushing us in here they might threaten our railway to Riet, or even cut our lines of communication with Swakupmund. We are glad to hear that the 2nd Kimberleys are there, a regiment of old veterans, also the Rhodesians and the I.L.H. Yesterday about a dozen armed motorcars were rushed through Swakupmund by train, to take part in this fight. It is an Imperial contingent, and it is said they were shipped from home thinking they were going to France, and that they did not know where they were going until they were landed at Walfisch.

The general has gone off to have a look at this fight, and we are hoping we may be diverted to take part in it. The 1st and 2nd Brigades have already left their camp at Nonidas, moving up the old line and the river towards Karibib. I visited my old friend the motor transport officer. He has more than trebled his output, and is now forwarding 1,625,000 pounds weight of stores for the troops per week. An advanced base has been formed at Riet, and there are "stacks" of stuff there.

The 3rd and 5th Brigades left Swakupmund in the early afternoon. We saw them coming towards us, over a distant ridge about five miles away, and into the intervening valley. It was a wonderful sight, for they came on at a great rate in a cloud of dust like a mighty serpent belching smoke. As the head of the column approached us, men were still pouring over the distant ridge. What a change from the lethargy at Swakupmund! All were now laughing, joking, and shouting. Each man carried his own belongings, just an overcoat, one blanket under the saddle, a haversack containing food and tobacco. Here and there a pan or kettle was dangling from a saddle, but beyond one or two pack-mules and horses, dragged by sweating, shouting natives, there was no transport. They swarmed past us on both sides in a cloud of dust as thick as a London fog, which even hid the nearest from us.

Out of the gloom an orderly rode up to me. "Colonel Mentz says you are to move on at once to Husab." And he vanished before I could reply. Evidently the German attack on our left had been beaten off, for our rush across the desert eastward was to be carried out. Our waggons were spanned in in quick time, and we followed hard on the heels of the column. As we climbed the road from the river, mountains appeared to the north and northeast. The formation of these is almost indescribable. Imagine a great cauldron of molten granite. A sudden explosion at the bottom of the cauldron would throw up the rock in every direction. Cooling, suddenly pointed, twisted masses of rock would remain jumbled together in a most irregular manner. The moon and other extinct globes must be something like this African desert. Silent, impassable, everlasting, weird.

The Boers always, if possible, choose moonlight nights for their trekking, and this one was no exception to their general rule. I have no doubt that General Botha waited for full moon before making this advance. Otherwise night marches in a broken unknown country like this would be next to impossible. The orders were for the whole column to be at Husab by dawn, and this night trek of forty miles was a series of nightmares. The *burghers* move in short rushes, and then rest, which is much less fatiguing for man and beast than just jogging slowly on. During the night we passed them twice, and they passed us three times.

As far as we could judge in the moonlight, the greater part of the country over which we were passing was a large plateau, and the *burghers*, riding over a wide front, could not be avoided when we lay down to rest a little. It was like two men locked in an embrace rolling over and over each other. Once I awoke to see tremendous horses, as they appeared in the dust, prancing over me. When we off-saddled the second time, we made little kraals with our saddles to avoid being ridden over by commandoes coming on behind. It was very cold, and the night was fine; but a great pall of dust hung over everything like a cloud, often obscuring even the moon.

The bivouacs of the *burghers* are very impressive. In the distance you would see a black patch on the sand, absolutely still and silent. This patch resolves itself into an orderly arrangement of men, saddles, and horses, perhaps arranged in long lines, each man lying with a horse and saddle at his head. Sometimes the horses are tied in circles of twenty or so, heads inwards, and the men sleep round. At other times the men would just dismount for a few minutes, and were leaning against their horses, quiet, motionless, and observant. Not a horse neighed or stirred, and on a dark night you might pass within 10 yards of a commando without realizing that they were there.

April 27.—About 8 a.m. we arrived at Husab. The *burghers* had all passed us during the night for the last time, and the ambulance was rumbling along sedately on a great flat plain, conscious that we were more or less up to time. With dramatic suddenness we came upon a yawning chasm, as if the earth had opened at our feet. This was Husab, just a volcanic fissure about 100 yards wide. Down the centre ran a narrow path, the sides studded with little *spitzkopjes*, irregular ledges of rock, and caves, all below the general level of the desert. Here our friends the *burghers* were resting. Men and horses were crowded up the slopes of the little kops like chamois. The effect of mirage greatly elongated the figures, the rocks, and everything. The chasm seemed to be filled with bright pink smoke, due to the sunrise upon the dust. Attenuated little fires crackled here and there, men as slender as telegraph-poles crowding round. It was as if one had come upon some distorted, demented dwellers of the nether regions.

There is nothing at Husab beyond rocks and sand, no shelter, and the water is three or four miles away in the river-bed. Consequently, all the animals had to be taken this extra distance for a drink. Without resting, I went on ahead of the brigade to Riet, the next stage, taking the motor ambulances with me. The same primitive mountains continue on the left, and on the right is a dreary plain, the Tinkas

Flats, marked on the map as a game reserve—I suppose to impress the Deutschers at home; for there never was, and never will be, any game on the Tinkas Flats, nor a blade of grass for them to eat, either. The road was hot and dusty, and the motors had all their work cut out to get through. The road here was dotted with dead horses, but, except for an occasional motorcyclist, we did not see a living thing, being well ahead of all troops now.

The endurance and skill of these motorcyclist despatch-riders[1] is truly wonderful. Freezing nights and broiling days do not deter them. In the bad places, to get through, they run the engine and also push with their feet upon the ground, zigzagging along at all angles with the vertical. How they maintain their equilibrium is a marvel. At Nabus the road enters the bed of the Swakup. Here I saw one or two acacias, the first trees of any kind we had come across in the country. The position the Germans had chosen to defend was very strong. To the south they had a great red granite mountain, Langer Heinrich; to the north the river-bed and a jumbled mass of rocks beyond. In front of the position a wide sandy slope extended for half a mile. They evacuated this place because their right at Jackalswater was turned.

Riet is a water-hole and a collection of fine trees in the bed of the river. There is but a single building, and this is only a tin shanty, now being used by us as a base hospital. The trees are quite a feature, and are a species of acacia known locally as the "*anna*." It grows as large as an oak, and the pods, the size of that of the broad bean, are used as food for animals. The river-bed here must be nearly a mile wide, the great trees giving it a park-like appearance; but the dust and heat are very trying, for the sand in the river-bed is of a light consistency, like flour, and the rocks on either side of the river, sweltering in the sun, seem to focus the heat rays in the river-bed.

It was two o'clock when our motors pulled up at Riet, and the *padre*, who was with me, decided that nothing short of a bath would restore him to the normal. We voiced this modest request at the hospital, but the best they could do was a small bucket. Padre, however, espied a foot-spray pump, and at once hit upon the brilliant idea of using this in lieu of a bath. So we took the bucket and pump to the well and sprayed each other until we were clean and cool. Here I formed the mental resolution that, were I ever responsible for the health of a body of men where water was scarce, a spray pump with a fine nozzle

---

1. *The Daredevil of the Army* by Austin Patrick Corcoran and *Despatch Rider* by W. H. L. Watson are also published by Leonaur.

should be a *sine qua non*.

Last night the enemy came down to attack Riet; but it was a very half-hearted affair, for on their way they had accidentally exploded one of their own mines, which had damped their enthusiasm considerably. Another attack is expected tonight, and the garrison, the Rand Rifles, hope to cover themselves with glory. Nobody here except padre and I seem to know there will be 6,000 *burghers* here before dawn tomorrow. But no doubt the Germans are aware of this, and are making themselves scarce. So that I think our gallant infantry will draw a blank among the cold rocks tonight.

It puzzles me why a *burgher* force has a sanitary service at all. The *burghers* certainly like to have doctors when they go into action, but they expect nothing elaborate. Just a bandage when hit, a little something out of a flask, and the assurance that they cannot possibly recover, satisfies. But that assurance must come from a real doctor, and they shout loudly until he comes; a Red Cross orderly suffices not. Transport of wounded, hospitals and operations are things that do not worry the average Boer general. If he has a docile Africander doctor with the commando it is enough for him; and for this kind of business his idea is not very far wrong, where mobility is everything. The reason why this Northern Force is such a medley is not far to seek. The fighting leaders have Africander ideas, and the administrative leaders have European ideas. The two at present are no more miscible than oil and water.

April 28.—The 3rd and 5th Brigades arrived at Riet early this morning. The bulk of them did not stay long, but watered their horses and moved on towards Salem. Later in the day the brigade trains came in, and our ambulance. After struggling through the sand for two days and nights men and animals were somewhat exhausted. Moreover nobody had had more than snatches of sleep, and we were in hopes that at least twenty-four hours' respite would be given us. But at 4 p.m. the order came to move on again to Salem. It was now gradually being borne in upon us that we were engaged in a neck or nothing rush, our objective Otjimbingwe, or even Windhuk, enemy permitting. Further, it was obvious that the transport would be out of it, for the heavy mule waggons could not be expected to live at this pace. At Swakupmund before leaving we had reduced our kit to an absolute minimum. Here again it was obvious that more things must be left behind, and we modified our ideas of what the absolute minimum was.

From Riet to Salem the river runs in a gorge with precipitous mountains on either side, and to get there at all is a matter of keeping in the river-bed, which is very sandy and loose. It was as much as the mules could do to pull the waggons through, and in addition the motor ambulances had to be towed. It took the transport four hours to do this stage of seven miles. Troops and transport trekking up the river gave it the appearance of a busy thoroughfare, although, instead of buildings on either side, we had the glorious *anna*-trees, and beyond the gold, the red and purple mountains. German graves were dotted here and there, generally indicated by a white cross and placed on a little hill. Against the skyline these crosses were very conspicuous, standing up like ghosts with outstretched arms pointing to man's brutal handiwork.

It was just getting dusk when we came upon a commando, off-saddled on one side of the river. Suddenly several men ran out from the group with their rifles ready, and we heard the bolts click as they crept stealthily forward. "A lion! a lion!" passed from mouth to mouth. "Only a old —— rock!" a laughing corporal predicted. And so it turned out, but we had had our thrill.

By the time we got to Salem it was almost dark. Several thousand men were trying to water as many horses at a long row of troughs. Pandemonium reigned; you could not see an inch for dust, nor hear yourself speak. In a trice I lost my bearings and all sight of my own corps. A lot of loose wire lay on the ground, horses were floundering and falling, men calling and cursing. As soon as I could extricate myself from this seething mass, I made towards some little bivouac fires on the mountain-side. Fortunately, the same idea occurred to most of our men, and by degrees, more by good luck than good management, we all got together again. Dry wood being plentiful, we lit fires on the mountain-side, and made hot drinks. The garrison, a company of the Rand Rifles, were camping in caves and so on. Their fires and ours looked like so many little infernos.

I was sitting apart, boiling a little water and waiting for my confreres, when the sergeant in charge of a picket came up and started a conversation. With very little encouragement, he began to talk about his family in Cape Town, and produced photographs of his children. He told me how he had saved a particularly delicate one suffering from diphtheria, after the doctors had despaired, his method being the application of recently killed and opened kittens to the throat. I think he said they must be black kittens. He continued in this strain to glorify himself, to the disparagement of my noble profession, until I offered him a cigarette, and as I held a match for him he was able to see that he was addressing an officer of the medical corps, when he suddenly remembered that his corporal was not very reliable, and German scouts were prowling about.

We entertained to supper two officers of the transport. They had been engaged in most tough and exhausting work getting waggons up from the coast. They assured us it would take nine days to get provisions up to Karibib or Otjimbingwe, and they disclaimed any further responsibility of feeding the troops. For the immediate future we must "live on the land." One of these officers was the D.A.Q.M.G. of our brigade. He said Karibib was our immediate objective. The 1st and 2nd Brigades, under Britz, were marching on this place. The 3rd and 5th Brigades, under Myburg, had for their immediate objective Otjimbingwe. Once there, the Germans would be in doubt as to whether Karibib or Windhuk was aimed at.

If the Germans concentrated against Britz, we, the 3rd and 5th, were to slip into Karibib from behind; if, on the other hand, they concentrated against us at Tsaobis or Otjimbingwe, Britz might take Karibib without fighting. In the event of Karibib being captured and our receiving little check, we were to spread out on the railway from Karibib to Okahandya, and threaten Windhuk from the north, not from the west. If we got hold of the line from Karibib to Okahandya, then the German forces would be cut in two. Those in the south would be between Botha's army and Mackenzie's, Berrangé's, and Van der Venter's, who were all concentrating on Keetmanshoop. The Germans in the north, if they did not offer battle, would retire to Omaruru, possibly to Otavi and Grootfontein.

At 11 p.m. we received orders to move on to Tsaobis, forty odd miles of river-bed and desert. There was no water between here and Tsaobis, and no doubt the Germans would destroy the wells or poison the water at this latter place. Ambushes and mines were highly probable. The troops had moved on towards Tsaobis at 6 p.m. The Germans were expected to defend it, so the ambulances must move up without delay. The base hospital from Riet had today been advanced to Salem.

It was now Wednesday night. Nobody had rested since Sunday. We had traversed eighty miles of desert, much of it on foot, every step an effort. In an exhausted condition we were called upon to do another forty miles to Tsaobis, possibly another sixty to Otjimbingwe. It did not need much reflection to realize that defeat or delay at either of these places would reduce us to a very critical state from thirst and fatigue, possibly from hunger, too.

Here our O.C. decided to push on with the ambulances, leaving the heavy transport behind to give the mules twenty-four hours' rest. As the road still ran in the river-bed, it was necessary to employ some of our mules to drag the motors through the sand until the road emerged from the river. We set off at midnight. The river was full of holes and gullies, and had it not been moonlight our waggons would very soon have come to grief. As it was, it took us all our time to get them along, and after an hour's hard work the two miles of river-bed were accomplished and a fairly decent road seemed to lie before us. We were quite without a guide, and had nothing but the spoor of the column to direct us. Scouts had told us that after leaving the river-bed the road was quite practicable for motors.

So we sent back the teams of mules we had used for the motors so far. The cars started off, and the rest of the ambulance followed. We had not gone more than a mile when we could hear that the motors in front were in difficulties, and we very soon came up with them in the river, again up to their axles in sand. Those of us who had the energy pushed them for three hours through the sand, finally emerging from the river again at 5 a.m. We were utterly done, neither man nor mule equal to another step. Referring to the map, I found that we had averaged a mile an hour since we left Salem. Two hours' rest were allowed. It was freezing hard, and the rocks we were on were like ice. In the confusion at Salem my orderly had mislaid my blankets, and I was much too cold to sleep at all, so sat drumming my feet on a rock, moodily contemplating the joys of a campaign without blankets.

April 29.—We had *trekked* so badly during the night that even our short rest had to be curtailed, and before dawn, without refreshment, we pushed on. A stiff climb brought us out of the gorge on to the high veldt, where grass and a few trees began to appear. The grass was perfectly white from the frosts, and, until it became light, was invisible. The trees were all stunted acacias, just one here and there. To our right were the great granite mountains, bare, cold, and desolate. An undulating plain lay before us, as far as the eye could reach. On the horizon, perhaps fifteen miles away, we could see a cloud of dust rising up to the sky, no doubt caused by the tail end of the two brigades in front of us. We pushed on with all eagerness, well knowing that every moment it was getting hotter and hotter.

At eleven we stopped a little while for refreshment, the sun being so hot that we were glad to have the shade of the waggons. We turned our horses and mules loose for them to graze. No doubt the animals would consider the word ' graze ' rather too euphemistic in this connection; for the grass, such as it was, needed careful looking for.

An *"indaba"* was held. Here we were, still thirty miles from Tsaobis, and our brigade, for all we knew, might by now be heavily engaged. Two officers were sent on in the motor ambulances, with orders to get to Tsaobis as soon as possible, to return and report to the rest of the ambulance if necessary. The O.C. and I with the mounted men were to push on as fast as we could. The dismounted men and the ambulance waggons were to do the same. This meant breaking up our unit most horribly, for our heavier transport was already twenty-four hours behind. It practically came to each man and each waggon making for Tsaobis as best he or it could.

We had not gone very far when a man stood up and stopped us at the entrance to a drift across a small river; he pointed out a mine area, and showed us how to avoid it. By making a *détour* we all passed safely over. After we had gone on a little way, it occurred to me that sooner or later a man left at a lonely drift to warn troops and convoys would either go to sleep, move on, or in some way or other fail to warn people of the danger. So I returned with the intention of putting up notices. Just as I got back to the drift, I was horrified to see an ambulance waggon making straight for the mined area, the leading mules being about where the contacts were supposed to be. It was tricky work getting the waggon off. The few brief moments seemed like an eternity. Past, present, and future were blotted out; my feet seemed to be the only things that mattered, and it was as if they were quite detached from me, and a long way away. "Look where you put your feet! Look where you put your feet!"' rang in my ears to the exclusion of every other sound. How strange to put my foot down next time, and not to see it, not to see anything, now or ever!

We made some danger-signals with red *bandanas* from the necks of two orderlies, and long splints from the ambulance waggons. Then we rolled big stones into the drift on both sides, scrawled notices, and put them up. Never shall I forget the trials of this noon and afternoon; the sun blistered even the sand. Being now far behind, I travelled on alone several miles. Nothing but sand, rocks, dust, intolerable heat, thirst, and fatigue. I overtook a vet. and a scout travelling together.

They seemed more woebegone than I. We pursued the endless track together. I asked the vet. how long horses would be able to endure these conditions without water. He thought three days, mules not so long. We began to see signs that the troops in front of us were in trouble. Dead horses lay in the road, sometimes with a brown patch beside them, showing how their agonies had been terminated. Men had discarded their rations, their blankets, their mess-tins, in the mad rush. These things were to be seen in the road, and particularly at spots where they had bivouacked; everything a soldier uses might be seen, except rifles and water-bottles.

We passed an old *burgher* escorting a young man who from excitement and fatigue had gone off his head; both they and their horses seemed *in extremis*. Without interest or notice of their surroundings, they were mechanically crawling along, the old man some 20 yards in front of the youth, whose wild and haggard aspect proclaimed his unhappy condition. I suggested to the old man that he should remove the lunatic's rifle, but he said it was not necessary, and it kept the youth quiet to think he was pursuing an enemy. I felt a little nervous that he might take me for the enemy in question, but he sat there clutching his rifle like an automaton without appearing to see us. Late in the afternoon I overtook the men of the ambulance struggling along, and we rested awhile under the shade of a bank.

The men showed great restraint in not drinking the water out of their water-bottles, and every man seemed to realise that he might be ten times more thirsty tomorrow. Blankets, haversacks, and tins of bully beef were strewn in the road more and more thickly the farther we went. I picked up a large twelve-pound tin of beef and fastened it to my saddle, but I could not persuade others to do the same. Salt beef without water seemed too great a mockery. The argument that they might be hungry tonight rather than thirsty did not seem to appeal to them. Under great privation men seem very soon to disregard the future or the making of plans concerning it; present miseries are all-absorbing. It is a dangerous condition to arrive at, and is speedily followed by the "let us lie down and die" state of mind if the circumstances do not improve.

Towards evening we began to overtake bodies of men *trekking* after the troops, engineers, ammunition carts, and so on. All were silent, and the animals looked ready to drop. At sunset we overtook our motorcars at Franke's Well. We had encouraged ourselves with the expectation of finding water here, but the stones we threw in fell down with a dry, dry thud, and, looking down, one could see the well had been partially filled in with rocks. The men in the motor-cars told us that Tsaobis had been occupied by our troops, but whether there was water there or not they could not say. The motorists had had a most gruelling day, frequently having had to push the cars, and when we came up they were engaged in pulling one of the cars up a steep hill with a rope.

When the sun went down we felt much happier, less thirsty, and more capable of effort. The unwisdom of *trekking* during the day was made most clear to us, but in this case, in our endeavour to keep up with the troops, we were bound to go day and night. Soon we saw camp fires blinking in the distance, but they never seemed to get any nearer, and it was nine o'clock before we rode into Tsaobis. There was only a single building here, a police barrack, looming large and white in the moonlight and dust. Men and horses were moving about like ghosts in all directions, but mostly towards the sound of a pump that we could hear going.

No music to my ears will ever resemble the rhythmic squeak of that little hand pump. But, alas! the sudden revulsion of feeling akin to dismay to find it dry! "Where's water? Where's water?" everybody was asking.

"There's a dam five miles away with plenty in," somebody said.

"No, that dam is dry; I been there," said another.

"It isn't; houses could swim in it half an hour ago."

And so on.

We heard that some people were digging for water in the river and getting a little. Like a man who has seen another fail to get his pennyworth out of an automatic machine, I tried the pump handle. Not a drop came. Stones fell down with even a drier thud than at Franke's. One of our men climbed down and reported it dry. I noticed a little water in a cement trough under the pump, and I scooped out a billy-tinful. It looked like strong chocolate in the moonlight. I strained it through a towel. It then looked like strong coffee. We decided not to drink it. My old horse "Joffre" sucked it up, tin and all almost, and swallowed it in one frantic gulp. I then took a sponge and mopped up another tinful muddier than the first.

I offered this to our sergeant-major's horse, and was almost trampled by the other horses in my efforts to do so. We decided to try the river. We climbed over some rocks and a dead horse or two to get into the river-bed. Men and horses—the latter at least half frantic—were struggling, slipping, and thrusting, in their endeavours to do the same. By going farther down the river-bed I found a hole already dug, six feet deep, the moonlight reflected at the bottom. I jumped down the sides, falling in as I tried to get to the water. By scooping away with my mess-tin I managed to hand up to the O.C. enough water to give ten of our horses about a gallon each. Then at dawn we desisted and lay down, our thirst slaked a little with water that appealed to the palate rather than to sight.

The Germans had managed to slip out of Tsaobis before our men got round them. As to their numbers I could gather nothing definite, but it is probable that there were not more than a hundred. The *commandants* had intended to remain at Tsaobis until tomorrow, but General Botha came up and ordered an immediate advance to Otjimbingwe. This was a very fine effort, and the tired troops moved out at 3 a.m. I was glad when they went, for some of their hungry horses were on the opposite side of the wall against which I was lying, and to hear them chewing at sticks and tree-trunks was not very cheerful.

April 30.—I suppose Tsaobis owes its existence to the fact of having a little water under normal conditions, for beyond this it has nothing to recommend it. The police camp and a pump are on the bank of a small river surrounded by a few decrepit-looking trees. Opposite the camp are three regular little *spitzkopjes* which give the place a quaint appearance. The greater part of the day was spent by us in getting water out of the river-bed. Hundreds of men were engaged in the same way, digging holes in the sand five or six feet deep, and then waiting for a little muddy water to collect at the bottom. Fortunately, the ambulance had spades, but many poor fellows were digging the sand with meat-tins, billy-tins, or even their hands.

At times there was a good deal of competition for the best situations, but on the whole the thirsty men exercised much self-restraint. I had found a good hole the night before, a long way up the river and among some secluded rocks. So I went there again, but was disappointed to see the tousled head of a *burgher* pop out of it, and so had to begin operations anew. By working all morning we managed to get sufficient water for our needs, and, by allowing it to settle for an hour or so, really decent drinking water was obtained. We treated some with alum, which quickly made it quite clear and limpid, although it detracted considerably from its palatableness.

There was no grazing for animals in the vicinity, and there were many hungry men, too. An officer in charge of the rear-guard came to us saying they were literally starving. After a little consideration I gave him the big tin of bully I had picked up, but we could spare nothing else. I said he had better open the tin before leaving. Great was the tension until it was discovered that the meat was fresh. During the day we fed several stragglers who seemed to be on the verge of collapse. In an outhouse, too, we found some men who were not well enough to proceed. We collected water, food, and bedding, for them, and left them to their fate.

Our transport turned up during the afternoon. One mule had to be shot. The condition of these animals made us set to work to lighten the waggons still further, and much useful kit and equipment was left behind here, including one of our operating-tables, tents for hospital, and much bedding. The colonel in charge of our brigade had gone off, leaving us only the vague instructions "to follow the spoor of the ammunition carts." Hardly liking to act upon such orders, we managed to get into communication with the chief of staff, who ordered us on to Otjimbingwe at sunset.

As soon as it was cooling and the animals had rested a little, we moved out on the Otjimbingwe road. This trek was almost enjoyable, although we walked the greater part of the night, our horses being so done up. From various distant hills we could see the Germans signalling with lamps to one another, and occasionally a rocket went up. General Botha with his body-guard was *trekking* immediately in front of us. He had six splendid mules in a Cape cart, and of course we did not expect to overtake him.

About 11 p.m. we halted in a nice open place among some acacias, where there was plenty of grass and firewood. We made a fire and enjoyed some chocolate, turning the horses loose. I gathered a big bundle of grass as well for my horse, and gave him a handful of mealies, the last he was likely to have for some while. We got a few hours' rest by a big fire, the night being as cold as the day had been hot. By 4 a.m. we were *trekking* again, stiff, tired, hungry and thirsty, and cold. However, we were cheered to see the country improving at every step, and as we neared Otjimbingwe saw indubitable signs of cattle and plenty of grass.

Chapter 5
Otjimbingwe

May 1.—Otjimbingwe, the old capital, is just a straggling village on the right bank of the Swakup. A Noah's ark church much in evidence, a store, an hotel, a windmill, a police camp, and a few houses, all looking bright and clean in the morning sun, constitute the place. The sight of the windmill actually at work, and horses grazing, cheered us greatly. So we stopped outside the town, cleaned ourselves up a bit, and marched on to the market square in review order. Lots of troops were camping about, but, as they were busy cooking fresh meat, they took very little notice of our imposing entry.

Not knowing where to go or what to do, we halted on the square. The general's ubiquitous Cape cart with its six splendid mules was standing near. The animals had done as much as we had, and probably much more, during the night, yet they looked as fresh as paint. "All a matter of feeding," observed our somewhat jaded conductor. Two or three batteries of field artillery were packed on the square. Their business-like appearance gave one a feeling of security, but I caught the eye of a gunner, and it seemed to say, "You gentlemen of the ambulance are a little bit late, aren't you?" And so we were, for the doctor of the 3rd Brigade, coming up, told us there had been an action yesterday, and we were to take over the hotel converted for the time being into a hospital.

The police barrack, next to the hotel, was also a hospital for the 5th Brigade; and our disappointment at not being in at the finish was mitigated a little by seeing on the barrack *stoep* the O.C. of a rival ambulance, his waggons and men still far behind, and, although he seemed otherwise engaged, he saw us all right. Seven wounded, four of our men and three of the enemy, were in the hotel in beds or on stretchers. Everybody had been too utterly exhausted to do much for them. The place was in an indescribable state of filth; the Germans must have used the rooms as stables, and the wounded were still in their dirty, torn, and blood-stained uniforms. A tired orderly was sweeping aimlessly, and two German soldiers with very conspicuous Red Cross brassards were pretending to take temperatures. There was nothing for it but to set to work immediately to try to get the place into order. Beds, sheets, and furniture, were commandeered, and by three o'clock we had a respectable hospital of three small wards and an operating-room in working order, and the wounds, which were all of a severe nature, cleaned up and dressed.

The whole ambulance worked with a will to accomplish this, and one felt very proud of the men, who, fatigued as they were, did their work manfully. We were soon to learn that we had others to deal with besides the wounded. As soon as it became known that a hospital was in existence, all sorts of stragglers worried us—men slightly sick, men without horses, men without food, men without heart. The resources of the hotel were commandeered for the hospital, practically only meat, fowls, and milk.

Hungry men were to be seen in all directions, leading what animals they might to the slaughter; but I think the authorities soon got these matters in hand, stopping individual buying or looting, and rationing meat in a systematic manner. Goodness knows we were tired enough this night, but rest was only to be intermittent, for, in spite of liberal supplies of morphia, there was much groaning and restlessness among the wounded. A guard, too, turned up to arrest our most assiduous, urbane, and obliging German orderlies, for it had transpired that they were wolves in sheep's clothing, one being a notorious mine-layer. They were unceremoniously routed out, and went off without protest, but were brazen enough to attempt to get away with the dressings, instruments, and drugs, the enemy had left.

May 2.—During the night two of our wounded died, both hopeless cases shot through the body. I am afraid that the Anglican *padre* attached to our brigade was disappointed that the deceased were members of the Dutch Reformed Church. During the *trek* he had but little opportunity of practising his avocation, for we were never long enough in one place for him to organise services. True, a native driver had been killed by a waggon on the way up, and the holding of a burial service over this poor unfortunate had encouraged our *padre* a little; for today he set about and arranged to have church in the afternoon; but it was not to be, for word went round that the brigade was to move on again at 3 p.m. Poor *padre!* I fear he will never come up with his congregation again; both he and his horse seem not a little discouraged.

This Sunday was another day of great exertion for the ambulance. Half the men were to move on, and half remain with the hospital; so there was much sorting, packing, and arranging to be done. Here, as at Tsaobis, a lot of equipment had to be left behind, and we who were remaining benefited, but the best horses and mules were to go on.

Water had been the problem on the march; now for us it is to be food. The place supplies water, meat, a little milk, and scanty grazing for the animals. We have three days' rations, and have about sixty mouths to fill in all. We expect relief in a week, but everything is so precarious and uncertain. The brigade trains may overlook us, and pass in the night, or the rations may be wanted more urgently ahead. The horses and mules, if not the men, will certainly have to live on the land.

I gathered a few scrappy details about the fight. Otjimbingwe is in the middle of a square, and at the four corners are Tsaobis, Karibib, Okahandya, and Windhuk; but a glance at the map will show that it is nearer to Tsaobis than the other places. When the 3rd and 5th Brigades arrived at this latter place, the Germans at Otjimbingwe signalled to Karibib for help. Karibib replied that, as they themselves were also threatened with an attack, Otjimbingwe must be evacuated. The Germans here never expected that our men would be able to attack them on Friday morning; but our men by a very fine effort pushed on during the night, and at dawn had partly surrounded the place, and would have done so completely had orders been carried out.

The attack was quite a surprise. An officer of ours blowing his whistle prematurely is said to have betrayed our presence. The Germans, less than a hundred in number, tried the various exits, but, being fired upon from several directions, finally broke up into small parties. One party, with great gallantry, charged direct at a dismounted commando at a distance of 50 yards, fired a volley, and literally escaped through our men. I hear they mostly got away towards Windhuk, dragging two field guns with them, one party of fourteen only being captured.

It is quite likely that, if our junior officers had remained in the positions assigned to them, all the Germans would have been taken; but troop leaders were constantly trying to better their positions, and consequently there was much overlapping. A fat old German "colonel" was under fire at 300 yards for a long time, but he seemed quite unperturbed. Finally he mounted his horse and rode slowly away. This sounds strange, but the explanation of such shortcomings is easily found, for the men had been tried up to the limits of human endurance. "There was not a sane man amongst us," was the comment of one officer. Men were to be seen asleep in the saddle or on the road, indifferent to the danger of passing guns and ammunition waggons. One poor tired wretch attempted to shoot himself.

Many had peculiar illusions, one of which was so common that it is worthy of mention. It took the form of large and beautiful buildings, often grouped together so as almost to form towns. I experienced the same thing in a minor degree, and think it was due to a tired, overwrought brain mistaking the images of blurred trees in the dusty moonlight for houses. So sure were these seers of visions about what they saw, so irritable and ready to argue about it, that it was wisest not to contradict them. Even two days after the fight, so jumpy and nervous were sentries, seeing Germans everywhere, that wise people kept at home after dusk.

May 3.—The feeding of our patients and our men exercises our wits day and night. The major bargains every evening with the hotel-keeper and his wife, and the latter is very keen. They are to supply the hospital as far as they can, and are to get a signed requisition form from us each day for things supplied. In addition they are to let us have 60 pounds of meat a day for the men. These people are very subdued and anxious to please. The old man particularly seems to be in a constant state of nerves, and stands before you hat in hand in a very pathetic manner. They have a married daughter with them, who has two little children, a girl of six and a boy younger, funny little square heads and not a bit shy. Their father is either a prisoner or still fighting.

The numbers of our troops passing through yesterday quite overwhelmed them all; they stood at the door awhile watching the troops passing, and then, unable to hide their despair any longer, went inside. The two brigades with their guns and ammunition waggons took nearly all the afternoon to pass. Occasionally one would see a *burgher* with a sheep or goat upon his saddle, and one man passed struggling with a live goat, his horse consequently very restive. They all looked rested and cheerful again, and the horses were wonderful.

Last evening, at supper, the major, after two or three ineffectual trials, ventured the mild protest that the tea was not very nice, that it tasted like pepper. I said, "Impossible!" and took a fair drink. It was a terribly pungent concoction, and it came upon me like a flash that I had in the dark given the boy tobacco instead of tea. Apart from the burning sensation we experienced in the throat, the loss of two teaspoonfuls of condensed milk was distressing. Then I remembered that I had mixed some of this supposed tea with our stock of tea, and the depression which followed was not wholly attributable to the effects of nicotine. I waited until today before looking at our tea supply, and there, sure enough, was the tea and tobacco mixed. We now spend our spare time trying to pick the tobacco out with a pair of surgical forceps.

The major is always nosing round for food and interviewing the few inhabitants left. In the middle of a conversation he will suddenly say, "I wonder if I could get any eggs!": I reply, "Considering the nervous strain under which the fowls of this locality must be living. I should think not." However, today he managed to get three at a tickey each. We decided to give one to the querulous lieutenant wounded in the foot, and two, one being broken, to a patient old *burgher* with a ghastly wound in the groin. "I have got a little butter," he will say, but how many kilograms I can't say.

May 4.—Today the 2nd Brigade arrived. They have had a terribly hard journey from Riet, practically up the bed of the Swakup the whole way. They certainly had better water that way than we had, but the going was very hard, and mines worried them considerably. Three men were killed by them. In one instance two men were blown to pieces, and a third is said to have been found at the top of a high tree, with not a scratch on him. Another mine blew up a water-cart and its driver on the ground over which an artillery column had already passed.

May 5.—Today the ambulance attached to the 5th Brigade moved away from the police barrack, leaving only their motors behind, having no petrol for them. Of course they asked us to take over their patients, which we did, though not with a very good grace, as they were leaving no rations for them. Judging from their weary and dejected appearance, I don't think they were taking very much with them, either; but they made no complaints, and did not ask us to help them, for it seems to be an unwritten law that each unit bears its privations silently and alone. Indeed, when you ask an officer of another corps to a meal, his distaste for food and lack of appetite is positively alarming.

As soon as they had gone, we swooped down upon the barrack like a lot of vultures, going through everything; but we found only drugs, dressings, bedding, etc. No food, of course, the carcass of a sheep that I had admired so much on a previous visit having disappeared to the last bone. The building is a large rambling place, and has terraced gardens, pretty and well arranged, with palms and trees, stretching down to the river. In these gardens our cook found the remains of some cabbages, just outside leaves and roots, but very acceptable. In the yard were two maxims left by the Germans. They were large things with limbers, and not mounted on tripods as ours are. Everybody who passed by helped himself to some of the cartridges or a movable part, so that before long, as weapons, they had ceased to exist.

The 2nd Brigade are a great worry to us, for their weaklings, their sick, and their lazy, try to get some or any benefit from the hospital. The Major is most polite to them: nothing would give him more pleasure than to take their sick in—but they must have at least four days' rations. As they have not four minutes' rations, the plan is very effectual. A burly quartermaster-sergeant, who was really ill, said he would rather die on the veldt than starve in hospital. Him we took in, on learning his occupation, and fed him on the fat of the land thinking of future benefits. We hoped we had seen the last of this brigade when they moved on this evening to a place called Uitdraai, where the grazing and water were said to be better.

May 6.—I went down to the town today. The place is deserted, for the only people of ours there are a sergeant and three men of Engineers. I went through the large store. This store, which had been of considerable size, belonged to a rich old man who lived on the premises with his married sons and daughters. Behind the store were the dwelling-quarters, and, judging from the amount of clothing, furniture, beds, toys, and utensils, scattered about, a large number of people must have lived there. I was told the old man had fourteen children and numberless grandchildren, but, hearing the "English" would send all women and children to Cape Town, the whole clan had cleared off to Grootfontein.

A very polite old German, who was only on a visit from Europe, and unable to return on account of the war, came to the hospital in the afternoon. He said he had lost everything while away from the house, even his return ticket home. It comforted him little to learn that a return ticket to Europe by the Woermann Line was not likely to be available for some time to come.

An old Rhenish missioner is a daily visitor at the hospital. He has a most venerable appearance, and is most courteous and mild. In fact, the behaviour and manner of all the old German people I have seen leaves nothing to be desired, and I have heard one of them say that he did not know what modern Germany and Germans were coming to. The aggressive, bumptious manner so general among the younger men seems to be a growth of the present generation.

When the 2nd Brigade turned up a few days ago, they were so short of everything that there was no keeping them out of the houses, though there is little enough here; for no supplies have come in since the war began, nine months ago, and the German soldiers had also removed all they could. It seems to me that it will be necessary to feed not only our own troops, but also what Germans remain here, to say nothing of the natives.

For a whole week we have had no news from anywhere, for no people are passing up at all now, and today our last communication with the outside world was severed, a branch of the Field Telegraph Service having packed up their wireless apparatus and departed, like the rest, northward.

The 2nd Brigade are still only seven miles away. They are out of touch with headquarters, and don't seem to know where to go. One of their officers was here today looking for cattle. He seemed quite worn out, and said the brigade was without food. The Major let him have five of the ten oxen he had commandeered.

We, too, are feeling the pinch a little, and, as our unit are mostly boys with healthy appetites, it is hard to get them to exercise restraint. Some of them have small private supplies of food. We would like to call these in, but fear such action would lead to further depression or panic. We cannot understand why the transport has failed us so utterly, and are haunted with the idea that possibly supplies are being forwarded by another route.

May 7.—Our horses and mules look very poor. We have nothing to give them, and the grazing near the town is very thin, one may say "tramped out." In these parts stock depend upon two things chiefly for food: a fine feathery grass, each plant growing separately, the stalks of which are very brittle; the other food is a low bush with bright yellow leaves and a blue flower. The tops of this bush are very succulent, and some horses prefer it to the grass. Low thorn-trees are fairly numerous, but not thick enough to make riding irksome. In every direction within a radius of three miles of the town everything is eaten down. I don't think our horses are entirely responsible for this, because lately, on account of the war and the unsettled temper of the natives, many German farmers have brought their stock into town for safety.

This evening we received a little news of what was going on outside Otjimbingwe. We were sitting on the *stoep* after supper, discussing the eternal food question, when two men loomed up out of the darkness, and asked unceremoniously for something to eat. They were very much exhausted, and said they had tasted nothing for forty-eight hours, and that they were trying to make their way to Karibib to join their corps of signallers. They brought the news that General Britz had occupied Karibib without resistance, and that the 5th Brigade had cut the line at Wilhelmstaal, a station on the line between Karibib and Windhuk; and, what was particularly pleasing to us, they said the 2nd Brigade had now moved on towards Groot Barmen and Okahandya.

This 2nd Brigade (Albert's) had been a constant source of anxiety to us, for they were rapidly depleting the town of stock, men coming in at all times to look for cattle, sheep, or goats. After hearing all this good news, we fed the signallers to the best of our ability. In fact, had the news been otherwise I think we would have fed them all the same, they were such tine fellows, full of grit, and regarding their privations lightly. As soon as they had finished their meagre supper, and with a biscuit each in their haversacks, they started off in the direction of Karibib, forty miles away, with nothing but the stars and their instinct to guide them.

May 8.—The wounded are all improving, and are beginning to take a little interest in things outside their own particular miseries. But their accounts of the recent fighting are contradictory and indefinite. It seems fairly clear, however, that only the Pietersburg commando and the B.B.S. took up the positions assigned to them. All the killed and wounded belonged to the Pietersburg commando. In fact, the wounded officer states that they all belonged to his troop, and he says that only from their side, a ridge to the north-west of the village, was the attack made. The Germans admit that they were taken completely by surprise, most of them being in bed when the fighting began. They say they waited with machine guns for us along the Tsaobis road until 3 a.m., and then returned to sleep; but, as usual, Brother Boer did not come along the road, but made the wide encircling movement his heart loveth, which, as I have said, was only partially successful.

Another of the German wounded declared that he was shot at a distance of five yards after he had put his hands up; but the man who shot him, and was himself wounded, said it was not the case. Among the German wounded is a nervous, aesthetic-looking clerk. His story is that he was taken from his office in Swakupmund, and a rifle put into his hands. He knew nothing about soldiering, and before he had fired a shot a bullet through the leg terminated his military career. From what he said, I gathered that the attitude of the regulars to the reservists was not too cordial, and mutual recriminations were rife.

I feel that today our spirits have reached a very low ebb, and, to cap all, eleven of our mules are missing tonight. These animals are taken out each day to feed, but as the bush is rather thick, grazing scanty, the drivers lazy, and I fear disaffected on account of their privations, it is not surprising that the mules go astray. Hitherto they have always been found, but today the drivers come in early in a very surly mood and report the disaster. I can feel that mutiny is in the air.

These drivers are mostly Cape boys with a sprinkling of *kaffirs*, and are intelligent and capable. They are engaged by the government for a fixed period, generally six months, and it is forbidden to officers in charge to administer corporal punishment. Consequently, to enforce obedience among them is not always easy, and tonight one of them flatly refused to kill a sheep. The conductor in charge laid violent hands upon him, and I, having first removed the offender's knife, stepped round the corner not to witness a very necessary breach of regulations. Afterwards, with a little persuasion from the O.C., the man slaughtered the sheep, and the incident had a very salutary effect upon all the boys.

Biscuits and coffee are now at an end, so that henceforth the men will have to live almost entirely on meat until we are relieved. Fortunately, there is a little rock salt on one of the waggons, and only those who have lived any length of time on meat only, without salt, can appreciate the value of this find.

During the campaign men lived for many days entirely upon fresh meat, in some instances as long as three weeks. All the men I saw who had lived so were emaciated and weak, shortness of breath and extreme lassitude being the chief complaints. One man declared that they became too weak to kill the sheep, so they used to wait for the sheep to pass, and then shoot them. We who have salt and the cabbage leaves aforesaid generally boil together the meat, salt, and cabbage, drink the fluid as soup, and eat the residual mush as joint. Soup without salt or vegetables leaves a full-empty feeling almost worse than hunger. The men who are continually moving often have to eat the meat quite fresh. I have seen the still quivering muscle being grilled on skewers of wood, with a resulting indigestible mass, charred outside and raw inside.

A much better plan, which is adopted when possible, is to cut the meat into ribbons and partially dry it in the sun. So treated it remains fresh in the men's haversacks for several days, especially if it has been salted a little. This meat is much nicer than the fresh meat, and causes less indigestion and discomfort.

May 9.—This morning I was up before it was light, and went off to look for grazing and the lost mules. Arguing that the boys and what men could be spared from camp would search for them where they had been lost, I decided to break new ground, and made for the mountains in the direction of Karibib. After going six or eight miles I found quite good grass and plenty of the succulent yellow bush, and I also saw one of the large conical ant-heaps which, although not very common, are a feature of these parts. These heaps are nearly always built round a thorn-tree, so that the trunk of the tree is hidden and the branches of the tree stick out on all sides. What can be seen of the tree looks green and flourishing, and usually the apex of the ant-heap exceeds the tree in height. They may be as high as 15 or 20 feet, having a diameter of 10 or 12 feet at the base. They are composed of a very hard grey substance which looks like a mica mud. They are inhabited by a little black ant, though I always found the larger ones deserted, monuments rather than dwellings.

This little ant is also a great road-builder. The roads they make are concave furrows in the sand about an inch wide. From one of the smaller heaps I traced one a distance of over 100 yards. It appeared to go straight to some destination, skirting obstacles often, but always resuming the original direction. Numerous branches were given off from the main road, generally at an angle of about 20 degrees. The ants were to be seen going along, some in one direction, some in the other, but never hesitating, turning round, or leaving the road. One felt sure they must have a General Botha directing and encouraging them in their efforts to cross their miniature desert.

Quite unexpectedly I came upon three white mules grazing quietly in a little hollow. I thought they would make off when they realized my evil designs; but, the halters and chains of servitude being still about their necks, they just looked up, as much as to say, "Why didn't you find us before?" and walked sedately back to camp in single file. That they were not our own did not detract from the pleasure of the find; for it transpired that they belonged to another ambulance which had moved on nearly a week ago. So that these mules, which looked in very good condition, must have been in the bush all the time without water; for the only water anywhere about is the well in the Swakup River, from which water has to be pumped.

The question as to how wild animals obtain water in many parts of this country is very puzzling; for one finds such creatures as buck, baboons, and birds, in areas where standing water is to be found only during rainy periods, and then only for a short time, for it usually sinks into the porous sandy ground very quickly. Occasionally one finds small pools in the river-beds, but they are few and far between. The atmosphere is so dry that, although the nights are often cold, the fall of dew is very slight, so that this source of moisture can hardly be considered.

The only explanation as regards *herbivora* seems to be that the food they eat contains sufficient water for their needs. As to how the *carnivora*, such as leopards and jackals, manage I can offer no solution at all. I have seen a jackal looking sleek and well thirty miles or more from the nearest known water, and that was in a deep well. Why he was there at all in the desert I could not imagine, for nothing living was to be seen except a very occasional lizard or beetle.

May 10.—A few Germans here, now that the troops have passed, are beginning to pop their heads out, and one is not a little surprised to see several able-bodied men among them. No doubt their uniforms are snugly hidden away somewhere, for here, as elsewhere, the conscience of the Hun is very elastic. He is soldier today, Red Cross man tomorrow, civilian and spy combined the next, whichever serves his purpose best. On more than one occasion I have been asked to release German wounded because they were "civilians." "Surely," said the German matron of a hospital, with affected surprise, when a batch of convalescent wounded prisoners was being sent down, "you're not going to send this man and that man with the prisoners? They are only poor civilians."

It was galling, too, to see the large herds of cattle and flocks of sheep appearing as if by magic, which had been hidden away in the mountains when the danger threatened. When our troops had asked for meat, the owners of all these animals had declared they had only a few old cows and goats. Now they have not only the effrontery to bring in their stock, but to ask in a most importunate manner for police protection and compensation. They declare they are in danger of attack from "wild" natives living between here and Windhuk, and make claims for large quantities of stock which they say we or the natives have taken.

No doubt the natives have made use of their opportunities, for they are now to be seen with small quantities of stock about their dwellings, whereas under German rule they were practically debarred from the ownership of cattle or sheep. A well-to-do farmer, who had entertained General Botha in his town-house during his stay here, sent the following letter to us, with the request that it might be forwarded to the officer commanding troops at a little place, Potmini, twenty miles away, on the Swakup River, and where his farm was situated.

> The order of General Botha is to protect every private property, to do not kill any angora goat, wool sheeps, or other animal of Potmini, and to do not prevent the animals of Mr. C. (himself), who presently is at Otjimbingwe, do his work on this place. On the 30th of April at Otjimbingwe the general has had the kindness to promise me that my private property at Potmini shall be protected. I afterwards heard from officers that perhaps before the general come to Potmini plenty of my cattles already were slaughtered. Directly after taking of Otjimbingwe I have offered all my cattles to General Myburg, because at the first the soldiers had no victuals enough. I only have invited not to consume my last cows, Australian wool sheeps, and the three hundred best angora goats there with I can breed again. Beautiful angora goats, merinos, and ostriches, are very scarce in this country, and must be imported again from South Africa. I beg the general to engage that the slaughtered animals be compensated, and the rest of the animals can return again from Potmini to the little water *hasis* in the next neighbouring, where in this bad year is a little more food. I should be very grateful if the general would permit me to go myself with a patrol to Potmini to prevent more loss of cattles, date palms and other trees, by the going away of my Damaras. Mr. C———.

He was allowed to send a native girl over to Potmini with this epistle, and we took the opportunity of sending a message as well, informing the officer in charge of the precarious state of the hospital. She returned in two days with the report that all the stock had disappeared from the farm. "I am a poor man!" wailed Mr. C——. "What shall I do now?"

What he did was to sit down and write a long rigmarole to the Minister of Defence putting in a claim of £1,600 for alleged losses. As for us, we received the laconic note:

> There are no troops at Potmini. Have informed Swakupmund of your position!

For any help Swakupmund can send us, he might as well have informed Timbuktu.

Today some enemy subjects were found in possession of two shot-guns and two sporting Mausers, although all firearms were supposed to have been handed in when the place was taken. We are very anxious to get hold of a shot-gun, or even a rifle, so that we may vary our menu a little. Boiled mutton and cabbage stalks are getting a little monotonous, and the latter are showing signs of coming to an end.

Tonight the welcome news is circulated that a brigade train is three miles away; but our joy is tempered with apprehension, for, not belonging to our brigade, they may be unwilling or unable to give us anything. It seems very curious and difficult to realize that we strong and healthy men are suddenly shut off from the common necessaries of life and all communication with the outside world. So far we have joked about being hungry, but the major leaves no stone unturned in his efforts to keep the place going. Yesterday he exchanged a sheep for 18 pounds of mealie-meal and 5 pounds of rice. Today he has been negotiating for a little milk for the men, but without success, for it would mean the patients and children going short. So far the wounded have lacked nothing, but the preparing and carrying in of their savoury meals must be a considerable strain upon our hungry orderlies.

May 11.—The brigade train of the 2nd Brigade has arrived. The Major, through the good offices of our patient the quartermaster-sergeant, managed to get two sacks of mealie-meal and a box of biscuits out of them, and this has heartened our boys more than a great victory would have done, although it only means one biscuit each a day and a little mealie-meal porridge. The inhabitants made attempts to buy rice, coffee, sugar, and mealie-meal; but, of course, they could not have any, for twenty half-loaded waggons seemed to be little enough for the 2,500 starving men waiting for them. It is to be hoped that this transport will come up with their brigade, for nobody here can tell them in which direction the troops have moved. We also heard with some concern that our own supplies have been diverted from this route, and are being sent direct to Karibib; but the certain knowledge that General Britz has occupied this place more than compensates us for this bad news.

The brigade train had experienced a most gruelling time dragging the waggons up the sandy bed of the Swakup for nearly a hundred miles. Whoever is to blame for failures in the Q.M.G.'s department, it is certainly not the men who are in charge of the waggons or motor-lorries. One and all have worked like heroes, day and night, with little expectation of *kudos* or reward. If I were a sculptor, I would design a great monument of men and animals of the transport, with a mule chafed and scarred at the top, and put it in front of the Government Buildings in Windhuk.

May 12.—It is becoming abundantly clear that we cannot maintain a hospital here much longer unless we get stores. We would very much like an explanation from the army medical staff as to why we are left here to live or die, without orders or assistance. If we had sufficient petrol, we would risk mines and chance of capture, and motor our patients over to Karibib; but without petrol and oil our four motor ambulances stand there useless, grim witnesses of their own limitations. However, by putting what little petrol and oil remains in all the cars into one, the driver ' thinks ' he will be able to do the forty miles between here and Karibib; and, the major taking his courage in both hands, they set off on what no doubt is a perilous journey: for the road is said to be mined, and as yet no vehicles have been that way.

All day long I hear explosions, and see bits of major, mechanic, and motor, flying skywards in my imagination. It is nine at night before we see, with feelings of great relief, the lights of the returning car, and presently hear it grinding its way through the river-bed and so home. "Nobody knows anything about anything," is all I can get out of the tired major. However, they got some rations and promises of more. General Botha, they say, has formally entered Windhuk today without resistance.

While the major was away I interviewed the garrison *commandant*, a sergeant of Engineers, in charge of a squad of three disaffected privates, the sole protectors of the town. He said they were put here to grind mealies; but as there were none to grind, as the supply of food was finished, and as his horses were daily becoming weaker, it was his intention to evacuate the town.

The idea of being without protection is very alarming to the German inhabitants. Already they declare that their native servants have refused to work; and if they are left alone, they expect that the "semi-wild" natives who live in the mountains to the east, and who exist upon game and roots, will raid them. Here, as elsewhere, the German farmer and villager are living in constant dread of natives, both Hottentot and Herero; and if an evil conscience makes people afraid, they have every reason to be so. Before the Herero rebellion in 1904, Otjimbingwe seems to have been a centre of these people.

The town itself suffered in the rebellion, buildings being fired and a few people killed. The brother of our present landlord was killed outside his own door, and his house gutted, as photographs in the possession of the family show. But the Germans here are reticent as to what has become of the natives in these parts; for although a large Herero reserve is shown on the map, none are to be seen except a few herds and servant-girls, all very subdued and tame, and given to the singing of German hymns. Ugly rumour has it that most of them were driven into the desert to die of hunger or thirst.

The climate here at this time of the year is on the whole pleasant. The atmosphere is very dry, and all the time we have been here I have seen neither cloud nor dew. Just before dawn each day a northeast wind begins to blow with great regularity. It gets stronger towards afternoon, and ceases at sunset. The days, especially the afternoons, are hot, the thermometer in the shade generally registering over 100°. As soon as the sun goes down it becomes chilly, and before dawn the temperature may be down to freezing-point; so that there is a diurnal variation of 70°, which is, I should think, rather exceptional.

Moon and stars are very bright in these parts, and both the Great Bear and the Southern Cross are visible. For the sunrises and sunsets alone the country is worth a visit. So still is the atmosphere at these times that one can often distinguish all the spectral colours, from the violet at the zenith to the red on the horizon.

Today I explored the bed of the Omusemu River, which joins the right bank of the Swakup at Otjimbingwe, cutting the town into two parts. As this so-called river is typical of a great number of watercourses in Damaraland, I will describe it briefly. The first thing one notices is the absence of surface water. Only very occasionally do these rivers come down, and then only for a short while. Two factors are responsible for this—the porous nature of the soil, and the comparatively slight rainfall; but they all have steady streams of underground water, often very abundant and good, and this at no very great depth, generally anything from 10 to 50 feet. The Omusemu varies in width from 200 to 600 yards; indeed, in many places its limits are very indefinite, so low are the banks.

But the most striking thing about it is the luxuriant vegetation. Away from the river there are only a few stunted thorn-trees and a little sparse grass. As soon as you get to the bank of the river this is all changed. Gigantic acacias larger than the biggest oak, and of the same spreading habit, which denotes strength of limb, fringe the banks at intervals, or grow, in family groups and sometimes singly, in the bed of the river. Thorn-trees of smaller varieties abound on the numerous islands, and there is very thick undergrowth in places. Several varieties of grass grow freely and to a considerable height. All this goes to create a very beautiful and park-like appearance. Viewed from a distant hill, a river like this is a very conspicuous feature of the landscape, a broad belt of verdure winding through a comparative desert, to be lost to sight in the distant mountains.

May 16.—A Cape cart arrived from Karibib today, bringing some stores and petrol. We also received orders to evacuate our hospital to Karibib, and to proceed to Windhuk via Groot Barmen without delay. With a little squeezing it would be possible to get all the wounded into the four cars, including the prisoners, one or two of whom were now almost well. As we had no escort, there was a possibility of the prisoners trying to escape, especially as they were never tired of telling us how they were looking forward to their visit to Cape Town. To prevent this contingency, orders were issued that they were to go clothed in pyjamas and overcoats, boots and water-bottles being withheld.

May 17.—We were up at five this morning, and had all the wounded dressed and fed by seven. To stow them comfortably for a long and rough motor journey was not very easy, especially as three of them had leg wounds and were unable to sit up. However, by propping them up with pillows and bags, and by suspending the splints from the frames of the cars with bandages, we got them all arranged to their satisfaction. Just before starting, each man received a good dose of morphia, including the Germans who we suspected might attempt

Transporting wounded to Karibib

to escape. All were in the best of spirits; even the man who had done nothing but whine and complain for the last three weeks seemed to be buoyed up with hope. In spite of the morphia, and in spite of the fact that we only travelled at the rate of ten miles an hour, the journey left something to be desired from a wounded man's point of view. The cars were much too heavily laden, the road very rough and uneven.

Consequently, the frames of the cars came down with a bang on the axles every few yards with great regularity, which was followed with equal regularity by a chorus of groans. It was almost humorous the way the poor beggars sat with a rigid, fixed expression, anticipating every bump, and occasionally, I thought, emitting the groan before the jolt occurred. For the first ten miles or so the road ran north along the bank of the Omusemu, when it crossed a loop of the river where, in a beautiful little dell, a deep well is situated, with its sides protected by masonry, and operated by means of a windlass, chain, and bucket. Turning westward through a *poort*, we came into fine upland country with plenty of grass, and near to Karibib passed a large farm enclosed with a wire fence, belonging to a wealthy Jew engaged extensively in horse-breeding.

Karibib itself is not an interesting place. Standing almost on the edge of the desert, it is very nearly devoid of trees. A high wind was blowing, and this combined with the movements of numerous troops and waggons caused the place to be almost obscured in a great cloud of dust, through which one could make out a few roofs, and a great mountain on the farther side. This place is important for its railway workshops. Here the two-foot gauge railway from Swakupmund ends, and a three-foot-six gauge railway begins the line for Windhuk, Keetmanshoop, and Luderitzbucht. With their usual thoroughness and attention to detail, our sanguine foes had constructed a large wire cage with sidings into it from both railways, wherein they hoped to, and possibly did, exhibit any of the Union forces who were unfortunate enough to fall into their hands. "Nothing I have seen during the whole campaign," said an officer, " has given me so much pleasure as seeing the ungodly Huns in their own pit; and if I had only had my camera with me the day I saw them in it, my cup of joy would have been full."

We took our patients straight to the hospital. Though the medical authorities knew four days ago that we were coming, the officer in charge of the hospital had not been informed; consequently our arrival was quite unexpected. Still, the hospital authorities did their best, though the patients had not the nice beds they had with us, and the rooms were small and unsuitable. The accommodation, too, was quite inadequate for a large base hospital, and all but the most severe cases had to be content with shake-downs in a large shed adjoining. A general order had appeared forbidding commandeering even for the hospital, and as a result many of our sick and wounded had to lie on the ground, although there were plenty of beds in the town. In fact, not only here, but everywhere, the general was most careful to protect the interests and property of the inhabitants.

I had occasion to visit headquarters, for the Rhenish missioner at Otjimbingwe had asked me to take a letter to the general explaining the precarious condition of the inhabitants, who were on the verge of starvation and expecting native raids. The chief of staff was most sympathetic, but explained that at present it was quite impossible to police occupied towns. But, with regard to feeding German civilians, arrangements were being made, and he gave me ten days' rations for such people as I could assure him were badly in need of them. And this, too, at a time when the troops in Karibib, General Britz's brigade and an infantry brigade, were on half-rations, if that, and we ourselves could only obtain half-rations for our trek to Windhuk. I think it can safely be said that General Botha's soldiers went short of food without a murmur, in order that the wives and children of men who were in arms against them might be fed.

The general military situation with regard to the Northern Army is now as follows: The infantry are along the line from Walfisch to Karibib, and the *burghers* are spread out like a fan, also along the line, but in a semicircle almost from Karibib to Windhuk, the left wing of the 3rd Brigade at the latter place, under Colonel Mentz, being engaged in capturing or dispersing the remains of the enemy east of the line. The *burghers* are occupying their time in reorganizing, which means, chiefly, trying to get their horses into better condition preparatory to making another rush. The Germans are watching us in a line parallel to ours, but some distance north, Omaruru being, perhaps, their headquarters and point of concentration.

Chapter 6
The Trek from Otjimbingwe to Windhuk

May 18.—Windhuk lies almost due east of Otjimbingwe, but there is no direct road connecting the two places, because a large waterless, irregular plateau known as the Komas Highlands intervenes. This region, which constitutes the watershed for the greater part of the whole country, must be skirted either to the north or south. The Burghers had taken the northern route, partly on account of the better water-supply, and partly to avoid having an extensive waterless and difficult region between themselves and their base, but chiefly in order that the wing marching on Windhuk should not lose touch with the rest of the army.

Now we were free to move on to Windhuk, and our orders, too, were to take the northern route and not to delay. Journeys in this country are dominated almost entirely by the water-supply, and the treks must be so arranged that the water-holes are reached at reasonable intervals. Further, *trekking* must be done at night, for two reasons: first, because the days even in the winter may be unpleasantly hot; and, secondly, because the horses and mules must graze in the daytime, so that they can be watched. In our particular case we are faced with additional difficulties. Our animals being in very low condition, they are not in a fit state to make long treks.

We have no food at all for the mules, and only 1 pound of mealies a day for each horse for five days. For the men, too, we have only food for five days. But, worst of all, we have no knowledge of the country through which we have to pass, and do not know where the water and grazing may be. Without a guide, we shall have to rely entirely upon the map, which is quite unreliable with regard to the waterholes, or, rather, with regard to the water in the water-holes. At dawn today we are ready to leave the place where we have spent three anxious and strenuous weeks, weeks that have seemed to us like eternities. The inhabitants seem to be sorry that the ambulance is leaving, and express their gratitude for the little we have done for them by making us gifts of foodstuffs, which we know they can very ill afford to do.

Soon B section of the —— Mounted Brigade Field Ambulance is on the road again, three ambulance waggons, three general service waggons, and a water-cart bringing up the rear. Men without horses walk to save the mules; men with horses walk to spare the horses. The road is very heavy, the wheels clinging to the sand with a grinding noise. Two or three hungry German dogs follow us, hoping thereby to prolong a miserable existence. The dust rises and hangs in the air, and as soon as the sun is up it becomes unpleasantly hot. The dust of many parts of this country is quite a feature, being often very light and powdery. This is due to the fact that it is composed very largely of mica. A moving column will raise a dust that ascends like steam or smoke, and remains in the air a considerable time. Troops or herds of animals are easily localized in the daytime by the dust they create, which is often visible for many miles, so that surprising an enemy during the daytime is generally out of the question.

During our stay at Otjimbingwe we had collected a good many stray horses, most of them in a most wretched condition, left behind because of their uselessness. Our orderlies would appropriate these animals, and make attempts to improve them, and also to acquire old and discarded saddles and bridles. Amongst our men were a good many from the towns, with no knowledge of horses and little of horsemanship. These were the very ones who had made such efforts to convert themselves into mounted men, and on leaving we were not a little surprised to see several of these gentry booted and spurred and mounted on these sorry nags. But before many miles were done they were all on foot again, the effort of propelling these animals, combined with lack of skill, proving more irksome than walking.

We continued to advance along the road parallel to the Swakup for an hour or two until we reached a spot called Uitdraai, where it was our intention to pass the day and wait until the evening before beginning the real trekking. We had been told that there were both water and grazing here. There was a little water in the river, but no grass was to be seen; for the 2nd Brigade had been here nearly a week, and had eaten up everything. The place, too, was a regular Golgotha, the bones and other remains of slaughtered animals lying about in great profusion. Dead horses and mules there were, too, in abundance. We spent the day under the trees, as far as possible from the unsavoury camp of Albert's men, and at five in the evening we spanned in, the order being to *trek* until 10 p.m.

This evening the travelling was very heavy, for the road leaving the river on the right rose higher and higher; the surface, too, left much to be desired, sandy patches alternating with rocks and boulders. With every step the country improved, and at ten o'clock everybody was quite ready for a little rest. The night was very cold and frosty, but with the aid of large fires and hot coffee we managed to keep fairly warm, and would have been quite happy but for the thought that at 2 a.m. we must be up and off. Of all the abominations one has to undergo in this country, I think nothing is so trying as getting up for the early morning *trek*. Cold and stiff, you rise more fatigued than when you lay down. With difficulty you mount a tired horse, and with greater difficulty still you make constant efforts to keep awake. In fact, I think it much the best plan to walk as much as possible at this time—at least, until you are thoroughly warmed and roused.

May 19.—About dawn the road ceased to ascend, and we began to cross a series of beautiful river-beds running into the Swakup from the north. Here the country is like a park; grass is plentiful, especially in the beds of some of the streams, and the thorn-trees are numerous and large. In the hopes of finding water, I rode up or down several of these river-beds for a mile or so, but in vain, for not a sign of water was to be seen. It was now about twenty-four hours since the animals had had a decent drink, and, although the sun was beginning to get hot, there was nothing for it but to push on to the water. To crown all, about breakfast-time the dissel-boom of the water-cart broke off short going down a steep hill. Our conductor, in despair, wanted to leave it behind, but of course the Major would not hear of this, and after considerable delay we managed to fix the water-cart on behind the last general service waggon.

My horse being better than most, I pushed on alone to Klein Barmen to search for the water. At noon I came to the spot, just a drift in a river, with two derelict buildings, but no sign of water or grazing. Hunting down the river-bed, I came upon a well of large dimensions, but it was filled in with rocks and the winding apparatus broken. Coming back to the drift, I saw two small notices, one in German,

"Neither grazing nor water here," and the other in Dutch, "I hear there is water and grazing three miles farther; I am trekking on." Cursing the mocking German, and blessing the Dutchman for his message of hope, I off-saddled my now exhausted horse, sat down under a tree, and waited for the ambulance. It was 2 p.m. before they arrived, the mules looking ready to drop.

I pointed to the notices. The conductor, after reading, said: "I must span out; I cannot go another step." Nothing for the animals, not even sufficient shade; they were just tied to the waggons. We made a little porridge and coffee, the first food we had tasted this day; but looking at the mules and horses, and thinking that we were probably going to try to urge them on another fifteen or twenty miles to Groot Barmen, made one too utterly wretched to have any desire for food or drink. Most pitiful is it, throughout these trying marches, to witness the endurance, patience, and sufferings, of the animals. A mule will pull gamely until it drops to rise no more and a merciful bullet puts an end to its career. One would see them trying to nibble bushes as they went along, or swaying out of the course to get at a little grass by the roadside.

Our great difficulty was that we rarely found grazing and water in the same place; for the troops preceding us had always eaten up the grass near the water, or, the water being near the homesteads of the farmers, the stock on the farms had done so. Often we would find good grazing, and the mules would be too thirsty to eat, or we dared not stop until we came to water. Then, when we arrived at the water, no grazing was to be found near. Attempts were made to gather grass as we went along, but the quantity obtained in the time at our disposal was never more than a few mouthfuls. Let no man lay flattering unction to his soul for his share in this war, but rather give the full meed of praise to the gallant beasts whose bones will whiten the sands of German West for many a long day.

Encouraged a little by the rest, but more by the Dutchman's message, we moved on again at 3 p.m. We struggled on three miles, four miles, five miles, in the heat and dust, without sign of water. The conductor, able to stand the strain no longer, and probably not wishing to see his animals give in altogether, came up and asked me to ride ahead with him to see if we could find water. In our anxiety we forced our horses into a gallop. Mine felt so weak under me that I thought he would never gallop again. Mounting a rise we saw a roof, then several, then some large farm buildings, and as we descended we saw a large cement dam full of water glittering in the sun, wherein several men were leisurely bathing and washing their clothes.

For the moment I think, if I had had a revolver, I would have fired upon those men, for they seemed to be fouling, with their filthy shirts, the water we wished to drink. But, as a matter of fact, there was water in abundance, and they were only washing in the place appointed for the purpose, for somebody had made arrangements for both drinking and washing. I turned my horse to a drinking-trough. He seemed to hesitate. I jumped down to taste it; it was quite hot. Later I made a careful examination of the spring. It came bubbling out of the soil at a single spot, whence it was led by furrows and pipes to drinking-troughs and the large tank. The water came out of the ground at a temperature of 49° C., and I could not maintain my hand in it at this spot, although grass was growing up to the edge of this spring and algae were there in plenty. I noticed also a water-beetle or two.

The water was quite odourless, colourless, and tasteless. I was told it is radioactive. A three-inch pipe carried the overflow away. It is in reality a little spa, and a shed at hand had two cement plunge baths in it, with the water laid on. We camped under some massive white granite rocks on the bank of the Swakup, within a hundred yards of the spring. The wide bed of the river, with vegetation down to its edge, the glistening rocks, and the distant mountains, all tinted a peach colour peculiar to African sunsets, made a serene and beautiful picture.

We had hardly outspanned when a commando rode up from the Windhuk road. They watered their horses expeditiously, and moved on at once by the road we had come. A dusty staff officer galloped up to our camp and saluted the major. "The colonel says you are to follow the wing immediately to Okasisi." Okasisi, fifty miles to the north-west! Excuses rushed to the major's lips: the mules, the horses, the men, his orders.

More to the point, he finally asked, "What brigade is this?"

"Colonel Collins' left wing of Colonel Albert's brigade, sir," replied the staff officer.'

"But I am the ambulance attached to Colonel Mentz's brigade," said the major in a tone of relief I have never heard equalled.

"In that case I have nothing more to say," replied the staff officer, putting spurs to his horse.

Thinking it rather strange that the troops were passing through in the direction away from the capital, I hailed a passing officer, and gleaned from him the following somewhat disconcerting information, that only a few of the Northern Army were now at Windhuk, and that a concentration was taking place towards Karibib. What troops were still in Windhuk he thought might belong to our brigade. He said that they had captured a German ambulance complete with nine wounded prisoners; about 300 Germans were still watching General Mackenzie's troops in the region of Gibeon, not knowing that Windhuk was lost, and Colonel Mentz was engaged in rounding them up; all fighting south of the Karibib-Windhuk line was now over, the German forces having retreated towards Grootfontein and the Waterberg.

When asked how the *burghers* had been faring, he said that at times they had been very much reduced from want of food; they had been in the saddle every day for twenty-five days, and often they had covered as much as fifty miles in twenty-four hours. Since he left Swakupmund he had received seventeen biscuits only, no coffee, tea, or sugar, and only very occasionally a little mealie-meal, so that they had lived almost entirely upon meat.

Our daily allowance of biscuits is six per man, so that these men had been, not on half or quarter, but on "tenth" rations, and, as a matter of fact, they had been out of touch with all supplies for twenty-one days. They had still a *trek* of forty or fifty miles to the line at Okasisi, and there was no reason to believe that they would get much when they arrived there. Both they and their horses appeared to have plenty of vim. They were cheerful and keen, although the less said about their clothing and toilet, the better.

The ambulance was now in a regular quandary. Orders were to proceed to Windhuk; but all troops, we were told, were now making for Karibib, preparatory, no doubt, to making a new rush northward along the line. The major was for obeying orders, no doubt a good soldierly precept. I, on the other hand, counselled remaining where we were until we could get fresh orders, arguing that since we had received orders the whole military situation might have changed. But we were very soon to discover that staying here was out of the question, for there was not a blade of grass for the animals to eat within four miles, and there was nothing for it but to move on first thing in the morning to Groot Barmen, where there was, so we were informed, both grazing and water, also a telephone-station.

May 20.—This morning I interviewed the manager of the neighbouring farm, a blond and communicative Hun mounted upon a mule. He was taking the imminent change of government in a very philosophical if not cheerful way, and prognosticated a speedy conclusion to the campaign. He said the war would last another five months, and then he dismissed an unpleasant topic with a shrug of the shoulders. This large farm, Klein Barmen, belongs to the German Farming Company, which was really Liebig's, but went under a German name in this country, London capital being at the bottom of the enterprise. At present they were milking 200 cows, making butter and cheese which they sold to the military.

Altogether there were on the place 4,000 head of cattle, and when the number reached 50,000 or 60,000 it was their intention to start Liebig factories. Labour was a great problem with him, especially, of course, since our arrival in the country. The natives, he said, are very "low-class," and only work if compelled. "For disobedience we give them twenty-five *sjamboks*, and then they are all right for another six months. It's like medicine," he added with a laugh. "We don't flog them ourselves, but just send them to the police with a note, saying, 'Kindly give bearer twenty-five lashes,' which is done without inquiry. Every native capable of working is registered, and wears a brass label with a number on, and the name of the town near which he dwells. When we require labourers, we simply ask the police to send them, and the natives have to come whether they want to or not."

The Germans must have had very large numbers of men and women so registered, for I subsequently bought a good many labels from natives, bearing numbers such as "Karibib Pass 8,376" and "Omaruru Pass 11,347." The natives themselves parted most willingly with these passes, as if they regarded them as badges of servitude, as indeed they are.

It seemed rather strange to see a man so well dressed as this manager, and controlling such large interests, riding a mule, so I asked him why he was doing so.

"Because I have no horse," was his trite reply.

Horse sickness being very common from here northward, very few horses were to be had, and they were very expensive. In fact, people often rode oxen, and recently he had sold 400 "good riding oxen" to the soldiers of the *Kaiser*. Land, he said, was cheap, the government selling good farms at 50 *pfennigs* per hectare.

Lizards are very plentiful in these parts. One small, very agile variety I noticed first in the desert between Salem and Tsaobis. The body is the colour of the sand, and the long tail a vivid transparent salmon colour. When disturbed it makes for cover like a streak of flame. Another very beautiful variety is found on the sunny rocks. The largest I saw was about 10 inches long, including the tail. The body is rather more squat than a lizard's generally is—halfway between a lizard's and a frog's. The head and neck are marked like a tiger's, but of lemon, yellow, and black. It holds its head well up, and looks about in a very perky way. It has scarlet epaulettes, and the body is grey marked with white. Its power of holding on is phenomenal, and I saw one running up and down the smooth cement side of a house, just to show what it could do.

Immediately after breakfast I was despatched to Groot Barmen, a distance of ten miles, in order to select a site for the camp, and to try to get into telephonic communication with headquarters. This short journey to Groot Barmen is along the Swakup River, which the road crosses several times. The white sandy river-bed, the great trees and mountains, combined to make it very picturesque. Mica here is very abundant, large flakes glistening in the sun like diamonds. Sedimentary rocks, not noticed nearer the coast, were in evidence on account of the strata being twisted and bent in a most marked manner. In one place a layer of sandstone could be seen following the ups and downs of the mountains with great regularity.

Groot Barmen consists of a farm, a deserted police-station, and a ruined Roman Catholic mission. At the farm there was a telephone, and we were able to talk to Okahandya. There is a hot spring here, too, the water being hotter than at Klein Barmen. "You can cook an egg in it," they say. On the farm was a young Dutchman who hastened to tell us that he was a "British subject." Subsequently it transpired that the farm belonged to a German who had fled north, and that he had got the "British subject" in at the outbreak of hostilities, thereby, no doubt, hoping to protect his property.

He possessed 300 milking cows, a thousand oxen, and several thousand sheep, all in very good condition. We were able to buy butter, cheese, and milk, in abundance, and our hungry orderlies were soon to be seen literally filling themselves with milk at threepence a litre. The police-station, or rather barracks, stands on a little hill with a very good view of the surrounding country. It has the appearance of having been out of use for years.

At a distance of about half a mile it is surrounded by four or five small buildings, which were no doubt blockhouses employed to guard against a surprise from the Hereros during the rebellion. The precautions had not saved the mission-station, which had been set on fire one night. Whether the holy fathers escaped or not I did not learn. We camped near these ruins under some giant acacias and date-palms. The church, of simple Norman architecture, is almost intact, only the roof, windows, and doors, having disappeared, a wooden ceiling, panelled, and supported by wooden pillars, being quite in a good state of preservation. The only article of furniture in the church was what I took to be the pulpit, but on closer inspection, it turned out to be a Berlin lucerne press. Two rude confessionals built of mud and stones, and whitewashed, stand at the west door.

The adjoining monastery showed signs of having been burnt, charred ends of the bamboo and fern thatched roofs and ceilings being visible. The building was large and rambling, suggestive of both poverty and toil, which no doubt the missionaries gladly endured until they were driven out by their own flock, to return no more. Bats innumerable inhabited the rafters, hanging in clusters like grapes, and I captured one with ease. They were of a small mouse-coloured variety, with tiny deep-set eyes, quite unlike those possessed by nocturnal animals generally. The ears, on the other hand, were very large and funnel-shaped, pointing forward. From this it would seem highly probable that bats rely chiefly or solely upon their sense of hearing for capturing insects at dusk, and, as their food consists only of the mosquito class, it seems all the more likely that this is the case. The sudden changes of direction these animals make in their flight lend support to this view, for they often alter their course at an angle which, judging from the position of their eyes, cannot possibly be in their line of vision.

May 21.—We stayed over at Groot Barmen the whole of this day in order to feed the mules and to give them a chance of recovering from recent exertions. Fortunately, there was an acre or two of ground round the spring, fenced off, so that we were able to leave them to feed during the night. The two nights we were here were exceedingly cold, the thermometer registering 4 degrees below zero Centigrade.

Four signallers belonging to the 2nd Brigade visited our camp. Both they and their horses appeared very worn. They told us that the road to Windhuk was very rough and difficult in parts, but with regard to grazing and water we would have no difficulty. Their whole brigade was on the way to Okasisi to reorganize, and the one wing under Colonel Badenhorst would pass here either today or tomorrow. We gave these men a few biscuits and a little coffee. They seemed hardly able to believe their eyes, and their delight and gratitude were quite touching. Later we had to send out an ambulance five or six miles to bring in a sick man belonging to this brigade, as they had no waggons or ambulance of their own with them. What the poor fellow must have suffered *trekking* from Windhuk, with his disabilities, I can hardly bear to think.

May 22.—Before we left, part of the 2nd Brigade turned up, and one of their scouts recognised a horse among ours which he said was his. It was a fine grey in good condition, but, as it bore the German Government's brand, we could not very well understand how it could be the legal property of a scout of Albert's brigade, and said so. The trooper rode angrily away, saying he would bring witnesses to prove his claim. He returned bringing witnesses who no doubt swore false witness; but the major was obdurate, and the man retired this time threatening us with his officer. He returned with his officer *plus* the colonel of the brigade. We meanwhile, fearing violent seizure of the animal, hid it away.

But the diplomatic colonel soon wheedled the horse out of us. "Of course," he said, "my scout has no title to the horse; but scouts are scouts, and they cannot scout without horses, and my brigade is now very short of horses."

"In that case," replied the major, "I will surrender the animal, although I am very short of horses, too."

Thus ended an incident which promised to be unpleasant, for the colonel told the scout to thank the major for "giving" him the horse, which the latter did with a good grace. Later I saw our man who had lost the horse consoling himself with a fine brindled bulldog, which he said the scout had given him for the horse. This remarkable dog had *trekked* from Swakupmund to Windhuk and back to Groot Barmen with the brigade. He became much attached to the major, following us all the way to Windhuk, where he unfortunately disappeared.

I had an opportunity of watching the *burghers'* behaviour while they were at this farm. They arrived in a famished condition, and, with the exception of helping themselves to a few pumpkins, they paid for everything they took. It spoke well for the docility and restraint of these men to see them asking the price of butter and cheese, and paying without cavil the somewhat exorbitant sums demanded. By four in the afternoon it was cool enough to make a start. The pleasure of travelling was much interfered with by the number of dead horses on the road. One saw dead animals as early in the trek as Riet, and they became increasingly frequent, until now one might be seen every few hundred yards. The corpses nearly always lay in the road, pointing to the conclusion that they had been ridden until they dropped.

We *trekked* this night to Davisdrohe, and most of the way the road was in the actual bed of the river, high mountains on either side making it impossible for a road to be constructed on either bank. In places it was only with great difficulty that the mules were able to pull the waggons through, for the river-bed here is composed of loose shingle interspersed with boulders and rocks. But, however the river punished us, nobody was ever heard to grumble about it. In or near the river there was always a road, there was always water for the digging, if not wells or springs, and there was always some grazing, even at Swakupmund. Had there been no Swakup River, the advance of the Northern Army could never have been made; the water problem alone would have baffled it.

At Swakupmund, Nonidas, Husab, Riet, Salem, and Otjimbingwe, the river and the river only had supplied us with water. Even after we had passed the desert we drew our water from the same source, for Klein Barmen, Groot Barmen, and all the water-holes up to Windhuk, are on the riverbank. At Tsaobis only did we rely upon other water, and this failed long before the requirements of the army were satisfied. The inexhaustible supply of pure water gushing out of the rock in a waterless waste, as at Riet or Salem, is as much a miracle as when Moses smote upon the rock in Horeb.

It is interesting to notice how the composition of the bed of the river changes gradually as one ascends from the mouth towards the source. At Swakupmund it consists of a fine impalpable mica mud which, when it dries, breaks up into laminated plates with curled-up edges and of considerable hardness. At Otjimbingwe the material in the bed is sand like that of the seashore; not a stone or pebble is to be seen in it. This gradually changes into a coarse gritty sand, and at Davisdrohe, as I have said, the bed is of shingle. Higher up still, boulders and stones predominate. One may conclude that a large stone starting at Windhuk is in the course of ages gradually ground down to powder in its passage to the coast. We get a faint glimpse of what geological time means when we are told that previous to this season the river had not been in flood for about fifteen years.

At Davisdrohe we were obliged to camp in the bed of the river, so broken or precipitous were the banks. It was very cold there, camping on low-lying ground, and whenever possible it is much better to choose an elevated spot to camp on during winter nights. Throughout the campaign cold nights were the rule, and many of the men were very ill supplied with blankets and coats. On some of the treks they were only permitted to carry one blanket or a greatcoat on their saddles. The infantry particularly suffered in this respect, and had not the supply of dry wood to make fires with been most plentiful, I am sure men would have died from exposure and cold.

May 23.—Not finding any water at Davisdrohe, it was necessary to make an early start, and we spanned in at 5 a.m., a heavy frost lying on the ground. During the night the mules had stampeded, and, although the drivers had searched for them all night, two were still missing. At 11 a.m. we came to the farm Otjiseva, where there was a good supply of water pumped up from the river by a gin into a cement tank.

The farmer here, who looked more like a Berlin clerk, did not receive us with enthusiasm. He told us most emphatically that this was a very bad place to outspan, and that good grazing was to be found at a spot three miles farther on. Disregarding his advice, I searched about, and found very tolerable grass nearby, much to his disgust, I fancy; so we outspanned near his house, and borrowed some of his neatly chopped firewood. The lady of the house, popping her head out of the kitchen door, said to her husband in German, "Are there some more of those things here? I thought we had seen the last of them."

Unfortunately for her, a sergeant nearby understood her remark, and on the spur of the moment could think of no better relief to his feelings than pirouetting his horse on her flower-garden until he felt cooler. After this our host and his spouse went inside, and we did not see them again. We left this inhospitable place in the afternoon, passing through rich pastureland along by the river. There were several empty dilapidated houses near the road, and on close inspection one could see that some while back they had been destroyed by fire, in all probability the work of the Hereros during the rebellion. The dust here was worse than any we had encountered. It was as light as flour, and lay on the road a foot thick. The drivers could neither see nor hear the waggon immediately in front of them, so that collisions were frequent, and the mules were constantly leaving the road.

It is quite impossible to do justice to the beauty of the country we passed through this night. The road and river were winding up a narrow gorge, frequently crossing each other. Giant acacias fringed the snow-white bed of the river, and extended to the greensward beyond. White rocks shone like silver in the river or on the mountain-sides, which towered high above everything. Down below on the road a slowly moving cloud of dust represented our cavalcade. All this, illuminated by a most brilliant moon, has left an indelible impression in my memory.

It is wonderful how soon man adapts himself to his surroundings. When we arrived at Walfisch we found walking in the sand most irksome; at Swakupmund we gradually got used to it, though one generally arranged one's peregrinations so that maximum use could be made of the wood pavement and the sleepers of the railway. Now we can walk for hours in the heavy sand with little fatigue. Many men have adopted unconsciously a shortened step and a high vertical lift of the foot. It may be inelegant and like a goose-step, but it is efficient and to be recommended. It seems especially to minimize that fatiguing backslide which is experienced when walking in sand in the ordinary way.

We found a nice wooded rise with an open space for the waggons to outspan on near Ongosi, and soon had a dozen fires going worthy of Guy Fawkes. Seven hours' fast, and most of it spent in walking in the sand uphill, made the despised clinkers with jam and butter most acceptable.

May 24.—The last stage to Windhuk was entered on with great enthusiasm by all, though the formal occupation had taken place nearly a fortnight ago. For five months the word Windhuk had been continually on our lips, and pessimists in Cape Town had told us that we would lose a third of our number in the attempt to take the place, that we would be ambushed in the narrow defiles, and that finally big guns would have to be faced and trenches stormed.

North of Windhuk are beautiful undulating highlands, rising higher and higher until within two or three miles of the town. The country here is well wooded with thorn-trees, and grass is plentiful, now bleached by the winter frosts. About here a few fences are to be seen, separating the farms, but, compared to what we have in the colony, of very inferior construction.

Windhuk lies in a basin on the top of the watershed of the whole country. To the west the land gradually slopes down to the sea, to the south to the Orange River, to the east to the Kalahari, and to the north towards the Kuneni River. It is the pinnacle of the country as well as of our hopes and ambitions. An irregular ridge runs across the basin from north to south. On the eastern side of this ridge is the hamlet of Klein Windhuk, and on the western side Groot Windhuk. The Windhuker Swakup winds through the valley on the eastern side, its source being in the Aus Mountains, which form the southern boundary of the basin. This range of mountains, the highest in German South-West, rises to nearly 9,000 feet, and is the most conspicuous feature in the landscape for fifty miles in every direction. On the west of the town is a conical hill, the Kaiser Wilhelm Berg, beyond which are the Komas Highlands, stretching away to the western horizon. Finally, to the north are the undulating hills through which we had approached.

The whole landscape had a dappled appearance due to the green thorn-trees scattered freely amongst the white grass and sand. The inevitable columns of dust were rising at several points, and the sombre aspect of things was only relieved by the bright red roofs and white walls of the houses. But what riveted the attention above everything else were seven slender black towers standing together in the plain west of the town. Five of these towers are 400 feet high, the other two being a little shorter. They belong to the renowned wireless station, or, as the Germans call it, the "*Telefunken*."

Chapter 7

Windhuk

The first building, or, rather, block of buildings, we came to was flying the Red Cross. We congratulated ourselves on coming to such a fine hospital. It was only the native hospital, however, and still under German control. A smiling caretaker directed us to the military hospital. Not understanding him, but seeing another Red Cross in the centre of the town, we made for that. This was a large building near a church, and in a third building, which looked like a school, we could hear children at a singing class. A nun came to the door. This, she said, was the Catholic Hospital for Women and Children; but again we could not follow her directions, only gathering that the hospital was a long way off. Away to the west, on a hill well out of the town, there was another large building with a flag flying, and with the help of glasses we made out the Geneva Cross again. We charged at this hill like *burghers* at a *kopje*. The building appeared to be a large private house, and a very neat nurse all in white gave us to understand that the soldiers were not here, as it was the Elizabeth Maternity and Nursing Home.

Utterly routed we again descended to the town, and for awhile wandered aimlessly about. Women and children there were in the streets in plenty, and not a few men, some of whom wore semi-military khaki; but they were all obviously Huns. At last we met a single ragged-looking man, carrying rifle and bandolier, and we assailed him with the Dutch and English languages simultaneously. He thought the hospital was away to the south end of the town, and directed us up a steep hill, at the top of which was a new stone church of the modified Noah's Ark type, taller than it was long, with a very high-pitched roof and a slender spire, a gilt clock-face reminding us that half-past three was well past our breakfast-time.

A little beyond this church is the Feste, a sort of old fort with a splendid equestrian statue in front of it; and here we had the first and only proof that we were masters of the place—namely, a cheap little Union Jack about the size of a handkerchief, which was fluttering at the end of a sort of clothes-prop.

The military hospital is at the south end of the town, and a new wing was in course of construction for fever patients. The German contractor was working away at this as usual—so convinced are they that the occupation of the place is only temporary. There is very little of modern construction about the hospital; the administrative block, built round a quadrangle in which are some small coniferous trees, seems to have been an old barracks. The two buildings used for the reception of patients are cold, dark, and cheerless, but the two operating theatres are quite new, and have every modern convenience, and there is a fine X-ray installation. Behind are several large buildings for stores and laboratories. There are good arrangements for sterilizing bedding, etc., and, what seems a little unusual to us, a large aerated-water plant.

We had heard there were vast stores of medical requirements here, but the things we found were not very useful. It seems that when the Germans decided not to defend the capital, the military removed all medical equipment likely to be useful to them; and after the soldiers had gone, civilians were allowed to come and take away anything they liked. Even after we had taken over, German ladies were in the habit of visiting the stores with baskets, and they always seemed to resent being told that everything in the hospital now belonged to His Majesty King George. Among the things in the pharmacy store were large quantities of hypodermic medicaments manufactured in Lisbon. These, the Germans said, had been captured at Naulella from the Portuguese, whom they claimed to have utterly defeated there.

We found nice quarters in the dispenser's house, within the hospital grounds; and having removed most of his mural decorations, which to us seemed a little depraved, we proceeded to make ourselves comfortable therein.

May 25.—Today our section of the ambulance took over the charge of the hospital. Although the wards, beds, and patients, were very clean, the sanitation and general arrangements had been much neglected of late. A German matron is in charge with four German nurses. These are assisted by a few ladies belonging to the Red Cross

The surrender of Windhuk

Society. We find the trained nurses very capable and self-reliant, for it seems that much more is left to them by the doctors than is the case with us. One nurse told me that she was in the habit of doing minor operations, and that she gave all the anaesthetics. When we had occasion to do an operation on a German today, this same nurse kept a careful watch upon the doctor giving the chloroform, feeling the patient's pulse and examining his eyes; but she subsided into her proper sphere when the administrator said to her in a loud voice, "I suppose you think that, not having succeeded in killing a German in battle, I am trying to do so on the operating-table?" After this she never questioned our ability to administer anaesthetics, although she seemed to be a little apprehensive at times.

Until today a German doctor had been in charge of the German wounded and sick, about eighty in number. Fortunately for us, he has quarrelled with the matron, and has refused to continue to attend unless she is discharged. As the major considered her the more useful of the two, he has been allowed to depart, and is now, we hear, spending his time accusing us and her of neglect of duty. Later in the day a petition comes in almost demanding the discharge of the matron and reinstatement of the doctor. We reply by running up the Union Jack and having sentries posted round the hospital. There are a good many German soldiers in the hospital suffering from typhoid, and they tell us it has been very prevalent among them, also that their inoculation against the disease has been a failure.

Up till now, on the other hand, the disease has been practically non-existent in our army, and among the inoculated men no case has occurred. This result is a striking testimony to the efficacy of inoculation, for our men at Swakupmund and elsewhere often lived for weeks together under most insanitary conditions. The German wounded, some forty in number, are now under my care. It seems they nearly all received their wounds in a battle they had with the Bastards near Rehoboth on May 8. The Germans claim to have defeated these people, but admit having lost a good many men.

The Bastards, although for the most part armed with rifles of 1871 pattern, seem to have done some very good shooting, one man under cover killing five Germans by shooting them through the head, while another rendered a machine gun useless. The wounds of the Germans also point to accurate marksmanship. Three men have superficial wounds in the back received when lying on their faces, while in the act of raising themselves a little to alter their positions. Another was shot through the right hand, as he rolled over a little, the better to open the bolt of his rifle. Apart from their wounds, these men are in very good condition, and do not look at all like men who have been engaged in arduous guerrilla warfare. Their uniforms, boots, and hats, are quite new, clean, and untorn. Herein is found a cue to their ill-success in this campaign; for, unless they were compelled to do so, they did not leave the railways or roads, and never moved without ample transport and food. Whenever they attacked us, they came down the line or along the road. They prepared fortified positions, and built light railways up to them, and whenever we captured them they had transport and food and drink in abundance. General Botha's men had quite different ideas about fighting. They *trekked* without transport and without sufficient food or clothing; they crossed deserts and mountains irrespective of roads; and the last thing they thought of was to make a frontal attack or fight when the Germans expected them to.

I cannot say that I am very much impressed with the German methods of treating wounds in this hospital. The healing strength of nature has been given very little scope, the surgeon apparently taking full responsibility. The wounds are plugged to overflowing with gauze and various chemicals in what appears to the uninitiated an indiscriminate manner. To say the least of it, the patients themselves are very uncomfortable with these dressings on, for under our simpler methods the complaints of pain and discomfort were immediately fewer.

The German soldier at home may be a stoic, but he certainly is not one here, and the way he endures his hurts does not impress one. I found him nervous and excitable, taking a morbid interest in his wound and in the minutiae of treatment. For the most part he sleeps very badly, and demands and expects to get an hypnotic for the asking. He knows the names of these, and prefers veronal or chloral. He is quite familiar, too, with the hypodermic syringe, and both the patients and the nurses in charge were surprised when I ordered that morphia was not to be given without my consent. I talked the matter over with the matron, and she readily admitted that life in the colonies did not improve the physical and moral fibre of the men. She admired the way our wounded behaved, and especially the nonchalant manner in which they came up for anaesthetic and operation.

I think it is not very far from the truth to say that the Germans here have lived in a constant state of dread and apprehension of the various native inhabitants, and this, together with every form of self-indulgence imaginable, has sapped their virility and confidence. "Poor man!" a nurse would say when a certain individual put up a very poor show during the dressing of his wound; "he is very nervous; he has been two years in the Kameruns, and has had fever." One felt like replying: "Maybe; but he eats too much and drinks far too much; he indulges in tobacco, and possibly drugs; his licentiousness is unequalled; and no doubt the dying agonies of the natives he has witnessed worry him a bit, too."

I believe the Germans here are heavy drinkers, although I must say that since I have been in Windhuk I have never seen one the worse for liquor. But there is very conclusive indirect evidence to show that they drink a lot. A small place like Swakupmund had over thirty hotels and beer-shops. Breweries and distilleries abound; I don't think it is an exaggeration to say that it would not be safe to walk anywhere in the country with bare feet, because you would cut yourself with broken glass. On the mountain-tops, in the desert or bush, you find bottles; you see buildings and walls made of bottles and mud; garden paths and beds are ornamented with them; and where German troops have camped you see regular pyramids of them. Whenever we captured their convoys we found quantities of liquor, chiefly rum of good quality.

May 28.—There has been a good deal of talk about mines since we have been here. To delay our advance, the Germans relied almost entirely upon this mode of fighting. On the line of advance to Karibib, in the bed of the Swakup, and along the road from Riet to Otjimbingwe, dynamite was placed in great quantity. Not only were these mines put in places where we were likely to go, such as drifts in riverbeds, or near wells, but the Huns also laid traps for us. A favourite ruse was to put a mine in a riverbed, and then near it to put up a notice, such as "*Wasser* 3 kilos." In these places we never found the water, but generally the mine. Another trick was to place a stick of dynamite above a house door, so that when the door was opened an explosion occurred. As soon as our men discovered this kind of practical joke, everybody was to be seen entering houses by the windows.

The number of mines the Germans laid was very great. In one place alone between seventy and eighty were taken out. At Tsaobis we slept within a few yards of a large one which was subsequently accidentally exploded by a native. It was cunningly placed between the well and the river, and hundreds of people must have walked over it. By putting down so many the enemy defeated their own object, for our men became very quick at finding and avoiding the places where they were. Later on, too, when so many failed to explode or did so little damage, we became more or less indifferent about them. In all only nine men lost their lives in this way, which was due in great measure to two causes, the first being the straggling, scattered way in which our troops moved, so that very few were near when a mine did explode; and, secondly, for some inexplicable reason, the mines generally failed to explode at all, or only exploded after nearly everybody had passed, as in the case already mentioned, where an artillery column passed over safely, and the harmless water-cart and its driver, following far behind, were blown up.

As far as I know, the well at Riet was the only place where the Germans might have done us real damage by mines. There after the fight, and when the Germans had evacuated the place, hundreds of men and horses crowded down to the water in spite of warnings. Had the large mine there gone off, 200 or 300 *burghers* must have gone into the air, which would have had a most deterrent effect upon them; for it was their first experience of mines, which, until they became familiar with them, they held in great awe. As it was, they regarded the incident as a very good omen and evidence of Divine intervention, a point of view their astute leaders made the most of. As a matter of fact, somebody favouring our cause had tampered with the wires, unbeknown to a German who was vainly endeavouring to explode the mine when discovered; as, of course, the Burgher leaders very well knew, but they wisely allowed their men to think otherwise.

The Germans employed both contact and observation mines, using the latter only at very important points where they hoped to do great execution. I only heard of observation mines at two places, Riet being one; the other was the narrow neck of beach between the sand-dunes and the sea just south of Swakupmund, the only way our troops could approach the town from Walfisch. Contact mines were arranged in various ingenious ways, the commonest being exploded by connecting an innocent-looking peg or stump to a detonator consisting of sulphuric acid and a mixture of chlorate of potash and picric acid. These chemicals were in separate glass phials, and when the peg was touched the phials were broken and the resulting explosion fired the dynamite beneath. Another kind consisted of a small wooden box with a hinged lid, which was buried in the sand, with the lid propped open a little bit. As soon as any weight was placed on the sand-covered lid, the box closed and an electrical contact was made which fired the dynamite.

If anything, I think the mines encouraged our men to fight rather than the reverse. They considered it a very unsportsmanlike way of fighting. On one occasion in the Swakup, when the troops were very much done up and discouraged, a mine exploded, destroying the eyesight of one man and partially that of another. The effect on the troops was magical; every man forgot his fatigue and thought only of revenge. From the German point of view, too, the indiscriminate scattering of dynamite about could only be considered foolish; for it had no military significance, and only irritated their enemies. On one or two occasions our troops were made so angry by these pinpricks that they were with difficulty restrained from putting Germans to death who happened to be in their hands at the moment.

May 30.—The Germans were very wise when they made a capital at Windhuk. Perhaps I should have said "manufactured" a capital, for the town at once gives one the idea of having been placed here in a new and complete state, and not to have grown, as towns are generally expected to do. Of course, what primarily brought them here is the water-supply, which seems to be inexhaustible. Wherever a borehole is put down, there water seems to be, and, besides these, the hot water gushes out of the rocks in several places, just as at Barmen. At one of these springs is a bathing and washing house where a hot bath can be had for the asking. Then the site is splendid; for although there are mountains on every side, the outlook is not in any way restricted by them, and, as the bulk of the buildings are on the irregular slopes of a well-wooded hill, there has been no difficulty in making the place very picturesque. The streets run north and south, more or less parallel to the hill and at different levels, and the broken nature of the ground has prevented the place taking on that rectangular arrangement which spoils so many colonial towns.

The main street, known hitherto as the Kaiser-Wilhelm-Strasse, is just at the foot of the hill. In it are nearly all the shops, stores, and hotels, as well as the bank and post-office. This street alone is well paved, all the others being still in a very rough and stony condition. Below the Kaiser-Wilhelm-Strasse are what one might call the "slums," and at its lower or northern end it opens out into a sort of square where the station, gymnasium, and gaol are situated. I had occasion to visit this latter place several times. Outside it is not so bad, surrounded as it is with an attempt at a garden and pepper-trees, but inside a more dismal, dark, cold, forbidding place it is difficult to imagine. The gaoler told me that, when he took over, the place literally swarmed with bugs, and that it would be the refinement of cruelty to put prisoners in many of the cells. Yet it was here that many British subjects, military and civilian, were confined for many weeks.

The governor's palace, the public buildings, and the residences of government officials and the well-to-do, are all built on the side of the hill. The palace is not much of a place, but it has beautiful gardens in which palms predominate, and is surrounded by trees. The houses in this part of the town are very nice, often perched on high rocks with winding paths leading up to them, and terraced gardens below. What strikes one about them is that no two houses are alike. Some of them have very fantastic shapes, especially as regards the roofs.

For a long time before Windhuk became the capital, it was a Rhenish mission-station, and the buildings belonging to this period can easily be distinguished from the more modern ones; for, instead of being plastered and of ornate design, they are built of plain red brick, and are of simple and severe pattern.

When Windhuk surrendered, not many able-bodied men were in the place; but there were a great number of women and children, mostly belonging to the poorer classes, who had come in from distant parts when the Union troops approached, or who feared to remain on the farms after their men-folk had left. Altogether there were about 3,000 young children in the place besides grown-ups, and the bulk of them were very badly off for provisions, and had to be fed by the Union Government. We were told that only those civilians who could provide themselves with three months' rations were allowed to retire north to Otavi and Grootfontein, which explains why so many people were left at Windhuk.

The shops are open from ten to twelve and from four to six, but, with the exception of the butchers, very little trade is going on, for the shopkeepers have little to sell and the people but little to spend. A certain amount of trade is being done with the military at very exorbitant rates, the provost-marshal not having fixed any tariff. The inhabitants pretend to go about their ordinary avocations as if we were not here. They dress up in the afternoons, and parade the streets or drive about in their cumbersome spiders. Men are to be seen in the beer-gardens making shift with one mug of beer, the supply of which is very low on account of the shortage of grain.

One cannot help but admire the way they brazen it out. The fact that they have been in a state of siege for ten months, the fact that we have taken their capital without a blow, and that their troops are scattering and fleeing before us, does not depress them; for they know that their Emperor's troops are on the way to relieve them. Meanwhile they kill us with looks or ignore us altogether, except a few dashing ladies whose duty it is to glean what information they can from our officers. In consequence of this sort of thing I hear, though how true it may be I do not know, that a general order has been issued forbidding all social intercourse with enemy subjects.

I am very much impressed by the German colonial woman. In spite of her somewhat flat feet, loose, rotund figure, and cold blue eye, she is a very fine animal, full-blooded, active, and self-reliant. In the absence of the men, many farmers' wives and daughters are managing estates, riding about among the natives, protected only by their own rifle or revolver, acting hostess and spy with a *sang-froid* which compels admiration. Her father, husband, brothers, and sons, are fugitives or prisoners, her larder and purse almost empty; but pride and determination alone are written on her countenance. She rears a goodly number of white-haired, sturdy little square-heads whom she will give to the emperor without qualm or regret. Fortunately for us and for civilization, her mate is rarely her equal. Past middle life, he is debauched-looking, flabby, and dyspnoeic; a *Landsturm* raised in Windhuk would be very small beer.

May 31.—Today I visited the native location, situated on a rounded hill a little distance west of the town, where there are said to be about 10,000 natives, mostly Hereros with a sprinkling of Hottentots. The place is laid out in a very orderly manner. The streets all radiate from the summit of the hill, where there are benches, an ornamental pond, and a flag-pole, the sides of each street being lined with tins painted white, in each of which there is a tree, either a pepper or a eucalyptus. At present these trees are only small, but when they grow the place will be quite imposing. But the huts themselves are the most miserable habitations imaginable.

In his natural state the Herero builds a circular hut about 10 feet in diameter, with a rounded roof, the whole thing having the shape of the upper end of an egg. These huts are normally built of long sticks bent over to form the roof, the intervening spaces being filled in with mud, and the roof thatched. Beaver-like, the Hereros have tried here to keep to this design, but, not having the necessary materials, they

Native location—Windhuk

have attempted to make the huts with any material that came to hand, such as roofing iron, petrol tins flattened out, bits of plank and sacking. The effect is very bizarre, and to most of these dwellings wind and rain must find a ready entrance.

For the most part the people are well dressed and clean-looking. The women are much more comely than Bantus usually are, and have very peculiar and distinctive figures. They are tall and thin; at least, viewed from the front or back they look very thin, due to a narrowness across the shoulders, which approaches deformity. They make up from before backwards what they lack from side to side; thus, their figures give you the idea of having been compressed laterally. The dress they affect accentuates these peculiarities, for they wear their waists just under their armpits, and they fold a handkerchief, or *duk*, the shape of an ordinary flowerpot, and wear it on the head.

Of the various peoples in the country, the Germans can only claim to have subdued the Hereros, who seem to be a very docile and peace-loving race. What are left of them the Germans have reduced to a state of slavery by a very simple and efficient means. They do not allow the Hereros to own cattle or land except under conditions which make it next to impossible. In order to live, therefore, these people must work, their pay being about 10 *marks* a month; and this they must spend at the German storekeeper's, the only place where food is to be obtained. There is no doubt whatever that the Germans have treated these people systematically with the greatest cruelty. Their lives are of little account; since we have been in Windhuk several bodies of murdered natives have been exhumed and their murderers brought to justice. One man readily admitted shooting a native. "But why make such a fuss about it?" he queried.

I have several times seen the shackles used by the Germans; they are very heavy, and remind one of those used in the Middle Ages. A common practice was to chain five prisoners together legs, arms, and necks in such a manner that if one wanted to move it disturbed the others. I have also seen photographs of executions and floggings, all very barbarous. Natives are generally hanged to trees with their arms free, so that they linger a long time, preventing suffocation by holding on to the reins with their hands. Around may be seen a group of German soldiers apparently enjoying the proceedings.

On one occasion our troops found some bodies hanging from a branch by means of barbed wire round the necks. Bodies, too, were found fastened together in graves, with every indication of having been buried alive. German soldiers and others had regular *harems* of Herero women, who, when they happened to have a child, were given a few goats and cut adrift.

An attempt was made by societies in Germany to prevent the obvious evil of colonising the country with "Eurafricans,": and large numbers of German girls have been sent out, ostensibly as barmaids, telephone clerks, and typists, but their fate is often little better than that of their African sisters. It is quite a common thing to find at the farms, not a *frau*, but a *fraulein*, living with the farmer. Her position, of course, is quite insecure, but the custom seems to receive social recognition, and nobody thinks any the worse of her.

June 1.—We have started an out-patient department at the hospital for the troops. Several units are here without medical officers, and in other cases the regimental doctors are engaged in chasing about the country doing post-mortems and attending exhumations of murdered natives. Every morning at nine the *burghers* flock to the sick parade in great numbers. About 10 *per cent*, have toothache, 20 *per cent*, a skin complaint which we call *veldt* sores, another 20 *per cent*, have intestinal complaints resulting from improper food, and the remaining 50 *per cent*, are malingerers or attend for a little diversion.

The unwisdom of allowing men with slight defects to go on active service is now very apparent, for men who are desirous of getting home use these defects as a means to that end, and, although they may be suffering no inconvenience, we have to believe them. One ingenuous man wanted to get a sick discharge in order that he might, so he said, go to Europe to fight. Among the men who attend are many fine old back-*veldters*, who nearly all fought against us in the Great War, as they call the Boer War. Most of them have wounds to show; one has eleven, with two British bullets still in him; yet he is now willing to extend the British Empire since General Botha is doing so.

These men will stand rifle-fire all day at 1,000 yards or so, but they are nervous about the big guns, and don't quite like the machine guns since the experiences at Jackalswater. Many of them are now armed with Mausers, which they prefer to the Lee-Enfield. They think it inflicts a more deadly wound, and this is the view the Germans hold, too. A few days ago a German officer attempted to blow up the line, but was shot and captured. The first thing he said, when taken, was, "Was I shot with one of our rifles or one of yours?"

On being told he was shot with a German rifle, he replied, "I am done for, then."

One thing I have certainly noticed with regard to the Mauser bullets is that, if they meet with resistance, such as buttons or bones, they are very easily stripped of their nickel casing, and the lead, spreading or breaking up, makes a very large wound; sometimes, indeed, there are several exit wounds.

The *burghers* never look like fighting men when off their horses, but now they look less like soldiers than ever. Much of their original clothing has been worn out, and the necessary substitutions have not always a military cut. Quite a number of men are entirely clothed in German uniforms, which may lead to complications if fighting should occur. A few days ago a motor-driver lost his life because he was wearing a German hat. He approached the farm of a Bastard, who, mistaking him for a German, shot him dead. The Rehoboth Bastards were much upset by this incident, and offered to shoot the man who had made the mistake, or hand him over to us for justice, so anxious are they to conciliate General Botha's armies.

The Germans about here are now broken up into small parties, which our men may be said to hunt. The present object of the enemy is to harass us by interfering with the train service between here and Karibib. Every few days they succeed in doing damage to the line; but it can only be slight, for the daily service of trains is rarely interfered with. We hear they nearly succeeded in blowing up the big suspension-bridge at Okahandya, a very fine effort, seeing that an infantry regiment was detailed to protect the bridge.

Six men of Hunt's scouts captured twenty-four Germans the other night. It was very dark, and the scouts heard some waggons lumbering along the road, so they lined up in the bush close to where the waggons were to pass. The unsuspecting Huns were riding on the waggons, some being asleep, and were quite taken by surprise when our men appeared suddenly out of the bush. Pointing their rifles at the reposing foe, with a "Come down out of that!" the thing was accomplished. Having no bayonets, the scouts mounted guard with the weapons of the prisoners, whom they put in a cattle *kraal* for safety's sake until the morning. The prisoners' disgust was extreme, next morning, when they saw how few their captors were, and they were inclined to be truculent; but a few prods with their own bayonets quickly rendered them docile.

June 4.—The army is now "reorganising"—that is, resting and getting fit for another dash northward. The headquarters of the various brigades extend from Karibib to Windhuk along the line; General Britz's brigade form the left wing. They are to advance left of the line towards Elosha Pan, and have perhaps the longest and most difficult march. Their horses have been sent down the line so that they can be more easily fed from Swakupmund. A large number of infantry are concentrating at Karibib: the Rhodesians and 2nd Kimberleys of Trekkoppi fame, also the 1st Durban Light Infantry. General Bere's brigade has been brought round from Luderitzbucht, consisting of the Pretoria Regiment, the Transvaal Scottish, and the Wit Rifles.

General Lukin's brigade of the South African Mounted Rifles have also joined the Northern Army, and are at or near Karibib. The Free Staters, under Marnie Botha, have their headquarters at Johann-Albrechtshöhe. The right wing of our brigade, the 3rd, is at Wilhelmstaal under Colonel Jordaan; Colonel Albert's brigade, the 2nd, is at Okasisi. The Rand Rifles are at Okahandya, and we, the left wing of the 3rd Brigade, under Colonel Mentz, are at Windhuk, although the bulk of it is to go to Okahandya to take part in the advance. It will therefore appear that, if Grootfontein be the objective, General Britz, on the left, will have to go farther than anyone else. We at Windhuk will not get very far, I fear, but remain behind in case the Germans break back. Nominally, Colonel Mentz's troops remain the garrison of Windhuk, but they may be relieved by General Mackenzie's Natal Mounted regiments, who are advancing north along the line from Gibeon, and whose scouts have already entered Rehoboth.

Some of Colonel Berrangé's Eastern Army who have *trekked* across the Kalahari from Vryburg through Rietfontein are also on the way up through Keetmanshoop. General Van der Venter's Southern Army turned back at Keetmanshoop, and have been disbanded with the exception of the heavy artillery under Colonel Devine, who are very slowly coming up this way from Upington. Practically speaking, our front can now be said to extend from Karibib to Okahandya, a distance of about sixty miles. I cannot say now how many troops are taking part in the final advance, for the Burgher brigades are being very much reduced, men being allowed to return home on very trivial grounds. We of the left wing (3rd Brigade) were about 1,400 strong at Wynberg; now I don't suppose we have more than 500 effectives. I don't think any of the mounted brigades exceed 1,000 strong, and the infantry 500 to 600 in a regiment, which would give a total of about 9,000 men.

A good many officers, too, some of high rank, have been given their *congé*. Some, we are told, are burning to take part in the political campaign. There is, of course, a strong political vein running through the whole *burgher* army. To some extent this is unavoidable, owing to the commando system. Naturally, the government appoint a man as commandant in a district who is one of their supporters, and who is more trustworthy than the Parliamentary representative? Either the commandant has become M.L.A. or the M.L.A. has become *commandant*.

In some cases this arrangement has worked quite well. Young men who proved themselves in the Boer War, and subsequently entered Parliament, have in not a few cases proved themselves good leaders now; but in other cases, I regret to say, men have been put into high positions purely because of their political status or command of votes. Even in the medical corps there are several members of Parliament, all holding the rank of Lieutenant-Colonel. In fact, I never heard of an M.L.A. holding a lower rank than Major. We have yet to acquire that altruistic spirit which compels men of note to shoulder the rifle as the French senators are doing.

In a scratch army like ours, soon to be disbanded, these soldier politicians can do little harm; but, unfortunately, the political element has been allowed to enter our permanent defence force. Beyers, the first Commandant-General, was a man belonging to a political party, and when the crisis arrived he abused his military position, with the disastrous results so well known. If recent happenings do not teach us that our defence force must be kept free from political bias, then many useful lives have been lost in vain.

The medical service is also undergoing reorganisation, for it is now abundantly clear to the authorities that the field ambulances are not sufficiently mobile for this kind of warfare. Medical officers are to have more horses, and a greater number of the orderlies are to be mounted and attached directly to the commandoes. Most important of all, the O.C. of the medical unit is to be attached to the brigadier's staff, instead of being with the tent subdivision of the ambulance, which is always in the rear. In this way it is hoped the ambulance will be kept in touch with the troops and get early advice of their movements.

On the way up we generally had to fend for ourselves, and were left without escort or even orders. Or we would receive a belated order, such as this: "Follow the spoor of the ammunition waggons." We were always forgotten until a few men were hurt, and then there was considerable outcry if we were not on the spot. But this lack of cohesion is evident all through, and is due to one cause, and one cause only—namely, a dearth of properly trained staff officers.

I wish to goodness they would "reorganise" the ambulance waggons, which are of bad construction and worse design, being much too light and furnished with bad springs. Moreover each one only holds two severe cases, and it seems to be a great waste of energy for twelve mules to be engaged in transporting two wounded men. Even when one feels well and strong it is pain and grief to ride in these ambulances, and an officer suffering from severe lumbago, who was invalided down from Riet after the battle, told me that he preferred to walk rather than ride in them. Never shall I forget the agonised expressions of some German wounded whom I brought in from the Riet affair. Time was pressing, we made the mules trot a good deal, and the waggons bumped horribly. When these men write their memoirs, they won't forget to mention their experiences of the ambulance waggons of the South African Medical Corps.

June 6.—Away to the south-east runs a very impressive and inviting range of mountains, known as the Auas, culminating in a point known as the Moltkeblick, to which the maps give an elevation of 8,141 feet. Together with an Africander colleague, I rode out today to make a preliminary survey of this range with a view to climbing it on a future occasion. The road passes east over a ridge into the peaceful hamlet of Klein Windhuk, where the chief means of livelihood seems to be vine-growing. The soil is very full of lime, and the grape seems to do very well. Good local wine is to be had at a convent here, although the worthy Sisters tell you that selling to the military is; verboten.': But in this as well as other matters here we do not respect the German *"verboten,"* for everything is forbidden to everybody everywhere. You see this vile word on every public building, in streets and parks, on mountain-tops and in the bush. If the Prussian system withholds most of the things worth living for from its own adherents, what will it be like for us when "the day" arrives?

Riding through this little village, where the younger Germans were attending Sunday-school and the older ones drinking beer, we arrived among the foot-hills of the Auas Mountains. It would have been the usual quiet Sunday afternoon but for the continuous reports of guns and rifles in the valleys around. It was as if an infantry battle were in progress, but in reality it was only *burghers* shooting guinea-fowl and any other game that was not entirely scared away. Guinea-fowl literally swarm in these parts, and one sees whole acres of ground along the watercourses scratched up by them, and resembling the surface of the ordinary circumscribed fowl-run.

We climbed a neighbouring hill which goes by the name of the Kudu Berg. The view from the top was very extensive, except towards the south, where the Auas Mountains towered above everything. One could not help noticing the arrangement of all the mountains within sight, which were on a very definite plan. The mountains hereabout are composed largely of a mica-sandstone, or, rather, what geologists call a mica-schist, with a good deal of intrusive granite. The strata forming the mountains have all been tilted in one direction, and all at the same angle. The angle the *strata* make with the horizontal is something between 15 and 20 degrees, and the dip is towards the north-west. The ascent of any mountain here from the north is easy; you climb at an angle of 20 degrees or so, but without fail, as soon as you are on the crest, you encounter a precipitous jagged descent of 70 or 80 degrees towards the south. The whole thing gives one the impression of a gigantic incoming tide suddenly solidified. The great and small waves all have the same shape and direction, the gradual rise to the crest and then the sudden fall.

As I have said, there is a good deal of granite scattered about among the sandstone, which, being the harder, resists to a much greater extent the softening effects of the weather, so that the final result is that not only the mountains and the valleys, but also the streets of Windhuk, are covered with loose hard pebbles of granite, which make walking and riding very tedious.

On the way home we called at the farm of an Italian living in rather a poor way. At first he was not inclined to be very communicative. He was under the impression that things were going very badly with the Allies in Europe, and that we were about to be bundled out of German West. The Germans had told him that London was in flames, Calais and Warsaw taken, and that England, Russia, and France, were *kaput*, a word we hear frequently on German lips, and equivalent to utterly destroyed plus damned. We assured him that none of these things were so, and then he came down on our side of the fence without reserve. "The Germans call us Italians 'dirty pigs' now," he said, spitting on the ground with great emphasis, "and will crush us under foot like beetles; but we will show them!" and he destroyed several imaginary Germans in a very quixotic manner.

To turn the conversation into a quieter channel, I asked him if an urchin standing by eating a tomato, and whose colour and hair suggested Bantu blood diluted with a paler mixture, belonged to him.

"Yes, but my two *sons* at home are *soldats* fighting for Italy now."

"Your wife is dead, of course?"

"Oh no, she is in Italy, too." And then, with a laugh, he told us he had also a wife in Brazil, one in Buenos Ayres, two in Cape Town, one in Okahandya; "and this one," pointing to a Herero woman standing by, holding a squalling brat. "The Herero is the best of the lot," concluded this polygamous father of thirty-three children.

"Hadn't we better be going" gasped the astonished and faithful Africander.

June 10.—Every morning at nine the able-bodied Windhukers turn up at the Feste for roll-call, and this morning all were there as usual. The provost marshal called out the names of fifty-five prominent citizens, asking them to step forward. "Gentlemen, the train for Cape Town leaves at eleven. You have two hours to prepare yourselves."

What a shock! Protestations, remonstrations, all in vain. One, a medical, pleaded a weak heart. "You, a doctor," replied the inexorable provost, "ought to know that heart disease does better at the coast."

Another pleaded: "I live at Klein Windhuk, and have only this thin overmantle."

"We will lend you some blankets," was all the satisfaction he got.

They were all at the station at eleven, their women folk seeing them off, a special guard of fifty soldiers and a Maxim looking on. An account of each man's offence went down, too, most being guilty of attempting to communicate with the enemy. On the whole it was a very well-managed affair, reminiscent of the Government's seizure of the strike leaders.

Standing about Windhuk Station are a lot of derelict locomotives; but there are some besides which are quite in good condition, but we cannot work them because the Germans have removed some of the essential parts and hidden them. Some genius hit on the following plan to recover the parts: German engineers were offered a pound a day if they would work the engines. Money being scarce, the lost parts were soon forthcoming, and the engines put into working order, when the services of the would-be drivers were dispensed with.

June 12.—Our military politicians are employing their best endeavours to find out what share the Germans took in the rebellion;

for it will obviously be a powerful weapon in the hands of the government if it can be proved that the rebel leaders were in league with the Germans. Judging from what leaks out, there seems to be little doubt that Beyers was plotting with the *Kaiser* as early as 1913. The *Kaiser* sent wireless messages to Beyers after the war broke out, which were conveyed to him through Maritz and a certain De Wet who was resident in the country. When matters seemed ripe, Dr. Seitz went down to Warmbad to discuss things with Beyers, but the latter did not turn up owing to the shooting of Delarey. A German in Windhuk who is in the know admitted that a certain well-known Africander was to have been President of the new republic, but "now we are in the mud he knows nothing about it." Unfortunately for truth, the wireless tapes at the *Telefunken* relating to these transactions are not forthcoming, although those interested have used every effort to find them.

There is every reason to believe that the Union Government knew well enough about Beyers' little game; but the evidence against him was too indefinite, and his seizure would, no doubt, have precipitated the rebellion.

Now, although the Germans fostered the rebellion, there does not seem to be very much evidence pointing to their having made preparations for invasion of the Union. There are people who say that the Herero Rebellion was a very much overrated affair, that the Germans kept it going so that they might introduce large quantities of stores and munitions into the country without exciting suspicion. The country is certainly very well stocked with war material; besides what we have found, the Germans have destroyed a lot, and probably hidden a lot more. In Windhuk, for instance, there was a tremendous quantity of horseshoes, sufficient to shoe all the horses in South Africa for four years, as one man put it.

Speaking generally, the roads in the country are very poor, often mere tracks following the lines of least resistance. But there is one road running east and west through Windhuk which, from the excellence of its construction, at once made us think that it had been made for a special purpose. It is very wide, and could accommodate four vehicles abreast; embankments and cuttings have been freely used, and the surface is well metalled. From Windhuk it runs east through Seeis out towards Gobabis, near the Bechuanaland border, and westward it passes through Hensis towards Otjimbingwe.

Of course, there is no reason why the Germans should not make good roads, but this one neither links up important places nor taps populous districts, and the conclusion which comes naturally to the mind is that the Germans had the idea of using it as a military route for the invasion of the Union. When the Germans were questioned as to what this road was for, the reason given was not very satisfactory. They said that when Herr Dernburg visited the country he expressed a desire to go in the direction of Gobabis, so they had the road put in order for him!

CHAPTER 8

To Otjihangwe

June 17.—There is much tedium in war; but it is like holding lottery tickets: the suspended hope of excitement or reward prevents *ennui*. Today I got a little change which was very welcome after three weeks attending to a lot of wounds which do not seem to get very much better. News came in that there had been fighting at a distant outpost, and, there being no regimental doctors available for the duty, I was deputed to go.

Nobody seemed to know where the place was, what the name of it was, or what had been the nature of the fighting. Besides our own motor ambulance, the O.C. motor transport kindly put a large 35 h.p. Chalmers at our disposal, and came himself, bringing with him a greasy little bantam driver whom they called Chipp. "It's seventy miles," says Chipp. "I can do it in three and a half hours."

"I can't do it at all: my radiator pipe is leaking," puts in the somewhat pessimistic driver of the ambulance.

However, with the liberal use of hospital plaster and string the leak is stayed. At noon we are ready to start, with a good supply of rations and plenty of petrol. The Chalmers looks very business-like, all bonnet and box-seat, the body being replaced by a crude wooden seat with a large sort of tray behind. Knowing the weaknesses of the ambulance well, I chose the box-seat of the Chalmers, between O.C. and Chipp, the pessimistic driver and our tried sergeant-major following in the ambulance.

"We ought to have had the Red Cross on this car," says the O.C. as we pass over the hill into Klein Windhuk.

"Hadn't we better keep close to the ambulance?" is the best I can suggest. For the first dozen miles or so our way lay along the main-road which runs through Windhuk towards Gobabis, near our border in latitude 22° S.

This road is different to any I have seen in this country. It looks like a road with a purpose, making for its destination regardless of obstacles. Such a road the Romans might have made. It is quite new; in fact, it does not appear to be finished. The O.C. voiced my thought when he said: "The Germans were making this road to invade the Union by." One was glad to leave it at Kapp and turn to the left, so as to get away from such an outward and visible sign of German purpose and design. So far we had skirted the northern slopes of the Auas Mountains, but here the range comes to a sudden end with a rugged peak called Auas Ende, and a fine plain opens out, stretching east as far as one can see. At the foot of the mountain here is a farm known as Swartz-Klip, where the Germans killed a lot of Hereros, and lost a few men themselves, as the graves show.

Skirting some *kopjes* to the left, we soon made Neudamm, which is a government farm with a beautiful natural dam among the rocks, orchards, and some substantial farm buildings. Here we picked up our *burgher* guide, who had ridden in after the fight to telephone for us. He looked very fagged, and well he might, for he had been two nights and a day in the saddle, with no sleep, little food, and the excitement of a fight thrown in. Even he did not know the name of the place we were going to, but said it was 120 kilometres. They all talk of kilometres in these parts; the word ' mile ' is not used. I, who have not learnt to think in the Metric System, translated this into seventy-two miles, but our speedometer subsequently showed that this was the distance from Windhuk.

We now entered the real upland bush country, flat, with *spitzkopjes* standing up here and there, the grass, bleached by the winter sun and frosts, standing knee-high. The country is well wooded with acacias, nearly all of the *wachteinbilje* variety. It is an ideal part for stock, especially cattle, and is full of game, such as buck of various kinds (especially *kudu*), zebra, guinea-fowl, partridge, ostriches, together with such *carnivora* as leopards and jackals. About 4 p.m. we came to a large farm, Mecklenburg, where a very big dam is being constructed. The two occupants spoke English well. I asked one his nationality.

He prevaricated: "I am a British subject."

"Where were you born?'

"In Cape Town," he replied. "I came here in August to manage this farm, and have not heard from home since."

It might be coincidence, but this was the third "British subject" I had found managing a farm for a German owner within a short while. The advantage of this arrangement to the farmer is obvious under present conditions.

The roads about here are really good, for the surface of the country is flat and the soil gravelly and porous. Pointed kopjes stick up here and there on the horizon; we were practically above the mountains. At sunset we came to another farm, Ongono Gotjari, a very bare-looking place where most of the Pietersburg commando were. Our destination was still eleven miles farther on, and we covered this in less than half an hour, so good was the road.

The *commandant* met me with, "I'm very glad to see you, doctor. They killed two of my men yesterday, and wounded three." His eyes looked tired, anxious, and angry, and a state of restlessness and worry seemed to pervade the whole place. I went straight to the badly wounded man. His white face was all I could see in the dark, stuffy little room. Shot through the stomach, and a leg shattered, his case was hopeless; but he was patient and reasonable, though obviously dying. As he was lying in an utter state of discomfort and filth, we tried to make him a little more comfortable. Another man was shot through the neck from side to side. How the bullet had avoided his spine was a mystery. He was fussy and restless, more frightened than hurt.

Speaking generally, the majority of wounded men seem to be in a peculiar psychological state, apart from the shock and collapse, which I can only describe as hysterical. This applies particularly to men who are shot quite unexpectedly, as, for example, those who are ambushed or shot accidentally. It was pathetic to see how gently and unremittingly their comrades tended the wounded. Nothing was too much trouble. Yet they, poor fellows! were played out with fatigue and anxiety. One old man refused to leave the dying boy. They were neighbours at home, he said, and the lad always asked for him if he went out. Our sporting guide, as if he had not already done enough, must needs also hang about and do his bit of the nursing.

As a sleeping-place the farmhouse was very uninviting, and I preferred to brave the elements, bivouacking with my men under the lee of the motorcar. The night was terribly cold, and this, combined with getting up at intervals to attend the wounded, put sleep out of the question. It was with relief and hope that I saw the morning star appear in the east about 6 a.m. I remembered it was the centenary of Waterloo, and the thought of what our forefathers did on that day warmed my benumbed limbs a little. Our blankets were frozen stiff;

the water in our water-bottles and a little milk we had were also congealed.

June 18.—During today I heard various accounts of the little fight, and how our men had been outwitted by the enemy.

A certain lieutenant of the Pietersburg commando with his troops had visited the farm a few days previously, and had been received and kindly treated by the farmer. He made arrangements to come again on the 15th and take over some mealies from the farmer. A German officer with a patrol was known to be scouting in the neighbourhood. On or before the 15th he sends a telephone message to the Pietersburg commandant, asking him to send patrols to Gobabis to protect German women and children from the natives. Our commandant feels he cannot refuse this request, which turns out to be a ruse to get him out of the way. While the bulk of the commando are on this wild-goose chase, the Germans double back to Otjihangwe, as this farm is called, to ambush the mealie-seeking lieutenant.

The lieutenant, however, having been told by some natives that four German soldiers are now at the farm, approaches with caution. He divides his troop into two parties. Twelve men under a sergeant he lines up in the river-bed, quite close to the farm, and he himself with the remaining twelve takes cover behind a large cattle *kraal* on the opposite side of the farm. For some inexplicable reason, and contrary to orders, the sergeant instructs his party to rush the farm buildings. This they do without taking any cover, and, running into the farmyard, they are met with rifle-fire from the five separate buildings which constitute the farm, and which are so arranged that our men could get but little cover by hiding behind the walls. Two men were shot dead immediately, and three wounded, including the sergeant, who had rushed up to one of the minor buildings and rather madly emptied his revolver through a window. The remainder of the troop withdraw, taking what cover they could, leaving their dead and wounded in the yard.

It seems the Germans were partly taken by surprise themselves, for the farm offers very little facility for observing an approaching foe, and, besides this, a warning from a woman who was on the lookout at the neighbouring farm miscarried, a native girl to whom she had given a note telling the Germans of our approach, falling into our hands. Had the Germans been advised of the approach, they would in all probability have shot the whole troop down, for they had loopholed the walls and doors, and their rifles commanded the position in all directions.

As soon as the *burghers* had retired, the Germans, about twelve in number, evacuated the place, and joined their main body towards the north. Before they left they had time to ill-treat the wounded, for the man who was shot through the neck told me that, as they lay in the yard, the Germans came out and kicked them. He was compelled to get up, and was bundled in a brutal manner into an outhouse. On the other hand, the farmer and a woman on the place did what they could, burying the dead and dressing the wounds. The woman was particularly assiduous in her attentions. Rather too much so, I was inclined to think, for no doubt they had taken part in the ambush, and as likely as not the farmer had shared in the shooting, for I found his sporting Mauser still loaded with soft-nosed bullets, with every evidence of having been recently discharged.

After the Germans had left Otjihangwe, this farmer went over to the Pietersburg headquarters, which were now at Ongono, eleven miles away, and told the *commandant* that the Germans had left, and that he needed help to attend the wounded. Fearing another ambush, the commandant moved all his men up to Otjihangwe, and when they were near the farm the adjutant made the farmer walk in front, covering him with a revolver, and promising him instant death if a shot were fired from the house. This farmer and his assistant were put under guard. I never saw two men in a more abject state of fear. They expected summary execution, but it speaks well for the restraint of our men that they were sent down to Windhuk instead of being shot.

There is a feeling of great insecurity in this place. An attack is expected at any moment, as we are only about twenty miles from a large body of Germans, and no communications can be established with any of our troops either by helio or patrol. Consequently everybody is a little "jumpy," especially at nights. The second night even the animals seemed restive, and a large number of cattle in a neighbouring *kraal* stampeded, and would have been over us, but for the friendly shelter of the motorcar. The horses too were uneasy, dogs barked the whole night, and the very fowls were affected with nerves. Challenges were frequent, and once "Who goes there?" was followed by a peal of laughter. A sentry had challenged a riderless horse wandering about.

June 19.—During the night the wounded boy died, and as soon as he was buried the *commandant* decided to evacuate the farm, as it offered no facilities for defence. He still felt very angry, and wanted to destroy the farm. I tried to dissuade him, with what success I don't know,[1] for we left directly after breakfast. The women and three little children who had been at the place through all this trying time were sent off to Windhuk in a waggon.

Although the farm was a rather dilapidated and poor-looking place, it was very well stocked with household goods and personal effects, for your German colonial is very fond of comfort and likes good things. There was enough clothing in the farm to stock a shop, enough cutlery and plate for an hotel. In the dirty little kitchen, the thought of which spoilt one's appetite, there were between forty and fifty aluminium pots and pans.

Serviettes, towels, and handkerchiefs, tied neatly in bundles and marked, filled whole cupboards. For three small children there was enough clothing for thirty, and the same applied to toys. There was so much clothing at the farm that most of the men were able to supplement their scanty wardrobes, and some, notably my guide, were entirely re-equipped in German khaki, of better quality than fit. My conscience allowed me to take all the sheets and bed linen I could carry, for our hospital at Windhuk was not too well supplied with these commodities. In one of the outbuildings we found a great quantity of maize and dried beans, but there was no sugar, tea, or coffee, or any of those foodstuffs which the country has to import. Indeed, the shortage of food, other than what the country supplies—which is not much besides meat—is being acutely felt everywhere.

June 25.—We are now getting patients from the south, General Mackenzie's force having reached Rehoboth, sixty miles south of Windhuk. The railway is now open running south, but delays and breakdowns are so frequent that the journey from Rehoboth sometimes takes several days. As the nights are very cold now and food scarce, the sick have a very rough time on the road. One man left Rehoboth with erysipelas, but when he reached hospital it was all over. They are sending them up to us in batches of thirty or forty every day. The men have no severe illnesses, but are suffering woefully from privation, many of them being utterly exhausted in body and mind. Most of them are suffering from dysentery, and their hands and arms are covered with scabby sores.

Both men and horses have reached the limits of endurance, and

---

1. The farm was destroyed.

latterly they have only been *trekking* five or six miles a day. Men tell me that they are incapable of the slightest exertion, becoming breathless after a short walk, and that they hadn't energy left to catch sheep and kill them, but would wait for a sheep to pass, and then shoot it. Ever since the end of March they have had no regular supply of rations, and for the last month they have existed on meat alone, often not even getting salt. Pathetic tales are told of their privations.

One officers' mess had a little flour in a bag which they used most sparingly. This precious bag was in charge of the quartermaster-sergeant, with instructions that he was not to let it out of his sight. The care of this bag was a great anxiety to him, especially at nights, when he was in the habit of using it as a pillow. One morning, however, he found the bulk of his flour gone, although he was still lying on the bag. Some hungry trooper had cut a hole in it, and scooped most of the flour out without waking him. One man was seen searching among some refuse in a cellar. He wished to keep his discovery a secret, because he had found a few little wizened potatoes not fit for pigs. Many seemed to feel the lack of tobacco almost as much as that of food. One ingenious man told me he was fortunate enough to find a tin of tobacco extract, used for dipping animals. Lucerne hay, soaked in this and dried, made, he said, a very good smoke. Others, less fortunate, had to be content with dried leaves.

The horses died from sheer starvation in scores, and many went suddenly blind, which, my informant said, was due to the same cause.

June 27.—I have already mentioned the range of mountains, the highest in the country and running in a north-east and south-west direction, about ten miles to the south of Windhuk. Every night I have watched the sun set on these proud and fierce-looking peaks, and every night I have registered a mental vow to hold my head for a few brief moments higher than they. I had met nobody in Windhuk who had made the ascent, nor anybody who advised it. The matron of the hospital said an officer had once climbed it, and taken two days, but he had said he would not do it again for 10,000 *marks.*

Today Colonel K—— and I decided to make the attempt. Our plan was to ride as far as possible, and then have a shot at the Moltkeblick. Unfortunately, we were rather late in starting, and we rode and rode over thorn-clad foot-hills without apparently getting any nearer. It was half-past one before we reached a point where it was too steep and rocky for the horses to go farther.

The northern approach to the Moltkeblick is through a magnificent gorge about three-quarters of a mile wide. On either side of the gorge, and quite detached from the mountain, is a mighty cone-shaped peak, both of them being nearly as high as the Moltkeblick itself. They stand before the entrance like giant sentinels, silent and everlasting. Our hearts sank when we saw the distance still to go, but we decided to climb for two hours, and then, if not at the top, to turn back. Skirting the right side of the gorge, the colonel led off at a brisk pace over level but very rough ground, and I instinctively felt that this was to be a race for the honour of being the first Britisher to climb the highest mountain in "British" South-West Africa. We crossed over to the left side of the gorge to follow a ridge running up to the summit, the Colonel leading easily.

And now the climb began. The mountain is covered with large stones of granite and sandstone which are very angular. They are loose and slip easily, and between them are tufts of grass and small mimosas. Consequently every step is grief, and every other one pain. The colonel zigzagged along at a killing pace, and, in order not to lose heart entirely, I soon ceased to look at him. About halfway up I stopped, on the point of throwing up the sponge; but I was much encouraged to see that my rival, too, was in difficulties, for he frequently stopped and turned round, ostensibly to admire the view, but in reality, I think, to get a little breath. Soon we were level. Near the summit we were confronted with 100 feet or so of almost vertical rock, and the Colonel edged away to the left, where it was less steep. I regretted my temerity halfway up this steep bit. Fortunately, however, the grass was firmly rooted, and I dragged myself to the summit and looked round. No colonel in sight, and the beacon only a few yards away. Jumping to my feet, I hurried up to it. In less than half a minute the colonel was there too.

"God save the King!" gasped I.

"Johnnie Walker first as usual," was his disappointed retort.

The outlook from the top of the Moltkeblick is simply sublime. This great ridge of broken sandstone runs east and west like the teeth of a saw. On the north it is accessible, but on the south, at the point where we were, it seemed a sheer drop of, I suppose, 2,000 feet, the rugged ends of the strata protruding a little like giant steps. To the south and east blue mountains bounded the horizon, what was apparently a great plain lying between, but no doubt containing hills of considerable height, indistinguishable at so great a distance. The white river-beds, fringed with green, could be seen meandering south or east as far as the eye could reach.

Northward the valley of the Swakup could be made out cutting its way through endless mountains; while a little to the west Windhuk was represented by a few white dots, the Telefunken station still visible; but man's handiwork now seemed insignificant, its great pillars resembling a little clump of black pins. Westward the mountains tailed off into the Komas Highlands, stretching toward the desert and the ocean like a sea of hills.

Following the usual custom, we had to think of something to leave at the summit. The most appropriate thing we could produce was a George V. 1912 shilling. Him we placed in a broken German beer bottle, and hid at the base of the metal beacon to watch over as much of the Empire as can be seen from any one point.

July 3.—Today there is official news that General Botha's troops have occupied Otavi, Marnie Botha's brigade and the S.A.M.R., to whom the I.L.H. are attached, being the troops engaged in the movement. Only a few Germans were captured, we are told; the others have retired north into the "fly belt." War breeds rumour even more than peace. One day we hear Franke has shot himself, the next that he has accepted our terms, the third that he is under restraint, suffering from delirium tremens; but the Germans aver that he has done none of these things. "Franke is a brave man" is their only comment. A junior staff-officer told us the following: The Germans have squared it with the Portuguese and retired into Angola; they will wait until our troops leave, and then take the country again. When told that this must involve Portugal with England, he glibly replied: "Oh! but we do things differently out here."

Yesterday and today the town has been crowded with men of the Central Force. They are nearly all British, and come from Natal. They are to go back immediately *via* Luderitzbucht, and are a little disappointed, after weeks of *trekking* under the hardest conditions imaginable, that they are not to have a share in the final drive. Many of them hint that the *burghers* are being favoured, but they have no real cause for dissatisfaction or complaint. Even if their services were required further, neither men nor horses are in a condition to undertake another long trek. They have borne the burden and heat of the day, and everybody knows they have played their part as well as it could be played. An old German soldier who fought at Gibeon said they were the bravest and worst-equipped soldiers in the world, and that he would sooner meet other troops once a day than meet once a year the men who chased him at Gibeon.

CHAPTER 9

Windhuk to Luderitzbucht

July 13.—All last week rumours of peace, or rather of German surrender, were floating in the air, and now these rumours have merged into established fact. Seitz, Franke and Co., have surrendered. It seems that Franke, who met General Botha at Otavi, was quite unaware that he was totally surrounded when he went out to ask General Botha for an armistice. The general said he was quite willing to grant one, but he could not very well inform his wings about it, as they were far distant. Franke smiled in an incredulous manner, but he was soon to learn that he was shut in north-west and north-east as well as south, General Britz being on one side of him and General Myburg on the other. They had no option but to surrender. True to British traditions, General Botha has given them very good terms. The regular soldiers, about 3,000 in number, are to be interned, and the reservists, mostly farmers, are to be allowed to return to their homes, and trading facilities are to be granted to them.

The cessation of hostilities is, of course, the signal for a general exodus, almost *a sauve qui peut,* the major and I having found substitutes among the foremost; and we are leaving for home today by train to Luderitzbucht, or possibly, if the line is open, we may go all the way to Cape Town by train through Upington.

A train leaves for the south each day now. It consists of a few ramshackle trucks, and possibly a van or two, generally drawn by a very unreliable German engine. A few days previously the major, hoping for a *quid pro quo,* had given a sergeant of the Railway regiment some bedding which he was greatly in need of; but the best the sergeant could do for us was a capacious van, a sort of cross between a prison and a cattle truck, which we were to share with several other officers. At 3 p.m., just six hours late, we steamed leisurely out of the station,

COLONEL FRANKE (IN THE CENTRE)—IN COMMAND OF THE GERMAN FORCES

followed only by a few envious eyes.

Going south the railway has to climb a pass in the Auas Mountains. Railway and road, for the most part side by side, follow a most tortuous course between precipitous mountains until the top is reached, 7,000 feet up. Some day, when the roads are good, the railway reliable, and hotels and hydros are dotted about, the luxurious sightseer will come and spoil the primitive grandeur of this wonderful gorge. In the meantime let those who love Nature in her ruggedness hasten to Windhuk and walk or ride over the mountains to Rehoboth, the centre of the Bastard country, standing amidst waving grass and sharp *kopjes*. These Bastards, or, as they proudly call themselves, the Bastard Nation, have a history worthy of investigation and record.

Some time during the nineteenth century, long before the German occupation, some Dutchmen and Scotchmen *trekked* across the Kalahari into this rich pastoral country, and, finding it very good, settled here. Many of them were men of good stock, Van Wyks and Mac-Nabs. They built houses, framed laws, and finally took to themselves wives from among the neighbouring Hottentots. Instead of degenerating, as such people generally do, they have done much to maintain European ideals and customs. They have a law-book written in Dutch. The early entries in this book are in High Dutch, but the language used has been gradually simplified in subsequent entries, until the later ones have come to closely resemble the Taal. They have some very quaint laws with regard to property. A man has a right to demand his neighbour's oxen, plough, or anything that he may require; but there is a fixed tariff for the loan of such things, which must be adhered to. If a magistrate makes a decision in court, and the existing laws do not cover it, then the decision is added to the statute-book as law.

These people do not encourage intermarriage with the native races, but they are open to receive white men on the following terms: A probationary period of six months' residence is insisted upon; if the would-be colonist acquits himself creditably during this period, he is allowed to remain, on condition that he marries a Bastard girl. In this way they have reduced the percentage of African blood in their veins, and in Europe, where people are less critical in this matter, most of them would pass for Europeans. Some of the older men have very large possessions, or, rather, had until the recent trouble with the Germans. They are keen on education, and one hears of girls going to finishing schools in Europe, presumably in Germany, and they have returned with pianos and other signs of *kultur*. The men occupy their time with pastoral pursuits and hunting. Each man carries a rifle, often of a modern pattern, and from all accounts they are marvellous marksmen. They have maintained their independence with great adroitness, and even the Germans have left them alone, or, rather, have only attempted their absorption by peaceful measures.

Whenever feuds or wars have been on, they have thrown in their lot with the stronger side. They assisted the Hottentots against the Hereros; they helped the Germans against both the Hottentots and the Hereros. Finally, they refused to fight against their compatriots from the Union. This led to misunderstandings between them and the Germans, until at last they came to blows. The Germans sent down a punitive expedition from Windhuk, but the Bastards more than held their own in a fight on May 8, near Rehoboth. They claim to have killed 140 Germans in this engagement, but, although this is an exaggeration, the number of German wounded in Windhuk hospital who admit that they were wounded in this fight shows that the Germans did not have it all their own way.

After this reverse the Huns, as usual, destroyed everything they could lay their hands on, burning and shooting in all directions. An old Bastard chief said they destroyed all his cattle and waggons, and killed his children and grandchildren before his eyes. The Central Force on their trek up to Windhuk found ample evidence of these doings, such as the charred remains of waggons and effects, whole spans of oxen still in the yoke lying dead, to say nothing of women and children suffering from bullet wounds.

During the afternoon the engine was frequently in difficulties, and short stops were made to effect repairs to the injectors. Sleep on the floor of a bumping, thumping van was fitful and unrefreshing, and, besides, it was terribly cold. How the poor men in the open trucks managed, huddled together in little groups to keep warm, I cannot imagine. Daylight found us at Marienthal, a distance of only 150 miles from Windhuk, our magnificent German engine having dragged us at the rate of ten miles an hour.

July 14.—At Marienthal the country is flat, uninteresting, and rather barren. To the east, at some distance from the line, is a structure, interesting geologically, known as the Kalk Rand. This ridge runs parallel with the line from below Reboboth for a distance of 100 miles or more. The face is vertical, and beyond is a level plateau, which, of course, being several miles away, cannot be seen from the line. The ridge does not vary in height; I should judge it to be about 200 feet. To the west of it is an absolutely level plain through which the railway runs. This plain is a veritable sea of granite pebbles sparsely covered with a little scrub.

Away to the west, and running a southerly course, is the Great Fish River. The direction of the river is roughly north and south, and it finally enters the Orange River about sixty miles from the sea. Unlike most of the rivers in the country, it generally has water in it, not running, but as large pools. The banks are lined with large trees, which in contrast to the arid plain form a very agreeable feature in the landscape.

After some delay the train moved on again, but at Grab, the next siding, we came to a final standstill, the engine being affected with incurable *valvular* disease. We were soon given to understand that we should have to wait here and chance our luck, hoping that an engine or train might turn up from somewhere. On the receipt of this news everybody bundled out on to the *veldt*, and those of us who had the wherewithal began culinary operations. In the next van to us were a number of Hottentots going to Keetmanshoop. There were so many of them—men, women, and children—that, had we not seen them emerge, we could not have believed that so many individuals and so much material could have been crowded into so small a space.

The adult women of the party set to work with great expedition to prepare a meal. They made a diminutive fire of tiny twigs; so small was it that it might have lain on the palm of a hand. Over this they placed a large cauldron of mealie pap. The women then sat in a circle round the fire, and fed it so dexterously with little sticks that it burnt in a continuous flame like a spirit-lamp. Their pot was boiling as soon as our kettle, although we had a fire ten times the size and much less water to boil.

The porridge, when cooked, was served out in various receptacles—pots, pans, pan lids, meat-tins, cups, or saucers. They had several spoons, but they seemed to prefer to eat with their fingers, which they did in a rapid and complete manner. A little lady aged about two had her share in a pan lid, and the deft way she conveyed the hot porridge to her mouth was little short of conjuring. Whether a morsel stuck to her fingers, palm, wrist, or knuckles, it was unerringly carried to her mouth, and her tongue seemed to have the mobility of a chameleon's. In about twenty seconds she was finished, and her platter was handed in. They had an old patriarch with them who was too decrepit to walk or stand. He was provided with a chair, and ate a good meal with a spoon. He desired to wash it down with some milk from an immense calabash, but he was roughly choked off by word and look from an old hag who could only have been his wife, so connubial were her words and gestures. He relapsed into that futile muttering which even younger husbands are wont to resort to.

His pitiable state greatly exercised the major's tender heart until I suggested that she probably had her reasons and knew what was best for him. Feeding finished, the women alone smoked, using a pipe which looked like a large cigar-holder, and which had to be held vertically to prevent the tobacco falling out. They had only two of these instruments, one of wood and one of tin, and these were passed from mouth to mouth until all the ladies had had a few whiffs. To get the smoke through seemed to require great suctorial effort, and, judging from the salivation induced, the fumes were fairly pungent.

Smoking over, the ladies proceeded to wash up and to titivate. One washed her face in a cup of water by scooping, or, rather, throwing the water up with the tips of her fingers, without losing a drop. She then arranged her hair and *duk*, just as "my lady" does. Subsequently a little coffee was made, and the old man aforesaid was again doomed to disappointment, rolling his bleary eyes and mumbling as before, this time at his wife's relentless back, for she only put the lid firmly on the coffee-pot and removed it out of harm's way.

About noon a train arrived from the south, and the engine ran up close to ours on the same line in an inquiring sort of way. At first the driver of this train did not wish to help us. His boiler was dry, his something-or-other entirely inefficient. But he finally succumbed to the shrill pleadings of our driver, and agreed to take our engine only back to Marienthal, if he could pull it so far; and the plan was that our own driver was to come back at 7 p.m. with the engine repaired.

We spent the afternoon getting the sleep we did not get during the previous night. True to his word, the driver turned up before seven. As he passed us on the siding, he shouted, "I have only half an engine," and proceeded to ruthlessly turn out the occupants of the hindmost trucks. We, fortunately being near the engine, were left undisturbed. We started off at seven, and were making good time, congratulating ourselves that this driver was a man better than his word. "Dinner" was just over, and we were sitting on boxes round a large leather trunk which constituted the table, and drinking a liqueur of our own concoction, when, without any warning, all the movable things in the van seemed to race forward on their own account in three successive and rapid jerky bumps.

One officer with his back to the engine outpaced his seat, coming in contact with the floor in a very undignified manner, and proceeded to attempt to jerk himself forward, while in a sitting posture, through the closed door at the end of the van. He was closely followed by the things off the table in fact, the contents of the coffee-pot finally overtook him. Nevertheless, with great presence of mind, he continued to hold a valuable wine-glass overhead after the fashion of Truth holding her lamp; the liqueur, however, mingled with the coffee grounds upon his nether garments. Then the train stopped and people ran to and fro shouting. We jumped out to the tune of "Engine's off the line; nobody's hurt," and stumbled forward in the darkness.

The engine was clean off the line towards the left, standing at a perilous angle on a small embankment. It appeared to be one mass of steam and flame, for the firemen were already drawing the fires and throwing the flaming coal and wood off in a very reckless manner. Hissing steam was emerging from all the usual and several unusual exits. The mangled remains of two oxen, the cause of the disaster, lay close to the line, bits of skin, flesh, and bone, were scattered about, and the intestines of one ox lay under our coach, the seventh in the line. The driver had gallantly stuck to his post, applied the brakes, and shut off steam.

One of the firemen had jumped at the last moment, when he thought the engine was going to turn over, and he was the only man hurt. The driver said he had run bang into a whole herd of cattle. A search was made for the wounded, but none were found. The engine had dragged the three leading coaches off the line with it, and in the middle of the train two vans were also derailed. The one containing two soldiers was lying on its side. It seemed a bit of a mechanical puzzle why two of the middle coaches had turned over; but it appeared that the vacuum brake did not act beyond this point, so that, when the brake was applied suddenly, the train naturally buckled between the stopping front half and the oncoming back half.

Before one could properly take in the situation, our friends the Hottentots were busy at the mangled carcasses, cutting off meat, as if a railway accident were the most natural thing in the world. They lit fires, and, joined by other natives, started a regular orgy. The ingestion of large quantities of meat often seems to have a most stimulating effect upon the brain, and these people soon became garrulous and quarrelsome as the feast proceeded. Finally, when they settled down, the Hottentot babies took up the tune, imitating caterwauling very perfectly, their discomfort being no doubt due in part to parental neglect, and in part to an overdose of tough beef. So that on the whole our second night in the train was little, if any, better than the first.

July 15.—Many of the men on the train were now beginning to feel rather hungry, for most of them had only two days' rations when they left Windhuk. Consequently, there were several visitors to the remains of the oxen as soon as it was light. They found little but the horns and the skin, for the Hottentots had taken everything; even the entrails under our van had been removed, and I noticed a woman preparing these for consumption, braying them a little in water, and then rolling them up. Cut into short lengths, these were cooked on the coals for breakfast. So that within twelve hours some forty or fifty people had consumed two oxen.

About 8 a.m. breakdown gangs arrived from Gibeon and Marienthal, and by dint of pushing some of the trucks off and levering others on to the line it was soon cleared. New lengths of line were put down with great expedition, and before noon all was ready for another start. Fortunately, the engine was so far away from the line that it did not interfere with traffic. The engineer who was in charge of the work told me that they had had great difficulties in getting the line into working order. In the first place, there was great shortage of material, and also of skilled labour. Many competent workmen had refused to come out on active service owing to the firm action the Government had taken with the strikers in Johannesburg and elsewhere. Between Luderitzbucht and Keetmanshoop it had been necessary to rebuild the line entirely, as the Germans had not left a single rail intact. Between Keetmanshoop and Gibeon they had blown up all the bridges, about twenty in number, and also destroyed the water-tanks and pumps; but little harm had been done to the permanent way.

Where the bridges were blown up, our engineers had made deviations and carried the line into the river-bed on an embankment. This, of course, could be only a temporary measure, for as soon as a river was in flood the embankment and line would be washed away. Supplying the engines with water was the greatest difficulty of all, and had not yet been overcome. This was especially the case on the section between Keetmanshoop and Upington. The rolling stock, he said, was in a very bad condition, and the German engines were old and our drivers did not understand them.

During the morning a train arrived from the south. On board were Colonel Berrangé, his staff, and some S.A.M.R., all *en route* for Windhuk, where the colonel was to take over the military administration. As it was only a single line, this train could not pass us, and during the afternoon we were dragged back again to Marienthal, where we were chagrined to see the train which left Windhuk twenty-four hours after us departing on its southward journey. Not until 7 p.m. did we again make an attempt to get on, this time with a S.A.E. engine provided with a cow-catcher. We went along intermittently, and woke up to find ourselves, not at Keetmanshoop, but only at Gibeon. Shortage of water, we were told, was the cause of the delay this time.

July 16.—It was just light when we arrived at Gibeon. The same Kalk Rand was to the east, the same sea of pebbles, the same dreary outlook, as at Marienthal. Near the station are the graves of the Natal Light Horse and the 2nd Imperial Light Horse who were killed on the line three miles to the north on April 27. There are about thirty graves in a single line, each with a little white wooden cross at its head. The name of each fallen soldier and his regiment are painted on the crosses in black letters. It all looked very simple, quiet, and pathetic, standing in the lonely desert. Major Watt and two other officers lie here. The major was found shot through the head, neck, and chest, still grasping his revolver. The circumstances which led up to the fight I have learnt from various sources, and I may as well put them down here.

For many months the Central Force had been unable to dislodge the Germans from their strong position at Aus, which is situated at the edge of the desert on the Luderitz line. At the end of March, with Berrangé from the east and Van der Venter from the south threatening Keetmanshoop, the German position at Aus became untenable. Further, by this time General Botha with the Northern Force had seized Riet, and was threatening Karibib and Windhuk. If the Germans remained longer at Aus, they were in danger of being caught between all four forces. Aus was therefore evacuated, and the Germans had left it a week before General Mackenzie's scouts discovered the fact. The Central Army then moved up and occupied the place, with orders, so I believe, to remain there. They, however, with their mounted men moved on rapidly through Kuibis, Bethany, Beersheba, and along the Fish River, with the idea of cutting the Germans off at Gibeon.

The Germans had retired slowly to Keetmanshoop, destroying the line behind them, and were now engaged in blowing up the bridges, etc., between Keetmanshoop and Gibeon. It is said that Sir George Farrar, who was Assistant-Quartermaster-General to the force, was greatly opposed to this advance, holding that the troops could not possibly be fed. He was, however, overruled. About April 24 or 25 our scouts tapped the telephone line near Gibeon, and overheard a conversation between some Germans. They learnt that the Germans were well aware of Mackenzie's advance, but also that the Germans did not think it necessary to evacuate Gibeon yet.

It was therefore decided to cut the line north of Gibeon, and attempt to capture the Germans in the place, who were supposed to be 600 or 700 strong. Colonel Royston, of the N.L.H., was ordered to place his regiment across the line to prevent the Germans from escaping north. Our people blew up the line on the evening of the 27th, and this put the Germans on the alert. For some unexplained reason the N.L.H. were lined up, not across, but along the line, and quite unexpectedly they were enfiladed by two machine guns which the Germans had in a culvert. Disorder prevailed in the darkness, men making frantic efforts to dig themselves in with the butt ends of their rifles; but, no supports arriving, the bulk of the regiment laid down their arms.

Here the Germans made their mistake, for, instead of making off with their prisoners towards the north, they remained, thinking they had captured our whole force. However, they were surprised to find themselves vigorously attacked. The Natal men chased them next morning, releasing the prisoners of the N.L.H., and also capturing a good many Germans. Unfortunately, in this action the captured N.L.H. were fired upon by our men, and several were wounded.

The Germans who were captured here declared that they would not have believed that men could ride so hard and fire so quickly as ours did, and they were sure the firing had been done without dismounting. I was told that some of our troopers got right in among the fleeing Germans, that two at least of the enemy lost their lives owing to inferior horsemanship; for when told to "hands up" they were not able to do so, as they were hanging on to reins and rifle to keep their seats, and were consequently shot with revolvers. A certain small pugilist was also said to have unhorsed two burly Germans with his fists.

The *trek* from Aus to Gibeon was a wonderful feat of pluck and endurance on the part of the men and horses, for over 200 miles of practically desert country had been traversed without transport. Roads there were next to none, and the men had hoped to live on the country; but there was little to live on save a few sheep and cattle, and dry scanty grass for the horses. Men and horses were utterly exhausted when they fought this fight, and they were yet to have two months of privation and exposure before they reached Windhuk. We of the Northern Force received most of the *kudos* for this campaign, but our sufferings never approached those of the Central Force, nor even, I believe, those of the Eastern or Southern forces who advanced to Keetmanshoop.

Among the passengers was a young Englishman who had been a political prisoner in the hands of the Germans. He told a pitiable tale of ill-usage, solitary confinement to gaol, and semi-starvation. One could see by his look that the iron had entered into his soul. He also told me that General Botha's attack at Riet was a great surprise to Franke, who that day was being entertained at a public luncheon in Windhuk, and that none of the staff were nearer the scene of action than Karibib. The bulk of the German supplies were at that time at Karibib; and had the Northern Force then pushed on, they would easily have captured the place and all it contained. After the reverse at Riet, the Germans were feverishly engaged for some days removing numerous supplies of all sorts farther north by rail.

The country between Gibeon and Keetmanshoop is on the whole barren and uninteresting. Conspicuous on the plain to the west is a high flat-topped mountain, the Great Bruckkaros, which is visible both from Gibeon and also from the hills above Keetmanshoop. Journeying all day, we never seemed able to get away from the thing. About Tses, opposite the mountain, the Kalk Rand dies out, and is replaced by broken hills, which nearer Keetmanshoop are of an ironstone formation, kopjes being built up of great red boulders, which are often so arranged as to resemble ruined buildings on a giant scale.

Keetmanshoop itself is a clean little place surrounded by ironstone hills very bare of vegetation. Its only claim to existence is that the Germans saw fit to establish large railway workshops here, and no doubt it will continue to be a railway centre, especially since it has been linked up with the colony *via* Upington. Here we decided to return to Cape Town *via* Luderitzbucht, and not to attempt the very uncertain overland route.

July 17.—We travelled well during the night that is to say, we jogged along intermittently at a little over ten miles an hour, and dawn found us at Schakalskuppe. A white frost lay on the ground, and it was terribly cold. Very few trees were to be seen, and very little growth of any kind. Sand, rocks, flat-topped *kopjes* looking like slag-heaps in the early dawn, all very desolate, surrounded us. Hereabouts the Germans had destroyed the line very thoroughly, for broken rails lay along the track in great profusion. Apart from the railway there was little sign of man or his handiwork. Here and there we saw heaps of bottles, sometimes large, sometimes small, where a German camp had been. Or, again, a collection of tins marked a spot where our men had rested and fed. Here, at any rate, beef had triumphed over beer.

Both from a scenic and strategic point of view Aus has a very fine position. It is placed in a gap in an inaccessible range of mountains running north and south. Advancing from Luderitz, you are bound to go over Aus Nek, for to the north and south of it is the interminable and waterless wilderness. There is quite a little town here, for there is water, and the place is a regular oasis. From here towards the coast there had been a very unseasonable fall of rain, and the young green grass and the white rocks glistening in the morning sun made a gallant show. From Aus the line winds down an ever-widening S-shaped funnel. Precipitous granite rocks bound this funnel on either side, and its floor is just sand, neither stick nor stone for men to take cover behind. Our advance from Garub could only take place into this winding, ever-narrowing funnel, in full view of the enemy. Further, the Germans reconnoitred our position every day by means of an armoured train or aeroplane.

Looking up towards Aus the view is sublime, and at the very apex of the funnel, where the mountains come together, is a great rock, the "Aus Needle," standing like a sentinel. It was here that De Meuillon, a reckless scout and a man known all over South Africa for his bravery, met his death. Several accounts of his last adventure are current, and I will merely give the story of his death as told to us by the Germans.

Between Garub and Aus, near the entrance to the funnel, a party of six German soldiers were engaged in destroying the line, when they noticed some horsemen advancing from Chankaib. They immediately hid in a trench they had dug near by, and the horsemen came on unsuspectingly. At close range the Germans fired a volley. De Meuillon fell at once, mortally wounded. Two natives were shot dead and three others were taken prisoners, while three white men escaped. De Meuillon died soon after, and they buried him on the northern side

Scenery near Luderitzbucht

of the funnel and hanged the natives on a tree close to the grave. And here the grave and corpses were found when the advance to Aus was subsequently made.

There is hardly anything at Garub now to show that it had once been a large camp—just a few tin shanties, a tent or two, and a pumping plant. The places where the stacks of forage had been are now, after the rain, beautifully green little lawns of stunted oats. A handful of natives gather up the *débris*, and when they have finished no sign of the camp will be left!

The desert now has a tinge of green, as if it had received a very thin coat of paint of that colour, which gives it a charm not to be described. A beautiful little heliotrope flower is growing, too, in great profusion, and I even saw a few birds.

Near Chankaib is an extinct volcano, and a little nearer the coast a pale grey lava enters largely into the composition of the desert. At Rotkuppe, and thereafter, although there had been plenty of rain, there was no sign of vegetation. As we approached the coast the country became more and more wild and weird. About Grassplatz it is utter chaos. Tumbled rocks of all shapes and at all angles intermix with the sand blown up from the coast. Mountains, hills, valleys, precipices, escarpments, gorges, ravines, fissures, without arrangement or order, fill in the whole landscape. The rocks are a dull grey, unearthly colour; even the sky looks grey and sombre. One feels here as if the end of the world were coming or had already come.

How the railway finds its way through this tangled mass is a mystery. It is nothing but curve and gradient, and you cannot see 20 yards ahead. It is here that they have such difficulty in keeping the line clear of sand, and to prevent it from blowing about somebody has hit on the novel idea of covering sand-hills near the line with canvas. One sees whole acres of dunes treated in this way, long strips of canvas several yards wide being sewn together, stretched tightly over the sand, and pegged down at intervals. Large gangs of natives are also engaged in constantly shovelling away the sand into small trucks run on light rails up to the line. It all seems a hopeless task, for the sand seems to come on in endless avalanches as fast as it is removed.

Kolmanskop, where the diamonds are, is a dreary waste of sand and rock. The diamondiferous gravel is collected into little heaps arranged in long regular lines waiting to be sifted. All this work is now at a standstill. The German Government had recently put down a lot of machinery here for working the mines, which is worked by electricity generated at the power-station in Luderitzbucht. There are a good many houses and offices for the workers, all well built and of large size; but it seems very incongruous to see human habitations in such a place, and I cannot imagine sane men living here even for the sake of getting rich.

The diamonds from this area are, generally speaking, small and of inferior quality, but they seem to be very numerous. I told a resident of Luderitz that I had heard of a soldier in a certain blockhouse having collected a pickle-bottleful of diamonds. "That's nothing," he retorted; "if he'd been energetic, he might have got a petrol-tinful." I hear, too, that attempts are being made in a systematic manner to get unregistered diamonds from Kimberley passed through as having come from Kolmanskop, but the difference between the diamonds from the two places ought to make the detection of such little tricks easy.

It is five in the afternoon by the time we get to Luderitz. Everybody is exhausted and disinclined for further effort. Our batman heaved our belongings on to the platform, where they constituted a respectable-looking mountain. For a while we sat and looked at it, and finally decided that some efforts must be made to find food and shelter, as it was cold and windy and getting dark. We set out to look for a place where we might lodge, but found the various places full.

At last a Good Samaritan appears in the shape of a sergeant mechanic known to me, and he shows us an empty house, of which, having put to flight many feline tenants, we take possession. There is some difficulty in getting water, for, although water is laid on to the houses, it all has to be condensed; consequently the supply is very limited, and the authorities cut it off at once from empty houses. However, we finally got a jugful from a shop still open. Furniture there was none in the house worth considering, but with the help of a few broken-down old bedsteads and our blankets we should have had a comfortable night if the cats had not made determined efforts at short intervals to recover the position.

CHAPTER 10

Luderitzbucht

July 18.—I don't suppose there is a more desolate, dreary, God-forsaken site for a town in the whole world than this, and nobody except extreme optimists like the Germans would ever have dreamed of trying to establish one here. There is not a drop of fresh water anywhere near, nor a plant nor tree of any description except seaweed. There is not even a flat space where buildings can be erected, and many are perched on pinnacles or in fissures in the rocks. Its only natural advantages are the sun, sea, rocks, sand, and wind. The town is at the foot of a great tumbled mass of volcanic rock which juts northward into the sea, and this mass is obviously continued in three islands with small shallow channels between them. In this way a bay is produced. Bias, who visited the place, but did not stay, called it Angra dos Ilheos—the Bay of Islets. Later it was renamed Angra Pequeña Little Bay. Finally the Germans changed the name to Luderitzbucht, after an explorer of theirs, Luderitz by name. All the rocks about are of the dull grey colour of pumice, and everything, including sea and sky, seems to reflect the same leaden hue.

The island nearest the town is now joined to the mainland by a causeway about 170 yards long, which the Germans built in 1907. The reasons for this causeway are two. In the first place it improves the harbour, and in the second it joins the island to the mainland. While an island it belonged to the Union, as all the other islands do along the coast; but when they joined it up to the mainland the German sophists argued that it was part of the mainland, and accordingly began to build upon it, erecting a fine hospital there and a lighthouse. Appropriately enough they named it Halfisch Insel—*i.e.*, Shark Island. One can hardly blame the Germans for jumping this island, for it is one of the few places where a road could be constructed so that the

Lüderitzbucht

inhabitants of Luderitzbucht might stretch their legs a little. It is upon this island that the Germans are said to have marooned a number of refractory Hottentots, where they might choose from among the following deaths—hunger, thirst, drowning, sharks, or a bullet.

The streets are sandy and rough, but are not to be compared with those of Swakupmund in this respect. Little railway lines run in all the streets, and in some places into private yards. The foreshore is utterly spoilt by base mercantile constructions—wharfs, yards, stores, fences, and sidings—all begrimed with coal-dust. There are four or five broken-down little jetties running out a few yards into the bay, but nothing in the way of a pier or landing-stage comparable to that at Swakupmund. The bulk of the buildings are substantial and well built, with granite foundations. Cement, bricks, and reinforced concrete, have been freely used. Most of the houses are of two stories. The bank, the Woermann Linie offices, the railway-station, and the hospital, are all good buildings, but there are a great many shanties and makeshifts. The house we are living in is a most inconvenient structure. There are seven rooms in parallel opening on to a *stoep*. There is nothing resembling a passage or a hall, and all the windows and doors look the one way. In front—that is, on the side where the doors and windows are—is a small yard surrounded by high walls and outhouses, so that both ventilation and view are not of the best.

The town was full of petty craftsmen living under conditions similar to those which their ancestors must have enjoyed in the Middle Ages. You find watchmakers, tinkers, dyers, cleaners, and sweet-makers carrying on a diminutive business in a small dark building which also serves as a dwelling-place for the artisan and his family. Next door to us a small ironmonger and tinker must have plied his trade. In front he had a little shop; behind was his dwelling and workshop, which was really one room divided into four, two bedrooms at the back with no light or ventilation except when the door was open.

These bedrooms opened into the living-room-workshop, and off this room, to one side, was the kitchen, size 8 by 4 feet, as dark as night, with a modern cooking range at the far end. Imagine what it must have been like on a hot summer's evening, the thermometer at 110, with Mr. Tinker tinkering in the parlour, and poor Mrs. Tinker frying the evening meal in the kitchen, and several little Tinkers rebreathing the foul air in the fusty bedrooms, to say nothing of the guests who no doubt were often there, judging from the number of wineglasses and other utensils, in the cupboard, for drinking and eating.

Indeed, Luderitz seemed to have relapsed into a state of medieval feudalism. Above were the great castles, not of Baron this or that, but of the haughty Woermann Shipping Company and Diamond Company, while below in their wretched hovels cowered Mr. Tinker and his equally submerged confreres.

Not only have the Germans a lot of wretched dwelling-houses in their towns, but altogether I was surprised to see how little attention was paid to sanitation. In Windhuk when we arrived there were epidemics of typhoid and diphtheria, yet no precautions had been taken to limit their spreading. We appointed a medical officer for the town, but he could get no help from the municipal authorities or from the local doctors. The sanitary condition of the hospital was distinctly bad when we took it over, and the gaol was also in a dirty state. A sanitary officer remarked to me that the Germans are clean in front and dirty behind, and this certainly applies to their dwellings and shops. A butcher's shop, for instance, would be scrupulously tidy, but his backyard would be the very reverse, skins, offal, and other filth, lying about. I remember going to inspect the back premises of one of the crack hotels in Windhuk, and finding a cesspool and a well side by side, the fusion of the contents being facilitated by other means as well as mere proximity.

July 24.—You can see all there is to be seen in Luderitz in twenty-four hours, or less. From the barren land we have turned our attention to the apparently equally barren sea, and for the last few days some of our party have been trying their luck at fishing, with very indifferent success. Seaweed is easily caught, and besides this the Major has bagged a few dogfish and young sharks. Crayfish are very numerous and large all along this coast. They are very voracious and easily caught on a bait tied to the end of a string. Curiously enough, although so plentiful on the west coast of Africa, they are not found on either the south or east coast.

July 26.—We have now been ten days in Luderitz, waiting for a boat, and I think we have exhausted its pleasures. With the town deserted, it is most dreary here, and, like those of marooned sailors, our eyes are ever on the horizon. Today we expected our boat to arrive. Another boat is in, but, as it is bound for Swakupmund, we regard it with impatience and loathing. For several days a tall thin man in white trousers, a black coat, and long-footed German boots has attracted my attention. Today he spoke to me in unmistakable English while I was scanning the bay for the boat. "You are going home?" he said.

"Yes," I replied; "I have been out six months."

His tired eyes searched my face, and I could see his form was spare and his gestures languid. "I have been a prisoner eleven months, and they are brutes!": he almost hissed. "I had been engaged in business in Luderitz for eight years. At the beginning of the war I was taken to Windhuk. There I had three months' solitary confinement, with half an hour's exercise twice a day in the prison yard. Food was scarce and the place overrun with bugs. When they moved us north, we were kept in a large *kraal*, and given very little and bad food. Two days before we were released the officer in charge said he could not take us with him, as he had neither food nor transport for us. Next morning there was not a German on the job. Fortunately for us, the *burghers* turned up next day."

"What are you going to do?" I queried.

"I don't know," he said; "my place here has been looted, and there is no chance of getting my money out of the German Bank."

He also said that, when the Germans saw how things were likely to go, the governor took all the available money and paid it out to the soldiers, giving three and six months' pay in advance. He then issued notes on his own responsibility, which, of course, nobody, not even the German Government, would honour. Seitz also advised the people to bring all their savings to him, and he credited them in Berlin by wireless. That is how the German settler prevented his savings from falling into the hands of the rapacious "English." A good many of them already realize that they were somewhat ill-advised in this matter.

War passes like a scorching brand over the land, and one is apt to forget the singed and squirming creatures left in its wake. The chief sufferers are, naturally, the weak—women, children, and the aged. In Windhuk several thousand women and children were left behind. Many of the women were young, earning a living as typists, teachers, telephonists, and barmaids. Their means of livelihood suddenly cut off, and the wages due to them in many cases unpaid their position has become desperate. Not a few poor girls have been driven into misfortune, and some have sold themselves for soldiers' rations.

Of course, lots of people, especially farmers who deserted their homes for the towns, have lost all their belongings—stock, furniture, and clothes—and they have been hard pressed to obtain sufficient food, although the government have been dispensing rations freely. Without work and assets, the prospects of the German community in the near future are gloomy indeed. All this suffering has come to a people who have only experienced the irreducible minimum of the evils of war. Its real horrors have been spared them. The behaviour of our armies towards them has been most exemplary, and everything has been done that could be done both by the authorities and by individuals to mitigate the sufferings of the civil population. The inhabitants of Luderitz are now flocking back to empty houses and empty shops, and the so-called "reservists" are in great evidence. They don't look a bit conquered, are rather jaunty, and not a little impudent. Many wiseacres are shaking their heads and prognosticating "trouble."

The German nature is bitter and unrelenting. To show mercy is not in their creed. The German nurses who stayed on at Windhuk, mainly to take care of their own wounded, were quite ostracized by their compatriots, and were almost afraid to leave the hospital. Even the matron's children came in for abuse. "Your mother is 'English,' and we won't play with you," said their former companions. I heard of a case of two women who tried to make the lot of some prisoners a little easier, and when our hungry troops arrived sold them some little things. One of them was a wife of three months' standing; her husband threatened her life, and finally gave her a revolver, telling her to go out and shoot an Englishman and then herself, as it was the only course left to her. These women dared not leave the house, and had to seek our protection.

One feels one is at grips with a madman, a madman stimulated by egoism and hate. It is most uncanny living among them. So sure are they of their superiority, their omnipotence, their Divine right almost, that one is at times almost persuaded and doubts one's own sanity. Today groups of their ex-soldiers parade the streets of Luderitz. "You scum!" "You filth!" flashes from their eyes. Comic enough this, behind the iron cage of defeat, terribly tragic were the circumstances otherwise. Intelligence without wisdom, strength without restraint, purpose without pity, egoism naked and unabashed—these are the forces civilization is up against. It is the subconscious realization of this cardinal danger which, as nothing else, has united the white, the yellow, and the black, to destroy the ogre in their midst.

July 29.—Our boat has come, and we are to embark today at noon; two or three hundred men of all ranks, regiments, and callings, somewhat disparagingly known as "details." There are besides 700 or 800 natives and a lot of horses, mules, and donkeys. For the last day or two, while the boat has been in the bay, we have behaved very like people unused to travelling, constantly running down to find out when the boat sails, to look if she has sailed, or to make arrangements for our kit. But the embarkation authorities know their work now, and everything is done in order: officers to embark at noon, men at ten; servants and luggage went yesterday. 11.30 finds us on the jetty, which is high. The tide is out, so it is a big drop into the waiting, wobbling barge below. One by one we brave it, and punctually a tug takes us out to the ship, followed by the feeble cheers of twenty men or so there to see us off and wish themselves off too, no doubt.

Getting out of the barge is ten times worse than getting into it. The lowest rung of the gangway towers above us. The barge sways up and down, to and fro. A stalwart sergeant-major comes down the gangway to help us up.

An officer whispers in my ear: "If you fall between the barge and ship, dive at once."

"Take your chances, gentlemen!" shouts the sergeant-major to the hesitating group below, as the barge swings up within reach. My turn comes too soon. My left hand seizes the ladder, the sergeant seizes my right; we pull simultaneously. For a sickening moment I am suspended in space, and then I am awaked to consciousness by my shins scraping on the ladder.

I shall not dilate on the pleasures of the trip to Cape Town, for they were discounted by several circumstances. The boat was slow, high in the water, and the decks crowded with superstructures for men and animals; the weather was cold and windy. Above all, we were all thinking of home, and the appearance of Table Mountain on the horizon was the thing we lived for. When it did appear, we watched it grow into form from a shadowy ghost. The greenness of Bobbin Island was almost painful to eyes inured to sand and rock. About three girls were on the quay to meet us—that is, some of us.

We were only details, the Cinderellas left behind to do the washing up, and a civic or other reception would have been out of place for such. And no doubt Cape Town was not a little tired of welcoming khaki. War had not scared the noble city. The same undersized, anaemic seminuts were in the streets; the same pleasure-seeking girls, bedecked a little differently, perhaps; the same intolerable hoot and clang of motor conveyances; the same tempting shops: all were there as when we left. And, thank goodness, above the turmoil, din, and smoke, the same glorious mountain raised its scornful head.

The Story of a Lion Hunt With Some of the Hunter's Military Adventures During the War

LEOPARD STALKING ITS VICTIMS

Contents

Introductory Note Concerning the Author	149
PART 1. PEACE: LION HUNTING	
En Route	151
The Okavango River	160
Nearing the Lion Country	183
At Grips With the Lion	187
PART 2. WAR: A SCOUTS' PATROL	
Unemployed	199
Intelligence Scout	202
My Fellow Scouts	207
"Bush-Rangers' Rest"	213
Lion Stories	217
A Capture	222
The End of the Trail	229
PART 3. WAR: CAMPAIGNING IN EAST AFRICA	
With the E.A.M.R.	235
Intelligence Department	240
A Capture	246
The Hunter Hunted	248

A Prisoner	251
My Escape	258
Back to Duty	264
Hard Times	271
A Fresh Start	279
The Last Phase	290

Introductory Note Concerning the Author

My brother Arnold, though born in Australia, was educated in England at Wixenford and Eton. The call of his native land drew him back to Queensland at the age of nineteen, but hardly had he returned, when the South African War broke out, and he promptly joined the Queensland Horse to serve throughout the greater part of that campaign as a trooper. In August 1914, as this narrative tells us, Arnold Wienholt was in Africa crippled by injuries suffered in his lion hunting expedition. Nevertheless he was quickly in harness again, serving till the end of the campaign in British East Africa in the Intelligence Corps, and winning the D.S.O., and M.C. with bar. That my brother was a well-known figure in the East African campaign, and that the enemy stood inconsiderable respect of him, may be gathered from the following letter, which he received from the German commander, General Von Lettow,[1] in December 1921:

(Translation)

Dear Mr. Wienholt,
Your very friendly letter of June has been handed over to me by Mr. Knoop of Bremen, and I thank you very much that you hold out to me prospects of your publishing a book about the East African campaign. It will interest me in the highest degree to be able to view the adventure from your standpoint; for, naturally enough, my own view is one-sided. It pleases me that you have read my own account with interest, also that you praise so much my conduct of the campaign. From your lips I attach considerable value to such an opinion, for I had heard

---

1. *My Reminiscences of East Africa* by Paul Emil von Lettow-Vorbeck is also published by Leonaur.

so much of your bravery and your daring patrols that I felt we were already acquainted to some extent before we met personally in Tuliani.

The unique nature of our campaign has brought it home to me that we did not keep enough records; and of the records we did keep, we were able to bring only a part with us to Europe. So that, alas! much is lost to us that is both valuable and unique. I am all the more pleased therefore, that I shall be able to supplement my personal recollections with your book. With deepest regards,

(Signed) Von Lettow,
Major-General.

Von Lettow himself, in his own account of the campaign, mentions how my brother captured and burnt a convoy containing *inter alia* some thousands of pairs of trousers, with the result that the enemy were left trouserless for months.

I have only to add that Arnold Wienholt in peace is actively interested in Australian politics, and sits in the Parliament of the Commonwealth as a member of the House of Representatives.

Humphrey Wienholt.

PART 1. PEACE: LION HUNTING

CHAPTER 1
En Route

Many and various are the things that man sets his heart upon. To become Prime Minister is one man's ambition; another would win the Derby or the Melbourne Cup; to hold a championship, be it of croquet or boxing, or any other sport, is sufficient for others. For my own part I have always thought that to shoot a lion was something quite worth doing. From earliest boyhood I had longed to go lion hunting, and had read eagerly every book on the subject that I could get hold of.

In August 1913 I found at last that the opportunity for that expedition to Africa to which I had for so long looked forward was mine. Many of the cattle ranches under my management had been sold, and having resigned my seat in our Queensland State House, to contest a Federal seat against the then Prime Minister, and suffer defeat, I was free for a time from political duties.

My desire was to get away from the common routes of sportsmen, and therefore I determined to try Portuguese West Africa, where, it was recorded, lions were numerous. I decided that the best plan was to travel as far north as I could by rail, through German South-West, a colony I was anxious to see, and then overland to the Okavango. This should bring me out well to the west of Angola, where I judged game and lions would be plentiful. A young half-caste stockman named Joe Barnett, from one of the Western cattle stations, a good, cheerful boy, fair bush cook, and satisfactory horseman and bush-man, accompanied me, and thereby I was saved in the event of accidents from ever being left quite alone.

On arrival at Cape Town I interviewed the German Consul-General, showed my credentials from the German Consul, Dr. Hirschfeld, in Brisbane, and was courteously treated. My object in going to G.S.W. having been explained to the consul, and meeting with no discouragement, I arranged to journey by the first boat. To the Portuguese Consul-General at Cape Town I also paid my respects.

The fortnight spent in waiting for the German coastal boat, the *Freda Woermann*, was taken up with getting rifles, ammunition, and other things necessary for camp that were not to be left to chance on arrival in G.S.W. A good light tent, mosquito nets and many small articles had necessarily to be specially chosen or made to order. Finally I got a .375 Mannlicher, a .303 Sporting Lee Metford, and a .450 Express (Martini action), all made by Westley-Richards, and at prices decidedly reasonable.

At length the old *Freda Woermann* was ready to start, and though she was but a small boat, the run up the coast was not unpleasant. True, the old *Freda* was a terrible roller. A much-travelled fellow-passenger assured me that a ship could not be said to roll until the trunks came charging out from under the bunks, and even this test was easily passed by the *Freda*.

With the desire to see as much as possible of G.S.W. we landed at Luderitzbucht, the plan being to go right round to Windhuk by rail, and to purchase there stock and plant, and also, if necessary, stores. From Windhuk we proposed to travel by rail to Grootfontein or Tsumeb, one or other of these places to be the starting-point of our *trek*. Little trouble was made at the Customs, to our pleasant surprise. The special permit from the magistrate required in the case of travellers with more than one rifle was obtained without difficulty, and another pleasant surprise was the discovery that the Customs duties were comparatively light. Luderitzbucht cannot boast of charm, for the sandy and rocky coast is quite bare of all vegetation; but the houses built of stone and cement all look wonderfully solid and well constructed, vastly different from our own wooden township buildings in Australia.

The hotels too were quite good. The town, of course, depends for its prosperity almost entirely on the diamond mines around; a remarkably lucky find for Germany these mines, for without them the G.S.W. Colony would have been an extremely expensive possession. Through the courtesy of the *burgermeister*, who held big diamond interests himself, and took a prominent part in the management of several mines, I was enabled to have a good look at the industry here.

From Luderitzbucht the country inland becomes even more desolate than on the coast; in fact, by the time the diamond field is reached,

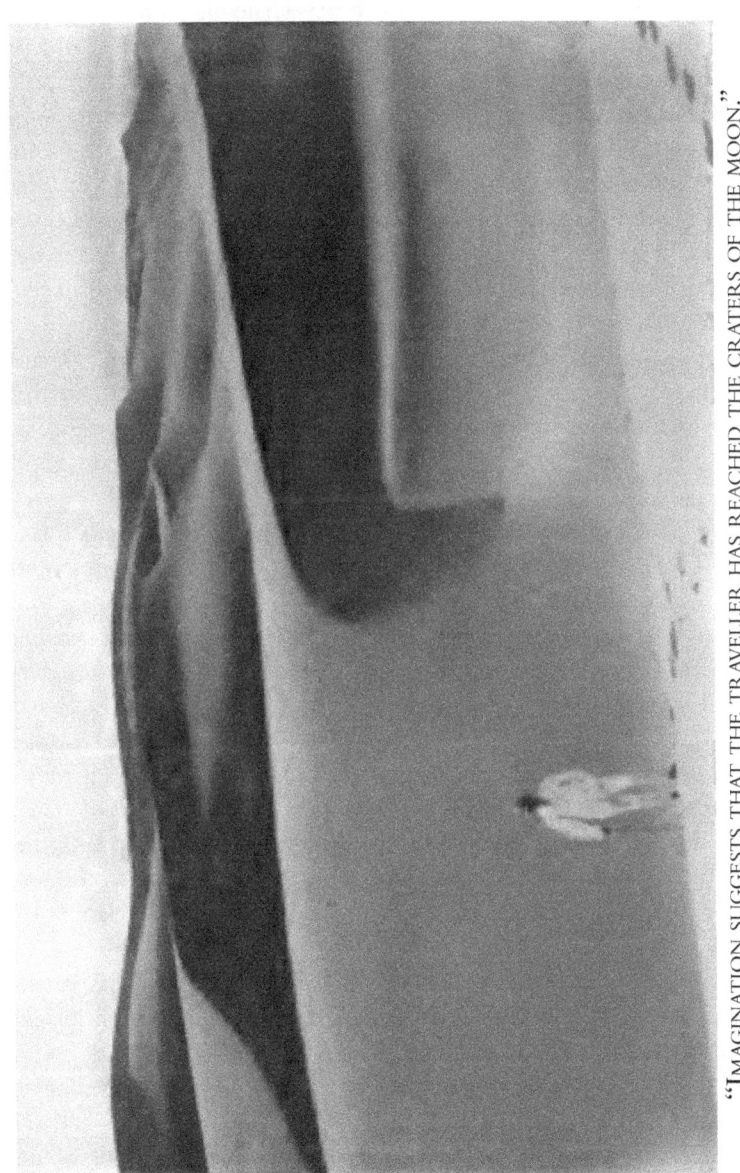
"Imagination suggests that the traveller has reached the craters of the moon."

imagination suggests that the traveller has reached the craters of the moon. The whole surface of the land, that is, the sand, down to the rock, which may be several feet, or only a few inches below the surface, is put through large hand-worked sieves, the big stones and small sand being drafted out. The remainder, perhaps a third, of a size to contain the rest of the diamonds, is from these sieves sent down to the washing mills. There, by a series of washings and concentrations, it is so reduced that the gems can be sorted out on a table by hand. The diamonds are rather small, no big ones have been found, but the quality is good. A large new sifter, to do the work of many hand ones, was then in course of construction, and the entire management of the whole of this field—it could not well be called a mine—was excellent.

From Luderitzbucht to Keetmanshoep was two days by rail, and soon there were many evidences that the colony, plainly a very dry one at anytime, was suffering from severe drought. Keetmanshoep was a pleasantly situated and well-laid-out little township with many good buildings.

Two days more in the train brought us to Windhuk, the capital, where I stayed some nine or ten days. The first morning I presented my papers and was courteously received by the governor and by the administrator. Dr. Hintrager himself was particularly kind and gave me permission to travel quite freely across their north-western districts into Angola. There is a good supply of water in Windhuk, obtained from warm springs evidently of an artesian nature, but the surrounding country is poor, and the small farmers close by who are trying to grow crops or vegetables with irrigation from these springs must have a hard struggle. I completed my plant and stock in Windhuk, with the purchase of a small second-hand wagon, sixteen donkeys, two horses, and two mules, the two latter, as it turned out, being the best of all my purchases.

By good luck, also, I picked up a driver—a Transkei *kaffir* called Charlie—a big fellow with a good open face, the real African black, much to be preferred to any native showing a white cross. Charlie could speak a fair amount of English, enough for our daily needs. But he never could grasp the difference between "this" and "that," and always mixed up those much-used terms. I remember one night, going down the Okavango, we heard the roar of two lions some little way off, and I asked Charlie, who was awake, which side of the river he thought the lions were.

"Master, the lions are *that* side of the river," said Charlie.

Next morning, when discussing where we thought the beasts had been, Charlie pointed back to our side of the river.

"Why, Charlie," said I, "I thought you said last night they were that side of the river."

"Yes, master, this side of that side, master."

In the museum in Windhuk, for me the most interesting thing was the skull of a lion which some time previously had been shot on the Okavango, after it had entered a German military camp at night and carried off a soldier. I heard the details of this adventure from one of the men who had been in the camp at the time.

A body of soldiers, consisting of about thirty mounted troopers, had made their camp one evening close to the river. In the middle of the night this lion had boldly entered the camp in spite of the number of fires about, and, seizing one of the sleeping troopers, started to carry him off. The man thus seized was, like his fellows, thoroughly tired with the wearisome ride through the sand, and did not at first grasp the position, so he merely called out to his comrades to desist from what he thought was their horse-play. However, he was soon thoroughly awake, and when he felt the lion's hairy chest, and sniffed the unpleasant and unusual odour of the great beast, he realised what had happened, and at once he began to struggle violently, yelling out for help at the same time. His cries roused the camp, and the soldiers rushing out frightened the lion sufficiently to make him drop his prey and disappear. But the following night this same bold customer stalked to camp again, only to be shot when about to seize one of the horses. The trooper whom the lion had seized was badly hurt, but eventually recovered in the hospital at Windhuk. The skull was plainly that of a very old lion, all the big teeth being worn down to almost blunt stumps. In this case it must have been old age and hunger that made him so daring.

In Windhuk the habit of closing all shops and suspending all business from 12 to 3 is remarkable. It may perhaps be a sensible and comfortable arrangement, especially as the weather is decidedly hot in the summer months; but to an Australian this establishment of the siesta is somewhat startling.

From Windhuk another four days in the train through the changing country brought us to Grootfontein, the terminus of the Northern Railway. Here, while the grasses, though very dry and bleached, still looked sweet and good for cattle, there was absolutely no surface water to be seen. This northern country of German South-West—and indeed the whole colony—seemed essentially a pastoral rather than a farming country; the total rainfall might be sufficiently heavy if it were spread evenly over the year, but, as things are, nearly the whole rainfall seems atone time—*i.e.* during the wet season.

The policy of the government was to encourage settlement by giving freehold possession. But I think the better plan is to grant long leases of areas of good size at a very small rent, and to reserve the right to resume up to half of these same areas (with, of course, compensation for all improvements made), should it be found desirable later, in the interest of closer settlement. At present the cattle business on purely pastoral lines and in big holdings seems the most likely way in which the colony can get a sound and productive start.

At Grootfontein we got our final supplies for the journey ahead. Two things, however, which were particularly wanted—bells and hobbles—could not be obtained, and the lack of these caused us much inconvenience later on.

It was at Grootfontein that I saw a patrol of some thirty German mounted troops go out on a bushman hunt, two white men, so it was said, having been lately murdered by some of the bush people. The Germans never had the knack of living on good terms with the natives under their rule, for both the Hottentot tribes in the south and the Hereros farther north had rebelled in previous years, in both cases putting up a desperate resistance before being crushed, and now it was the bushmen who were described as giving a great deal of trouble. Throughout the colony, too, the sullenness and depression of the native population was apparent. The British, no doubt, have had their own difficulties in ruling subject races, and critics can point to risings in India, Egypt, and South Africa against British rule. Nevertheless, it remains true that the Germans were particularly unhappy in their relations with the native peoples of South-West Africa.

When we were told that the roads up to the Okavango would probably be closed from want of water until it rained, there remained just a chance that the road to Kuringkuru by Tsinsabis might still be passable, and we elected to try that road. By making a detour, which took us a few days out of the road, I was enabled to visit several pioneer farms on the way, and to accept the hospitality courteously offered by German farmers.

The want of a few good bullock bells for the donkeys at night was now brought home to us, for twice they wandered away and thereby made us miss the trek for the following day.

Eight days later we were at Tsinsabis; outside the last farms and with nothing before us but bush to the Okavango. Our difficulties began at Tsinsabis, for we were faced with the prospect of 120 miles of a dry stage without water; though according to report there was reasonable hope that a little water might be left about thirty-five miles up the road in two big *vleys*, called Gumtsas and Gumtsaup. This meant a ride ahead to learn the truth of the report; and so, after fixing up our camp, I left in the evening on "Tommy," a young grey gelding purchased in Windhuk, to see what the track was like through the sand belt. Not a drop of water was left in either of the big *vleys*, and it was late before I got back to camp the next evening. Nothing now remained but to wait till some storms should bring water and open the road, and storms were already brewing every alternate day. As a matter of fact, it was nearly three weeks before the first water, on the road about thirteen miles out, was sufficient to enable us to push on.

During the spell at Tsinsabis we shot a fair number of small buck to keep the camp in meat, and there was also bigger game as well, for one morning a beautiful white *koodoo* cow passed me quite close. The dog I had bought at a German farm, and which we had patriotically christened Dingo, came in useful in procuring partridges for the pot, as when flushed they invariably took to the top of the tree. Joe was a great hand at the partridges. One morning when he returned with two partridges only, though I had thought I had heard him fire three times, I said to him, "What, only two birds, Joe, from three shots?"

"Oh," said Joe, "mind one of them was running."

Poisonous snakes were fairly plentiful about here, and an enormous brute—his length must have been at least ten feet—came in pursuit of a species of rat quite close one morning before Joe shot him. It was apparently what is called a cobra in Africa: an awful brute with "a head on it like a kangaroo dog." I saw several black Mamba also, very wicked and bad-tempered looking fellows these, and more aggressive than our Australian brown snakes.

My second Cape boy, David, left us at Tsinsabis; he had heard of, or had been stuffed with yarns concerning, the danger ahead of us from lions, bushmen, etc., and wanted to go back, which he did, greatly to Charlie's disgust and amusement.

We were off as soon as this first water was on the road; and by camping the wagon and riding ahead myself with a water-bag to find water, we managed to work up across the former dry stage easily

THE AFRICAN PUFF-ADDER.

enough. As storms were now falling nearly every day, the latter portion of the track to the Okavango became all plain sailing, although in places there was a good deal of work to be done, clearing the track of fallen timber, etc. Our German axe came in for much hearty cursing from all hands, and I heartily wished for a good British one in its place. With all the talk of late years of British manufacturers dropping behind, I am convinced that British-made articles in many departments of industry are still the best in the world.

The only people we saw all the way to the river were two small parties of bushmen, who bolted with fright immediately they caught sight of us. When we got near the river and were in the neighbourhood of lions, I was careful to *kraal* the donkeys with thorn bush close to the wagon every night, and to tie up the horses and mules close to the fire. For as Charlie, who is an authority on donkeys, assured me, "De donkey, master, not frightened for de wolf (hyena), but he very frightened for the lion; he think the lion no good for him." Charlie also told me that "the snake cannot come on the hot ground, or him brand"—*i.e.* get burnt.

CHAPTER 2

The Okavango River

Beautiful was the first view of the Okavango, the great blue river rolling along between green banks. On one side stood the pretty little police station of Kuringkuru, surely the most remote of all the Kaiser's outposts, while across the river was Angola, and the Portuguese post Kuangar. Wonderfully pleasant was the camping by the river-side that night after the long trek through the sand *veldt*, but though we were tired enough, the unusual rippling of the big stream seemed to drive sleep away. It was a typical and glorious African night, with every star showing: a night to lie a-thinking. No matter how vast the number of stars visible, a powerful telescope would bring more and ever more new worlds into the vision. Charlie said he heard the roar of a lion a long way off across the river that night, and I heard the noisy barking of dogs at the Portuguese fort in the early morning.

At the police station there were three German police and about a dozen Herero troopers; also about a dozen mules, but no horses. Received and treated very courteously by the Germans, I wished I had thought of bringing up mails for them, for I found they had been without news for over five months. During the afternoon I paid a visit to the Portuguese fort across the river, where the Portuguese *commandant* also received me very kindly. After the presentation of my credentials, I explained that my plan was to work through Angola towards Rhodesia, for the purpose not only of seeing a new country, but more especially of hunting lions; elephants I had no desire to shoot, and, apart from lions, I proposed to kill only the buck necessary to keep my camp in meat. The *commandant* at once gave me full permission to carry out this plan, assisting me further with a letter of introduction to his posts farther down the Okavango. As to any payment in the matter of a licence he simply would not hear of it at all. A thoroughbred

Portuguese gentleman, this Lieutenant Duron, the *commandant*.

Next day we crossed the river with our whole camp, pulling the wagon to pieces and then floating it over, with our other belongings in canoes, and swimming the stock. This was the first experience of swimming donkeys across a river, and a nice handful they were too. I swam old Billy—my old grey horse—myself, with the two mules following like a pair of big foals. I had bought a team of oxen for the small wagon, as we thought it would be much easier travelling with oxen than with the donkeys. The younger gelding, Tommy, was swapped in part payment for the team with the German trader from whom the oxen were bought.

Tommy was quite a nice-looking horse and had done well enough the principal work—riding ahead to find water in the sand belt—for which I had bought him; I thought, however, he would be sure to die of horse sickness if taken on with me through the wet season ahead, whereas the trader who bought him wanted him to ride back into civilisation straight away. This left me alone with the one horse Billy, a good sort of old grey, grade Arab: a terribly lazy old slug, but with a wonderful constitution, and although he met with a sad fate later on, he was such an annoying old pig that I fear he never gained any sympathy or became very popular. In fact, Billy was voted "generally beastly" (the common and final accusation of schoolboys when a more specific charge is not available). A couple of Ovambos, a somewhat unattractive-looking couple, were procured at the crossing to accompany us.

That night we camped close to the wagon of a German trader who had come up the river from the Quito. He looked, poor fellow, very shaken with fever, and mentioned that on the way up his best ox had been seized and so badly bitten by a lion that it eventually succumbed from the mauling. This piece of news was decidedly exciting. The next few days, happily spent in travelling down the Okavango, were interesting if uneventful. Tied neither to time nor to anything else, we just travelled or camped when and as we felt inclined.

So the weeks sped for us—travelling slowly down the beautiful river: drifting down the river of life too, I suppose, without thought or worry, and with the sheer physical enjoyment of being alive that each day brought. In places the track would be quite close to the river, by low banks and flats; then, as the valley closed in, we would climb long, red, sandy ridges, from which glorious views were often to be seen. Some of our camps on these low ridges were places of real beauty:

vast green plains of grass stretching below, and the great river, with its wide overflow lakes spreading through the flats. A few big buck might be seen out on the grassy flats, but to the eyes of a cattle-man there was room for thousands of cattle. There is a story of an old squatter who made a tour in Europe and gazed on the scenery that has become classic for grandeur and beauty.

On his return he was asked by a friend: "After seeing so much of the world, what do you consider the finest sight you have seen?"

To this the old squatter replied, "Why, five hundred fat Herefords feeding on a ridge beats everything."

We passed odd little Ovambo settlements from time to time. I had no difficulty in shooting what meat I wanted on the road, and one morning some reedbuck let the wagon come so close to them that, while still camping on the ground, I shot a beautiful stag from the seat of the wagon, the buck making no attempt to move even when Charlie stopped the bullocks. Wildebeestes and *sassaby* were fairly numerous also, and I shot an odd one of each kind: there were too many of the native population about for any chance of the meat being wasted.

There came a day when we saw the spoor of four lions. They must have travelled along the track for several miles, after a thunderstorm, and one of the four, it was plain, was a very big male. Numerous were the crocodiles we saw in the river and pools, and the sight of one of these fellows cruising slowly about will discourage the most enthusiastic bather. It was very hot weather, and, but for these brutes, we would have enjoyed many a good "bogey" in the warm blue water. We noted, too, as we began to get down towards the Quito, a good deal of elephant spoor along the frontage, though none of it was fresh; in one place what must have been a fair-sized herd had apparently been holding a kind of *corroboree* across the track in the wet.

When the small Portuguese posts of Bunya and Sambia (at each of which two Portuguese white soldiers and half a dozen natives are kept) were passed, we had worked down as far as Diriko, a Portuguese post at the junction of the Quito and Okavango. The fort is splendidly situated on a high ridge, the big Quito River running round three sides of it. I was anxious to cross the river as soon as possible and get beyond the low-lying flats on the opposite side, for if once the wet season set in, it might mean being detained for months. A Portuguese lieutenant was in charge of the fort, and, with the assistance of his coloured soldiers and a big iron boat, we managed to cross our wagon

Group of Ovambos

Herero Family Party

and belongings without much trouble.

With the stock we had more difficulty, as the currents ran strongly against our side, and it took us three tries to swim the cattle across. The donkeys were more stupid and stubborn than ever, and had to be dragged across, one at a time, behind the canoes. Old Billy I swam across as before, the mules following him like dogs; in fact, it was only by my kicking their noses that they were discouraged from trying to climb on top of the old fellow in the water, so determined were they not to let him get too far away from them.

At Diriko I let my Ovambo boys go home, and engaged some Hereros. These Hereros impressed me very favourably—in fact, I consider them quite the finest of all the native races I have seen in South Africa; big, tall, bony men they appeared to be: not so handsomely made perhaps as some of the East Africans—Zulus or Swazis, for instance—but grim and determined-looking customers; and grim and determined they had previously proved themselves against the Germans. Though very dark in colour, there seems a distinctly Hamidian strain in the Hereros, and they are never given to joking or laughing in the fashion of the average negro. In addition to those who were engaged to accompany me, another small contingent of native Africans were of our company as far as the last Portuguese fort at Mucusso. I suppose they came with us for the sake of companionship and perhaps for safety, and quite possibly for the chance of plenty of free meat. They all gave a hand with my own boys in making the thorn-bush kraal for the donkeys, and in other work.

On two nights before reaching Mucusso, we heard lions. Once the sound was fairly close to the camp. I notice that stock seem to take little notice of the roar of a lion, the sound apparently not conveying much to them: in striking contrast to the uneasiness and fear which they show with the slightest taint in the wind. Much has been written about the roar of a lion by old and experienced hands, but when I first heard wild lions, my own impression was that the actual noise was disappointing and by no means so loud as I had anticipated. Still, it must be admitted the sound has a peculiarly penetrating and even menacing tone. Even when one is accustomed for months to the frequent roaring of lions, it is impossible to wake up at night and hear the roar without a thrill of interest.

Later on in the trip, when I had picked up enough of their language to be able to talk a little with my Mombakush hunters, and through them with the bushmen in the camp, we often discussed the

CHEETAHS ON THE TRAIL.

"A LONELY OUTPOST OF THE CHURCH"

habits of lions, and especially when and why they roared. The psalmist of the Bible says that *"the lions roaring after their prey do seek their meat from God,"* but I doubt if this is strictly true in natural history, since a lion would hardly start his night's hunt by uttering so general a warning. Some of my hunters told me that a lion would roar after finishing a meal, if that was the last of the buck he had killed; but if he had killed a big buck, meaning to return to the same kill two or three nights running, he would only roar after the last and final meal off that particular animal. Perhaps they were trying to "pull my leg." At times I have heard lions make a short, grunting noise, probably to keep in touch when hunting or trying to drive game to one another.

We made fairly good time from Diriko to Mucusso, the last Portuguese fort, and the farthest east outpost in Southern Angola. On the other side of the river is the German mission school, a lonely outpost of the church, where the mail only arrives once a year, when the wagon goes down to Grootfontein for supplies in May after each wet season.

We camped several days at Mucusso, and I was able to purchase some flour and a few other supplies at the fort. As from now onwards there would be no road or track of any kind, it was a matter of doubt in which direction to strike, which route would provide the most interesting trip and the best game country; the best game country would certainly mean the most likely place for lions.

Libebe, the principal Mombakush chief, had his *kraal* on an island in the middle of the river, and there I paid him a visit. The island is very rich, every yard of it being cultivated outside the *kraal* itself. Libebe in response came over with about twenty of his retainers to return the visit, and to arrange about supplying me with some boys of his. After we had discussed things, I decided, in spite of hearing that we might find it difficult to get water on the way, to strike across country to the big *kraal* of the chief called Mokoya, which was situated on the Luiyanna River, perhaps 100 miles north-east from Libebe's *kraal*. I was told that we might find lions anywhere in that country, and my own idea was that now the first storms were bringing water in the back country, the game would probably work out that way from the frontages: just as on our far western stations in Australia the cattle after a bad time at once abandon the neighbourhood of the permanent waters directly rain has fallen in the back country.

One old Ovambo tried to persuade me instead of going towards Mokoya's to keep down the Okavango, and then strike out easterly

GAZELLES

A DISCUSSION WITH A MOMBAKUSH CHIEF

from the river, where he said I would find lions very plentiful. He described the latter in true native fashion: pointing to the sun as standing about eight or nine o'clock in the morning, he imitated the lion, "*Whoof, whoof, whoof—neemai!*" (the lion); then showing the sun still up in the late afternoon, "*Whoof, whoof, whoof,*" he called out again, "*neemai!*" (the lion); this was his way of explaining that the lions about there were so plentiful and bold that even well after sunrise and before sunset they are still roaring, and, as Wellington said of the French cavalry on the ridges at Waterloo, "*walking about as if they owned the place.*" However, it was settled that we would work up to Mokoya.

Having arranged for three of Libebe's boys to come with me as far as Mokoya, we made our first camp about ten miles away, where a little local storm had left water in a small *vley*. There I shot a couple of *sassaby*, and sent back the meat of one as a little present for the old chief. The previous season's crops in this district had apparently been only moderate, and as the inhabitants were not too well off for food, a large and self-invited family soon collected round me: at one time as many as forty-four persons travelled with me on the chance of meat.

About this time a two days' run of particularly vile shooting occurred, and unaccountably I missed several easy shots at big buck. The waiting and expectant niggers in camp could hear the rifle-shots in the distance, and returning empty handed made me feel more than a little ashamed before the many reproachful and hungry eyes of the Ovambos: it was as bad as returning to the pavilion after being out for a duck. However, the luck changed, and the white man's shooting reputation was cleared by my very luckily killing stone dead a big old solitary *wildebeeste* bull at 300 yards. It seems to me that the blue *wildebeeste* (or gnu), if not quite a true bison himself, must yet have a very close relative in the American buffalo or European aurochs.

Surface water was very scarce on the way across to the Luiyanna, in fact we only struck open pools in three places; but by digging down about five feet we could get plenty of water in the beds of the big dried *vleys*, and by making a small trough with an oil sheet we had no difficulty in watering all our stock.

Near one of our camps I found the remains of a splendid bull *koodoo* who had been killed by a pack of four or five lions. The lions had been drinking at a small claypan close to their kill, but had apparently not found the water in the little pool where we had our camp, for they had travelled on when the claypan went dry. If the *koodoo* had been found three or four days earlier when freshly killed, there would have been a good chance to get a shot at a lion, for lion spoor was all over the place. The *koodoo's* horns, a very big pair, I kept as a memento. A German down in the colony had told me of some place in these districts where all the native huts have to be built in the trees, so greatly do the inhabitants fear the lion. If this were true, the land should be a paradise for the lion hunter, but I "ha'e ma doots" as to its existence.

It was in this district I saw my first herd of zebras on the road and shot a stallion, a horrible thing to do, although of course every scrap of the meat was eaten. Unless actually compelled, I shall never shoot another. The dead beast was a very handsome animal, considerably bigger and stouter than either of my two mules, and very fat. Zebras seem too heavily made and too coarse in front to be able to raise much pace, and this, with their sleepy disposition in hot weather, makes them an easy prey and a favourite food for lions. Compared with the fleet and watchful buck, the zebra must be a simple capture in spite of his splendid, hard-looking legs, with fine bone and big joints: any "horsey" man will understand what I mean. The black and white stripes, extraordinarily well defined and clear cut, are carried right down to the coronet. In a country where horse sickness is so prevalent, it is a pity that these animals cannot be of more use to man; for though the zebra may be only a "donkey with a football jersey on," he certainly is the king of all asses.

On the road across to Mokoya's I struck some old wagon tracks going north, made, as far as I could make out, many years before by a party of trek Boers. It is rather strange that the Boer never took a fancy to the land in this region, land that was now getting more open, with patches of big open plain. In spite of being sandy, it carried a big crop of grass with plenty of water, obtainable even in the dry season by digging in the *vleys*.

One morning, whilst looking for a blind ox that had strayed away at night, we made the acquaintance of a little party of four unusual-looking bushmen—tall and dark, quite different from the little red or copper-coloured men in German South-West, or the bushmen whom I met and hunted with later on. Whether it happened that these four merely had a negro cross in them, or whether there is a different race or tribe of bushmen in this district, I do not know. These bushmen, who carried bows and arrows and spoke apparently the usual bushman's clicking tongue, were a little shy at first, but I soon made friends with them, giving one of them my Mannlicher to examine and taking his bow and arrows and pretending to suggest an exchange. They ran up the tracks of the lost ox very quickly and helped to recover the beast.

We went out hunting together the same afternoon, and I was well pleased that I had decided to ride my mule when I saw the way they stalked along. Although we were unlucky and struck no game, it was a delight to watch the savages. The bushman who took the lead, a young fellow of perhaps twenty-one years, over six feet in height and quite dark in colour, with a wonderfully pleasant and attractive face, was a fine specimen of humanity; a beautifully made man, with the litheness of the racehorse or the tiger. Even his manner and speech seemed well bred and soft; the kind of man to make a champion swimmer or boxer, or a second Tom Richardson, yet with hands and arms that an actress might envy. All four walked lightly, and with graceful movements, like highly trained thoroughbreds, and my only regret is that I was unable to have any real talk with them.

All these bushmen tribes are in the truest sense savages, as are our Australian aboriginals. Honey getters, root eaters, and snarers of small game, nothing comes amiss to them, even the remains of a lion's kill, but they toil not, neither do they spin. It must take both skill and pluck to live and to hold their own as these bushmen do, and at times it must often be a hard struggle for them. Where lions are thick and bold, they are dangers just as real to-day to these bushmen as the sabre-toothed tiger was to our cavemen ancestors.

Beautiful trackers are these bushmen, the sand with all its footprints being their newspaper, which they read as they travel along. Nothing escapes their notice; everything is an open book to them. Let them cross the big bullock-like tracks of a giraffe ("*garvie*," as they call him), and at once they know all about the big beast: how long ago he passed, and whether he was feeding, or was going fast, or was perplexed and anxious. They know immediately whether it is worth while to run up the tracks or not.

One morning the savages were extremely amused at my shooting a hawk with an old shot-gun. This bird, a particularly cheeky beggar, kept making swoops at our meat which was drying on a shrub close to the wagons. A yell from Charlie under the wagon at the critical moment of each swoop caused him to shy off the meat like a rusty beast passing you in a stock-yard, but as the swoops became closer and bolder, Charlie complained, "That bird he like the meat, master"; and after yet another swoop, "That bird he come to spoil our meat." So the judicious use of a shot-gun became necessary. When the hawk fell, there was a rush of astonished natives, puzzled apparently on not finding a bullet hole.

About the 14th day from Libebe we reached the Luiyanna at Mokoya's *kraal*, and after fixing up my camp, I paid a visit to the chief, or "*capitaine*," as they called him. There was something of a Lobengula about the fat old ruffian, who kept up a strict ceremonial, requiring all his men to approach him only on bended knees. Interviews with the chief were very tedious affairs, and only in a very roundabout way could conversation be carried on. As usual, I asked him if there were lions anywhere about, and tried to get information as to the best route to travel. Mokoya had several modern magazine rifles, including a Lee-Metford and a .375, and, of course, he wanted cartridges. Now I happened to possess cartridges for both the Lee-Metford and the .375, but as nothing would ever induce me to give rifle cartridges to native Africans, it took a little tact to convince him that all my rifles were English and his German, and that consequently none of my cartridges would be of any use.

At last the old villain sent for another weapon, which proved to be a shaky old No. .12 shot-gun, and as I had plenty of shot cartridge with me, I gave him two boxes of twenty-five each. This pleased him immensely, and in the evening he sent me down all the grain I wanted for my boys, and also a very acceptable little present of a calabash of honey. As I had decided to keep down the Luiyanna river as far as a place called, as I thought, Mafoota (though later I found it was the name of a white man and not a locality), I only stopped one day at Mokoya's.

Storms now set in every few days, and it was evident that the wet season we had been expecting had begun. There was a fair amount of game as we worked down the river, but I think most of it was then moving back towards the *vleys*, which were getting filled by these storms. In many places there was a profuse display of wild flowers, very pretty to ride through, especially a kind of big pink daisy, and in the higher country a large red flower, something like a fox-glove, which the bushmen called "*am'deava*." I used to gather bunches occasionally, if only to adorn the cheek straps of my old riding mule. The mules had turned out a good purchase, for they had kept their condition well, had weathered the horse sickness, and were quite passable enough for riding after game or for riding ahead in search of the best way for the wagon to follow. Still, it is impossible to get fond of a mule as we get fond of a horse, the mule being neither "flesh, fowl, nor good red-

WILD SOW AND YOUNG

HIPPOPOTAMUS

herring." The dismay of a hen hatching out a brood of ducklings must surely be equalled by the anxiety of an old mare at her long-eared, half-neighing, half-heehawing progeny.

During the whole eighteen days we were working down the river to Mafoota's, we neither saw nor heard any lions, nor indeed met a fresh lion spoor. Joe was suffering intermittently from fever, so we travelled slowly. We met and made friends with two or three small parties of bushmen on the way down. One morning I shot two *koodoo*, but one of them was only wounded, clumsily enough, in the fore-shoulder. I had only a young bushman boy of about fifteen years with me at the time, but he ran the trail for fully three hours ahead of me, and finally the poor brute worked round close to my camp again. After some lunch and an hour's spell, picking up two other young bushmen and again taking up the spoor, I got another shot late in the afternoon, and finished the wounded animal. Apart from the satisfaction of not having let a wounded beast go, it was an interesting business watching these three red human bloodhounds at work. It would be by no means so interesting to be hunted by them.

A fair number of hippo were in that river, and for a long time one afternoon I watched two of them in a smallish isolated pool. When just the head shows, the hippo resembles a big draught horse swimming, and after seeing them it was easy to understand how they got their name "river-horse." Beautiful is the command they have of the element in which they are so much at home!

But I am afraid I became unpopular with a small local faction of the inhabitants when I left the hippo unmolested.

In places along the river there were a lot of giraffe, and what pantomime animals they are! They must be seen in their wild state to be appreciated fully as the freaks they are. When disturbed they seem to start galloping in three parts, the neck going one way, and the front and hind legs galloping, apparently out of step with each other. Every minute it looks as if they would fall over or break their necks in the trees, though, as a matter of fact, it would take a smart horse to catch up with them. To the Mambokush, a giraffe, I think, represents absolute perfection in the game line: a big mass of meat, with plenty of oily fat, and, above all, no danger or risk in the capture of these most harmless of animals.

The native Africans are certainly not sportsmen. Their word for buck is "*nyamm*" (meat), and when pointing out a buck they always use the one word "*nyamma*," "*nyamma*." My hunters could never understand what the object was in wanting to shoot lions, and at different times they assured me, "*Morena, neemai badiko nyamma, badeka nyamma, morena*"—"Master, the lion is not meat, is no good for meat, master." I think their astonishment finally reached its height on the day an old lion skin was proudly brought into camp by some natives who wished to sell it to me. On my explaining to them that, as I had not shot the lion myself, the skin was of no value to me, and that I did not want it, they were utterly mystified. Probably they were thinking, "He does not want the meat, and now when he can get a skin without any trouble or danger, he does not want that either. What in the name of goodness can he want? Truly the ways of a white man are mad and inexplicable! "

We were now nearing the far south-east corner of Angola, moving towards the point where "three Empires meet," for North-West Rhodesia, Angola, and German South-West Africa all meet at a point somewhere below the confluence of the little Luiyanna with the Quandoo River. It was before we reached Mafoota that we suffered the loss of old Billy—"Billy the pig," to give him his full title. In spite of being tied up all night close to the wagon, Billy had been getting fatter than ever, though only eating grass, and it was but the evening before he died that I remarked to Joe, "I wonder after all if this old fellow is going to prove immune to horse sickness; he has never looked better."

At daylight next morning, however, when I let him go to feed around the camp, for the first time since we had had him Billy would not start eating, and by the time we were ready to move off camp, the old horse was puffing hard and evidently had the sickness. Before we had gone a quarter of a mile the poor old chap was too bad to lead. I knew that he was such a crying and whinnying old brute when left a moment alone, or apart from the mules, that if he possibly could he would follow of his own accord; but when the bridle was taken off him he lay down very sick. Still, when he saw the wagon and mules gradually leaving him, he got frightened at being left behind. Three times he made a gallant effort on his own to struggle up, the third time just succeeding. Slowly and gamely the old horse came pottering along after the wagon, but gradually fell behind and was lost to sight, a grey dot in the distance.

We only made a short stage of a few miles and then camped, half hoping that the old grey would come crawling into camp. In the afternoon boys were sent back to report how old Billy was, and when they found him he had already been dead some hours. Lying right on the track, he had followed as far as he could. That night we heard the hyenas howling his *requiem* in the distance.

What an appalling thing this African horse sickness is! It does more than anything else, I think, in Africa, to check progress. From the pastoral point of view especially, it is a frightful drawback. As a cattleman accustomed in Queensland to plenty of cheap and good horses, I cannot see how any of the country in Southern Africa can be successfully developed till this cursed horse sickness is stamped out or cured. No cattle will do well unless they have a free run, can feed and water when and where they like, and are able to withdraw to the ridges in cold weather. To be compelled to *kraal* cattle regularly every night is not only to encourage disease, but to make it impossible to expect any satisfactory result. But then if cattle are given the necessary freedom, they naturally become too lively or too flash to be handled on foot and must be worked with horses. All the cattle countries of the world—of course, I am speaking from a ranch or pastoral point of view—and especially the Argentine, Western America, and Australia, have, as a necessity, a plentiful supply of good horses, for without such a supply the cattle could not be economically worked.

About the eighteenth day we reached Mafoota's, where I had the pleasure of meeting Mafoota himself—otherwise Mr. W. Keys. He has made his home on a red sandy ridge overlooking the Quandoo, a beautiful though lonely spot on the edge of the Sepango forest, a forest that consists of very light, open scrub intersected by waste spaces. It was pleasant to have a good yarn with another white man again, and especially with Mafoota, an old African pioneer, with great knowledge of the country and its peoples. Mafoota (the native name comes more easily than the English) told me that at the time when his camp was farther up the river, he passed three years without seeing a white face. From him I learnt also that quarantine regulations would prevent me taking my stock through either Rhodesia or the Caprivi Sipra; information that decided me to strike west again and make a settled camp somewhere for a month or so; by which time I judged the wet season ought to be over.

After sending a few boys across to Livingstone to bring back my mail and a few other necessaries, we fixed our camp twenty-five miles west of the Quandoo. No sooner was the camp fixed, than the wet season started with fairly heavy rains, and a chapter of accidents opened that gave us rather a bad time. Both Joe and Charlie went sick, and then I fell ill myself through foolishly riding all day in the wet in search of some missing stock (the boys having lost a lot of the oxen and three donkeys) when I was already feverish. Joe and Charlie soon got right, but my recovery was a hard struggle, and it took me about seven weeks to pull through.

The most difficult part was the effort to keep a grip on oneself mentally, and so escape becoming delirious. I remember one evening, when the boys were trying to catch the mules, and the said mules—all with their bells on—were running about between the tents, being greatly worried by an almost overwhelming feeling that the thing I ought to do was to crawl to the door of the tent and shoot the bells off the mules as they ran past.

Misfortunes never come singly, and a strange native, seeing one of my mules in the long grass some distance from the camp, stalked it and shot it with an old Portuguese muzzle-loader under the belief it was "*nyamm*"—eland or something, I suppose. He had never seen a mule before and knew nothing of my camp. It was maddening, this loss of a good riding mule; but the poor devil of a native was terribly distressed, and there was nothing to be done. There is an element of humour in the accident, though at the time I completely failed to see it. Along the *vleys* near this camp, wild duck, evidently migrating from the rivers in the wet season, were in abundance; and very good eating, too, they proved, as also did the big black and white geese, when not too old.

As soon as I was sufficiently recovered from the fever, the camp was moved back again towards the Quandoo, about seven or eight miles from Mafoota's. I found I was now reduced to riding an ox, as the only mule that remained had got a terribly sore back after Charlie had ridden her for a day. However, the little black ox which became my chief mount was very much better than nothing, for I was not yet strong enough to walk more than a mile or so at a time.

One day I got a grand eland bull, luckily quite close at hand, and so big that it took two pack-ox loads and eleven boy loads to bring the meat into camp. Its dressed weight could hardly have been less than 1,100 lb. This eland meat was enormously fat, especially on the brisket, but yet was not at all coarse. In fact it was exactly like that of a big prime bullock, and, in my experience, the eland is by far the best buck meat there is. The eland can, perhaps, claim to share with the moose the sovereignty of the deer tribe.

The health of Joe and my *kaffir* driver was poor at this season, and

Riding ox

as both men seemed very homesick and in low spirits, I decided to send them to their respective homes. Their going left me quite alone in my camp, save for my local boys, and the solitude, of necessity, made me begin to pick up more quickly the native language. As a matter of fact, I particularly desired to master, at least to a slight extent, the bushman speech, that extraordinary though not altogether unmusical language of clicks.

The weather was by this time glorious, the nights cool and the days warm and bright. The grass was drying very rapidly, and I was able to burn patches in the neighbourhood of my camp, so that the early green spring in the grass might bring the buck on to the freshly burnt feed near my camp. Gradually, too, I was getting stronger and recovering from the effects of the fever.

A native hunter named Tatello visited our camp during my sickness, and volunteered to show me, on my recovery, where lions were plentiful—a somewhat unusual incident, as the inhabitants of those districts generally did not share my enthusiasm for the particular game we were seeking. However, I told Tatello that when I was strong enough, and had got the stores which were expected from the Zambezi, I would be prepared to go out on a hunt with him on the strict understanding that as far as he was concerned it was to be a case of no lions, no pay.

We were hearing lions quite frequently about this time, and, in particular, two had passed my camp one morning grunting in daylight, whilst I was away in another direction. There were also a fair number of that beautiful and graceful buck, impala, in the neighbourhood, and I shot several good stags. As we were then being visited by crowds of natives, many of whom came to trade with grain, pumpkins, etc., and held nothing more acceptable than meat, I shot occasionally an extra buck over and above what we needed for the modest requirements of our own little camp.

These weeks of steadily returning strength and the awaiting of expected stores passed very pleasantly. Now and then I would drive my own team of oxen for a load of wood, though Mafoota, to whom I sometimes gave a lift, would always rudely insist on getting out and walking when we got in amongst the timber.

With increasing knowledge of the language, it now became more interesting to talk to my boys—who never could be got to understand why, as I had told them, there was no game in my country (Australia).

"*Badeko hefu* (no eland); *badeko thovoo* (no wildebeeste); *badeko lefoouu* (no *sassaby*); *badeko mapi* (no *deiker*); and *badeko fumbo* (no sable)"; but when I reached "*badeko fumé*" (no rhinoceros), there was a chorus of astonishment and surprise, and "*badeko fumé,*" "*badeko fumé*" resounded: though why they thought it particularly wonderful that there were no rhinoceros (of all things) in Australia, I cannot imagine. When I started to make a little vocabulary of Makwengo (bushman), the spelling on particularly phonetic lines gave curious results. Hyena, for instance, I could only best put on paper as "oooo," a case, I think, of onomatopoeic spelling.

Old hands sometimes deny the bushman any keen sense of humour, but the natives of these parts could certainly enjoy a joke. Once, being intently watched by some twenty natives whilst sitting on top of the wagon, I pretended, after appearing to examine my discarded trousers (which, though old, had not yet reached the "given away" stage), to pitch them away. With one bound the whole mob of spectators leapt forward in the direction to which I appeared to be throwing the coveted garment. The laughter that followed when they found the trousers had not really left my hands was, if disappointed, quite good-natured.

Another day, having shot a *sassaby*, I fastened the horns (which I had chopped off) under the bridle on the mule's forehead, leading her back to camp with this unnatural growth. This, too, seemed to tickle the camp followers as something particularly funny.

A third instance: Amongst my boys there was a harmless lunatic. Mafoota, on a visit, caused considerable laughter by saying, "I notice your staff now consists of three men and one baboon."

I confess to a liking for these savages who have never yet been spoilt by civilisation and are still really children in most ways. What a happy disposition they have, and how few things seem to worry them! After all, the savage is fairly near the surface in all of us, and primitive instincts are still the basis of everyday life. Who is there that does not like honey? Does a woman ever look better than when she is wearing furs? I have read of a multi-millionaire who, when asked at the end of an interview by a reporter, "Now, Mr. So-and-so, may I ask you what you find your greatest personal pleasure?" replied, "To sit in front of the fire in my bedroom with my clothes off." Anyone who has knocked about the world, enjoying the good times and enduring the hard, experiencing, in short, something of many sides of life, realises that there is only a difference in degree between the ten-course dinner at a luxurious hotel, and a plain meal of cold corned brisket, fresh damper, and a pot of tea. (Personally I much prefer the latter.) The sum of life's happiness remains whether we live in a stone mansion or in a comfortable weatherboard cottage; whether we are adorned with a frock coat and bell topper, or clad in a soft shirt and moleskins. What does matter is the absence of a sufficiency of good food and clothes and of a comfortable home. There should be opportunity, too, for pleasure and relaxation, for it is not well that life should be one continual grind of labour.

Further, it is well to feel that one's children will have such education that, should opportunity offer, and their characters are equal to the burden, they may hold even the highest positions in the State. Perhaps, above all, it is good to know that in case of sudden death or accident, neither wife nor children will be left totally unprovided for. I think that any young man by the time he is twenty-five (quite apart from any particular gift of brains or other possessions), as long as he is a worker and not a drunkard, should be in a position to marry the right girl if she will have him, and enjoy life with her in happiness and comfort. These are some of the things that seem to me of real importance, and I believe that in Australia our ideas and politics will yet follow the lines of sturdy individualism rather than of Socialism. For Socialism, even if it were possible—by first killing individual effort and personal spirit—would soon bring national disaster at the hands of some more vigorous power.

At last the long-expected supplies came, and we had a three days' trip down the river and back in canoes to get them. Everything was now ready for a start after the lions. It was decided to hunt for a couple of months west of the Quandoo, and then to work in towards the Zambezi, with the hope that on the way we might meet Mr. Venning, the Native Commissioner at Sesheke, and with him try the pools known as M'gwezi, this side of the Zambezi, where lions were said to be pretty plentiful. Leaving the camp about the middle of July in charge of my little boy Sangallegwa and two smaller *piccaninnies*, I started out west with Tatello, three other hunters, four bearers, and two young boys.

We worked back towards the Okavango, but it was some seven or eight days before we began to find many signs of lions. Game was plentiful, and there was no difficulty in keeping our camp in meat; by shooting an extra buck or so, in particular one very big eland bull, we had no trouble in procuring what grain was wanted from the scat-

"Lex Talionis"

The Gemsbok

tered Mombakush *kraals* in exchange for meat and fat. I had made friends with a little party of bushmen that we came across, by shooting a wildebeeste for them, and I took two hunters from amongst them who rejoiced in the names of Qumano and Boombo respectively. In both these men the Mongolian type was evident, while the younger bush children are very pretty and very like Japanese babies.

CHAPTER 3

Nearing the Lion Country

We now began to find fresh lion spoor about, and in one place the bushmen ran for a short way up the tracks of a giraffe that had been chased by a lion—the tracks of both galloping animals being plain even to a white man. The giraffe had been "scratching gravel," yet I doubt a single lion holding or killing such a big beast as a giraffe. Perhaps he had chased it more out of play than anything else. Two or three times we had run up fresh tracks only to lose them, but it seemed we were getting closer to some sport.

Whilst hunting round for fresh lion spoor one morning, with little Qumano in the lead and some other hunters, we came quietly on a great bull eland standing under a tree in a little open patch. Qumano was at once all tension like a pointer. Getting off my mule whilst the boys squatted on the ground, I sat down to watch the noble fellow. As we already had sufficient meat for some days ahead, there was, of course, no wish on my part to molest him; so after enjoying the sight for some time, I mounted to ride on. Poor Qumano could not believe his eyes when he understood that I did not intend to shoot the eland; his expression of horrified astonishment and disgust at thus seeing meat and fat in the shape of a huge buck being left on the *veldt* was really ludicrous, and I should like to have been able to translate what his excited chatter meant.

My boys never could understand the pleasure I took in merely watching, without any desire to kill, the big buck. On this last trip in particular I fear I got into bad odour with my hunters for stalking close up to and watching a little herd of giraffe without shooting one. There was a magnificent bull in this particular mob; a still prettier sight was a cow with a quite small calf at foot, the tiny fellow striding alongside his mother like a little thoroughbred.

At last, one morning before sunrise two lions began to approach the camp, or rather, I expect the *vley*, some 100 yards or so away, keeping up a continual and steady roar. I used to camp generally fifty or sixty yards from my mob of natives, with, of course, a fire of my own. It was necessary to get some distance from them, as they always kept up a continuous chatter half through the night. Between my fire and the various fires of the boys we used to tie, for safety, the old mule and pack ox. I was lying awake that night listening to the noise of the lions, which seemed to be coming steadily nearer, when my little cook boy, Secumba, came running across to where I was lying (I took no tent on these expeditions), crying, "*Moraina, moraina?*" ("Do you hear the lions?"). He spoke in his own language, for in these parts not a word of English is known.

"Yes, Secumba," I said, "I can hear the lions."

Now, it was Secumba's duty always to keep my big enamelled billy full of water, so I added, "But, Secumba, I think the bucket is empty." It was quite dark and the water was some way off and that unpleasant moaning noise was getting closer and closer, so Secumba evidently thought my little joke in bad taste; but a very sickly grin came over his face, and he, making up my fire, returned to his own without any reference to the state of the water supply.

These lions seemed to turn back before they came to the water, though they continued roaring as they drew away. After an early breakfast, taking the two bushmen and other hunters, we set off to try and pick up and follow the trail of our last night's visitors. A hundred yards behind the *vley* Qumano picked up the tracks, crossing a bit of newly burnt country, and the pleasurable excitement of following up two big male lions, as they appeared by their tracks, now began. My hunters told me that these lions had not killed anything during the night, and on my being somewhat sceptical, they referred me to Makwengo.

These little men, however, only confirmed the same opinion, "*Ambi kocho—ambi kocho*" ("no meat"), for when it came to a dispute on the matter of tracks, etc., a bushman's verdict was final, even with the other natives. It was a long walk following the spoor, travelling fast where the sand was fairly heavy and the tracks plain, but losing time when we got amongst thorn bush or on the harder white sand and ant-bed country. There was a feeling as of electricity in the air when the tracks became very fresh, and even the little mongrel *kaffir* cur of Tatello felt this; for, when my leg once brushed him unexpectedly, he jumped sideways, doing it so comically, with a frightened yap, that we all burst out laughing, the boys seeing the joke too. The younger bushman, Boombo, always took the lead when the *spoor* was straight ahead, going quickly, his eyes glued to the ground. I followed him and the remaining boys in a line behind. If he got checked, then Qumano and the others would help to pick up the tracks again.

After a while we came out suddenly on a more open patch, with a thorn-bush scrub on our left and a little patch of bush around an ant bed straight in front. We were quite close up to the ant bed, Boombo with eyes on the ground, when there was a quick, excited chatter from the boys behind. I turned to see them all excitedly pointing to something directly before us, and at that moment two splendid big male lions appeared, doubling back into the bush with a "whoof, *whoof*," the half-angry, half-frightened noise a lion makes when suddenly surprised. Of course, the boys bolted immediately; Boombo simply disappeared.

This was my first sight of wild lions, and I fear, though it is unpleasant to make the admission, that I must have been a little excited also. I had two very close, though necessarily quick shots, one at each lion as they broke across the open patch one behind the other, but hit neither. I felt certain afterwards that had they been two big buck instead of lions I should have killed them both. We burnt the two lions out of their patch of bush with a fire, and later on burnt them out of another patch as well, but in both cases they broke on the side opposite to which I had posted myself. Thus we never caught sight of them again, and finally, getting into a patch of thick bush where the grass had already been burnt, and having no dogs, we were forced to leave them. Airedales have the best name for this sort of work, but I am looking forward on my next trip to taking with me some Australian cattle dogs to see how they shape: I think they should be just the thing. No dog with a bull strain in it is of much use, for its nature inclines it to make a rush on the lion, which means inevitably a sudden end.

The dogs are wanted simply to tease and attract the big beast's attention; moreover, at night a camp is not really quite safe without a dog. A good pack of dogs would have made all the difference to us on this expedition, and I had counted on picking up some in German S.W.; but they were simply unprocurable there, and the boys that I had sent in earlier from the Quandoo to try and bring out a collection of dogs (I had written to agents in Livingstone asking them to procure such a collection for me) were so frightened when they reached the

Zambezi, that they fled to their *kraals* without telling me. It is not, of course, every dog that cares to face or bail up a lion, or even follow the scent.

I felt delighted that at last I had seen wild lions; they seemed bigger and darker than one had imagined. It was satisfactory too that the plan of following up their tracks with these bushmen was turning out so promising a way to get some sport. At the same time I was horribly vexed with myself for having shot so hurriedly and badly.

On the following night I heard a solitary lion grunting in the distance; the boys said that later on—after I had fallen asleep—he passed quite close. However, through some mistake or dispute, we did not manage to cut his tracks next morning. Accordingly we shifted camp some miles south to the neighbourhood of a little *kraal* called Lekasi, and I shot a *sassaby* in the evening. What beautiful buck they are! It is not to be wondered at that Frederick Selous, that mighty hunter, counted them as belonging to the fleetest of all buck. They seem made for pace, with a lean, thoroughbred-looking head, beautiful sloping shoulders, and high withers; while the somewhat drooping hindquarters and finely turned hocks must all help to give them their great speed. Graceful movers, too, they are when travelling fast. If one could only breed such a racehorse, what a flyer he would be!

Chapter 4

At Grips With the Lion

Taking Qumano and a few other boys with me next morning, we started a look round, though no lions had been heard during the night. Two miles from the camp we hit some fresh spoor, and this, after examination, was reported to me as being that of three lions who had gone that way during the night, and the word was at once given to take up the track. It was not easy country to follow the spoor in, but eventually we found a place where the lions had pounced upon and killed a young two-year-old wildebeeste. According to their custom, the lions had dragged away the offal and scratched sand over it, the carcase itself having been removed and eaten close by. Hardly anything remained except the hide, with the bony part of the legs and skull attached to it, and Qumano proudly cut off the miserable hind legs above the hocks and transfixed them on his little spear. In vain I tried to explain to him that there were heaps of meat at my camp, that his carrying such a prize was surely a slur on his master's commissariat, and that he would make me indeed appear a "hungry master." The little bushman was bred in a hard school of *waste not, want not,* and stuck to his meatless, lion-slobbered hocks.

We soon found that the lions had been camping quite close to their kill, and on hearing us had galloped off, as their tracks showed. Taking Qumano with me, and the other boys following, we started again on the track as hard as we could, the spoor leading through light sand where the tracking was good. After about a mile or so we got our first glimpse of the lions on the move, perhaps a quarter of a mile ahead. I now took Tatello alone with me, and telling the others to follow well back, we set off in the hope of catching up the lions. As we followed them, we had glimpses of them from time to time, ahead between the broken bush, half walking, half jogging, their heads held somewhat low, for all the world like three huge mastiffs. They seemed anxious, and at times would stop and look back over their shoulders. Finally, when I judged we were nearly parallel to them, I ran up alongside a big ant heap.

The lions were now crossing a bit of open country ahead at possibly 400 yards distance from me, a big male in the middle with two lionesses; they were all on the move and I made up my mind to have a shot at the lion while I had the chance. My bullet hit him hard, knocking him right round, and thereupon he gave a violent display of bad temper, tearing up the ground, staggering about and roaring, his tail straight out behind him. He behaved, in fact, just like an ill-tempered buck-jumper finishing up an unsuccessful set-to. I thought, "I should not like to be too close to you, my boy," but little imagined the same big rascal would so soon be on top of me. The two lionesses had halted immediately and were both staring hard at me, or rather perhaps in the direction whence my shot had come, for it is doubtful if they could have seen me. Except for throwing in another cartridge, I sat quiet.

The lion's performance having carried him behind a little broken tree, which prevented me getting a second clear shot at him, I refrained from firing at either of the lionesses lest I might have a second wounded beast to manage. Presently the lion himself worked more into the open and I got a second shot at him, but my bullet merely passed under his stomach, throwing up the sand between his four feet. At this all three cleared off immediately in different directions into the bush, and to my disgust the big fellow appeared to move as briskly as the others. The rest of the boys, having heard the rifle shots and the roaring of the angry lion, now came up, and Tatello described in true native fashion the whole performance to the new-comers, showing off the actions of the principals concerned.

I had an unhappy feeling that about the worst thing that could have happened had really taken place, and the absence of all enthusiasm on the part of the boys when I prepared to follow up once more the track of the lions fully confirmed the idea. The ground was scratched and bloodstained where the lion had been hit, and we followed up the *spoor* very carefully. The lion, we found, after moving about 200 yards and being evidently pretty sick, had then laid down underneath a bush, leaving a pool of blood where he had stopped.

It was rather dangerous and ticklish work I felt, and a good pack of dogs was badly needed. The faithful dingo had disappeared one night a month or two before, probably taken by a leopard, and I had been unable to get any others. The boys were frightened, but still kept together pluckily enough and slowly followed the spoor. Qumano, however, had evidently shot his bolt; he drew the line at following a wounded lion, and he is not to be blamed, for nobody knows more about a lion than these little wild men.

The spoor now showed that one of the lionesses had come in and joined her wounded companion, and when the double spoor presently took us into a nasty thick piece of thorn-bush scrub, I decided, in accordance with my boys' views, to leave the lion for that day and to pick up the tracks again next morning; we thought that by that time there was every chance that we should find him dead.

So, leaving the spoor, we made our way back to camp, which was not far off, for the lion had taken that direction. That evening I turned in with a somewhat mixed anticipation that perhaps a lively time was coming. Next morning, after breakfast, having seen that the cartridges in the magazine were all clean and ready, we set off to take up once more the tracks of the wounded beast. Starting, according to my custom, when ready without saying a word, I was pleased to note that all my boys, bearers as well as hunters, fell into line behind me, with, of course, the two bushmen.

The dozen natives, all armed with spears, and following in single line, looked quite formidable, though I was aware not much reliance could be placed on my army. Little Boombo, who was not with me the previous day, now walked last of my followers, and I sung out for him to come to the front with me. He came up the line with a somewhat jaunty swing of the shoulders, receiving encouragement and probably chaff from the other natives, and from his expression it might be inferred that he judged the honour somewhat doubtful.

We soon picked up the tracks of the lions, but it was wretched country for the pursuit. Twice the boys cleared out with a false alarm, and it was plain they were all a trifle "jumpy." The second lioness had joined the other two, and we saw where they had been lying down, the big male leaving signs of blood at his stopping-place. Presently the tracks led out of the thorn bush, and away back right over the same country and over nearly the same spot where I had shot the lion the day before. The boys were naturally anxious and slow, and I think did well to stick to the tracks at all. Finally, after some hours on the trail, the tracks again began to take us into thicker thorn-bush country.

It was all rather close work, and as it was becoming hot and I was getting tired, and there was no certainty of how far off the lions might still be, I began to think we should have to give the hunt up. However, just ahead of us was a patch of more open bush, once an old cultivation plot (or "lands" as it is called in Africa), where natives had grown mealies or other grain, now abandoned, the light reddish soil having been exhausted. This patch had three or four years' growth of young bushes scattered over it, besides old stumps and grass. Giving one of my boys my box of matches and telling them to start a fire, I myself made a circle, followed by the two bushmen and one or two of the other natives.

When we had gone round to the far edge of the old lands, I thought I would wait there in some good position on the chance of getting a shot at the lions as they came past me from the fire, that is, if they were still there. No sooner had I decided that we had reached a good position, than my boys showed me fresh lion tracks, which I had crossed, showing that the lions had got on ahead of us. This seemed a finishing stroke, and I sat down to wait for the remainder of the boys before returning to my camp. In the meantime I asked the boys to see how many lions had gone on, and they, after investigating for some time, held up their fingers and showed me that two lions only had passed.

When Tatello and the remaining boys arrived, we held a discussion. I told Tatello that as there were only two lion tracks here, I thought they must have missed the track of the wounded lion during the morning, and that he was perhaps lying dead a long way back in the bush. This Tatello had hardly begun vehemently to repudiate, when a noise like the squalling of a huge angry tom-cat brought the discussion to an abrupt end. The noise came from the lion himself, and, stuck between us and the advancing fire, he was clearly in a very angry and perhaps excusably bad temper. Immediately there was a wild hullabaloo and a general rush amongst my boys, and in very much less time than it takes to tell I found myself alone.

Thinking the wounded lion was following along the spoor in the same direction the lionesses had taken, I quickly got about a dozen yards to the right of the track. This left a fairly clear view to my left, and there I waited, kneeling behind a stump and bit of bush. The boys had rushed away to the edge of the old lands and had climbed into the trees; though, in fairness it must be mentioned, one of them stopped and ran a few yards back, touching me on the shoulder and saying something before hastening to rejoin the others. What he said I do not know, but I suppose it was something in the way of a warning.

At first I expected the lion to show up at any moment, but as the minutes passed and he did not come, my tension slackened a little, and I glanced back over my shoulder to see where my boys were. Perched up in three or four trees, some fifty yards to my rear, they all were, and the twelve niggers thus settled on the branches, one above the other, like a flock of great blackbirds, presented a distinctly comical appearance. They are not to be blamed for bolting. It was not as if I had been suddenly attacked and seized by the lion when they were with me. Their attitude now said quite plainly, "We have done our share in bringing him up to the lion; if the white man likes to remain down there looking for trouble, well and good; it's his funeral, not ours."

One more angry whine came from ahead, but nothing more, and there was no other sign of the animal. The fire in front was still burning and crackling, but only somewhat spasmodically, through the thinner grass of the old cultivation patch. I kept quite still, anxiously watching my front; but after a time I began to feel tired, and to wonder what should be the next move. I really could not stay there all day. It had been anxious and close work from the time we had first taken up the spoor of the wounded beast (for I knew there was a risk of having to stand a savage charge almost at any moment), and I did not feel too game: at the same time I wanted to finish the hunt. I did not like the idea of throwing up and turning back at the last moment.

Besides, the lion must have been very hard hit to have stayed behind when his lionesses fled, and for all I knew he might be so far gone and so weak as to be almost helpless. It was only the previous evening in camp that I had been rereading some of my favourite poems of Adam Lindsay Gordon's from an old battered copy that I always carried in my tucker box. One poem in especial, *Lex Talionis*, always appeals to me. In this Gordon says that the only excuse for the enjoyment of shooting such game as pheasants, hares, etc., and the other animals that cannot hit back is, that a man must also be prepared, when necessary, to take his chance with dangerous game.

> *Shall we, hard hearted to their fates, thus*
> *Soft hearted shrink from our own.*
> *When the measure we mete is meted to us,*
> *When we reap as we've always sown.*
> *Shall we who for pastime have squandered life,*
> *Who are styled the 'Lords of Creation,'*
> *Recoil from our chance of more equal strife,*

And our risk of retaliation?
Though short is the dying pheasant's pain,
Scant pity you may well spare,
And the partridge slain is a triumph vain,
And a risk that a child may dare.
You feel when you lower the smoking gun
Some ruth for yon slaughtered hare,
And hit or miss in your selfish fun,
The widgeon has little share.

But you've no remorseful qualms or pangs
When you kneel by the grizzly's lair,
On that conical bullet your sole chance hangs,
'Tis the weak one's advantage fair,
And the shaggy giant's terrific fangs
Are ready to crush and tear;
Should you miss one vision of home and friends,
Five words of unfinish'd prayer,
Three savage knife stabs, your sport ends
In the worrying grapple that chokes and rends—
Rare sport at least for the bear.

These lines came into my head while I waited kneeling. I thought of the beautiful buck I had shot from time to time, and "Hang it all, here goes," I said to myself; "I must have a cut at this." Of course, it may seem very foolish now, but that is how I felt at the time.

Hardly was my mind thus made up when I distinctly heard the lion. Plainly he was lessening the distance between us, and I could hear him breathing as though in distress, like a horse gone in the wind. Slight puffs of breeze (the wind was blowing almost straight from the lion to me) made me lose the sound of his breathing, and then as these puffs died down I could again pick up the sound. It was impossible to see him, but at any rate I could now locate roughly the direction in which he was lying.

Another longish wait followed, and now it seemed that he had stopped, for the sounds came no closer. Expecting every minute to catch a glimpse of him through the low bushes, I began very carefully and slowly (with a "the headmaster wishes to see you after twelve" feeling) to work my way towards where I heard him, stopping to listen every time a gust of wind deadened the sound of his breathing. Slowly and with the greatest care I advanced some ten or twelve yards, expecting every second to see the lion, and feeling that if I could just get time to raise my rifle and cover him it would settle the matter at once. I had just worked up to a straggly young thorn bush, and was crouching behind it, when in a flash I saw the lion, moving, and moving rapidly, towards me. With poor generalship I had got into a bad place, since, though I could see him plainly, the thorn bush was too high to shoot over, and no one would dare attempt to shoot through it.

I could neither run away nor remain where I was, so I had to step out clear of the bush, almost towards the charging beast. He was then quite close, within twenty yards perhaps. There was no time to kneel and get a sight on the broad chest: I had simply to throw up the rifle like a shot-gun and shoot straight into him. Where I hit him, or whether I missed him entirely (which was possible enough, for I expect my rifle went off more from fright than anything else), I did not know.[1] I only realised that I had fired, that he was still moving, and was now nearly upon me. This certainty that he had not been stopped brought a nasty tightening up sort of feeling, which was perhaps the most unpleasant part of the whole affair.

I tore back the bolt of my rifle, threw out the empty shell, and tried to jump back behind the bush out of the lion's way. He had charged in absolute silence, coming very fast, not in great bounds, but with a sort of run along the ground. Now he came round the bush like a flash, knocking me down, and throwing me several yards behind the bush. I do not quite understand how he actually knocked me over, for I was not clawed in any way, and I heard afterwards that I had broken one of his forelegs. I only know that when he reached me I was off my balance. Anyone who has done or watched much boxing will understand how a man, caught retreating off his balance, can be knocked over with quite a light blow—a blow hardly felt; it is a very different matter to receive a punch when advancing towards it.

Something similar to this, I think, happened in my case. After knocking me down, the lion rushed in on my right side, and instinctively I tried to ward him off by shoving my rifle, which I still had hold of, up against him. He bit savagely on this several times, biting right through and cracking the thin part of the stock. Then he seized me and bit me several times through the wrist, breaking it badly and

---

1. I found long afterwards that I had broken his front leg, as a wounded lion with a track showing a front leg broken was a day or two later lying in the reeds, near the neighbouring Lekasi waterhole, and frightening the women from drawing water. Johnson and West told me this afterwards.

splintering some of the small bones. These bites hurt like fury at the moment: it was like a nine-inch nail being continually driven through one's hand. The lion bit very quickly, but with a horribly silent ferocity. He would have done better, I think, if he had taken more time over it. Then came several bites above the wrist and a big bite cracking the bone of the forearm below the elbow. My biceps caught the next bite, which cut clean to the bone, the muscle opening out like a cut in a leg of mutton. A bite through a muscle on the shoulder followed.

As weakness made me lower the rifle, the lion, with a quick shuffle of his forefeet, closed up with me, whipping down his big head and biting me twice on the chest. These bites too, though not very bad, hurt badly, and the sight of his big, hairy head, so near that we almost rubbed noses, was unlovely and offensive. Suddenly, after biting me on the chest, he whipped round and cleared out of sight back in the bushes. I should like to describe him as staggering away to die, but as a matter of strict truth he appeared to make off fairly briskly. Why he left me in this abrupt and unexpected way I do not know. I have at least no grudge against my adversary, for had he not behaved in true British fashion? Bailed up, he had reserved his strength for a final grim charge, and, having overthrown his attacker, he retired still undefeated.

My old helmet, much patched with grass, and four Mannlicher cartridges somewhere in the sand, remained on the field of battle as tokens of his victory. Nowadays, when modern rifles are so excellent, it would be ill to grudge a wild animal an occasional victory, no matter how unpleasant that victory may personally be to the defeated person. As in politics, and in everything else that really matters, those who hunt dangerous game must be prepared, like the Romans, to be equal to either fortune.

I had heard it said, and even had read the same opinion in one of the books of that splendid and experienced hunter, Frederick Selous, that bites from a lion may not be felt at the time. I can only say my own experience is vastly different—the bites through the wrist in especial hurt like the devil.

My first impression when the lion left me was a feeling that, anyhow, I was still alive, and not so very much hurt either. My next thought was for my rifle. The bolt being open when the lion seized me, all the spare cartridges had sprung out of the magazine in the shaking it got, and there was blood and dust inside. Hurriedly with my left hand I picked a cartridge out of my top shirt pocket and shoved it in the rifle, only to find I was unable to drive the bolt home through the pain of my broken wrist and lack of strength. It now dawned on me that with a wounded and angry lion still somewhere near at hand and an unloaded rifle, the sooner I got away the better. So, carrying my rifle in my left hand, I walked to the trees where the boys had been perched; but the birds had all flown, though I could hear them chattering in the distance. It was on seeing the lion catch me that they had all got down and cleared out. Probably I must have been a bit rattled or stupid from the shaking I had received, because instead of moving away and joining the boys, which was the obvious thing to do, I stopped under the trees which they had climbed, and tried again to get a cartridge into the rifle. But the broken wrist was hurting badly, and, putting down the rifle, I rubbed my wrist against the rough bark of one of the trees in the hope of stopping the pain.

Presently the boys, all much frightened, came creeping back to me in ones and twos, seeking to induce me to go away with them from danger. Now, though I certainly could not have used it, to get my rifle loaded again had become an obsession, and the one thing I must pigheadedly insist on. I kept handing my rifle to different boys, trying to show them how to clinch the bolt for me, but they were so frightened (and drenched with blood as I was I expect I cut rather a ghastly figure), that it was only after several had fumbled it about, putting it down or handing it back to me, that I got one of them to shove the bolt in. Then immediately I felt faint and sick, and everything seemed to go cold and black, though I managed, with the help of some of the boys, to walk a few hundred yards.

I now felt that I must lie down, but the boys persuaded me to keep going, exclaiming, "The lion, the lion; he's too close." A few hundred yards more, and I knew I could not walk all the distance home, but must needs lie down. When I told the boys that two of them must go at once to the camp and bring my old riding mule to meet me, a great argument arose as to which two should go, for they all seemed frightened at the thought of being separated from each other. I could hear them discussing who should go: "Marpo must go. No, Marparonga must go. No, Shara must go," etc. etc. Finally they decided that two Makwengo must go to the camp for the mule—of course the worst two who could be picked; not that it made any difference, for the two little bushmen had not the least intention of going.

All this jabber made me so mad, that suddenly I felt quite strong again, and, getting up, straight away I managed to walk home to my camp quite easily. My boys were terribly frightened, and I knew there was a chance—especially if they thought I might die—of the whole lot bolting and leaving me alone in the camp; the fear of being blamed for a white man's death, and perhaps some superstition as well, might quite easily make them clear out *en masse*, simply through pure fright.

On the way back to the camp we passed close to a tree bearing a small fruit with a taste not unlike that of an apple. The bushmen called this tree "*naharnie*," and Qumano and Boombo, like the children they are, forgetting temporary troubles, immediately ran to gather some handfuls of the fruit. It was always a source of amusement in my camp that I should be so anxious to pick up and occasionally air my knowledge of the bushman language, so I called out to the older bushman, "*Qumano, naharnie.*"

"*Uun*," said Qumano.

"*Naharnie tséka*," said I.

"*Uun tséka*," said the little bushman. This short interlude seemed to cheer up my scared boys and they started chattering again, thinking perhaps that things were not too bad with the white man if he still had a joke in him.

When we reached the camp I washed the wounds with a cake of carbolic soap—to which proceeding I expect I owe my freedom from blood-poisoning—and bound them up as best I could with pieces of calico. I had received altogether twelve bites, and my hand and arm by this time began to feel as if they had been through a chaff-cutter. The native African, I believe, accounts for the poisonous nature of most lion wounds by declaring that it is the *breath* of the lion which is the cause of the trouble, and in order to expel this breath, the injured person must be dosed with some barbarous concoction. I have no doubt that the fit of sickness brought on by this treatment may, after all, do good indirectly to the patient.

On the fourth day I reached my main camp near the Quandoo, my boys having carried me down on a rough stretcher made of saplings. A day or so later Mafoota arrived, and very kindly stayed at my camp, several weeks till I pulled through the worst part. He also had a supply of that indispensable stuff, permanganate of potash. I set the broken wrist and injured arm on a piece of pine board, and all except the wrist wounds healed very quickly, in spite of lack of medicines, the violation of the laws of hygiene and the routine of hospitals. Over and over again the same bandages were washed and used, but no signs of blood-poisoning appeared.

The long night hours were the worst part: even then, lying there crippled, a certain unending charm in the beautiful African nights brought compensation. All night one could hear the hippo in the pools—sometimes quite close; frequently a lion or a leopard, with at times the shrill whistling of a frightened reedbuck. It was just as well, if only on account of my old mule, that no lion paid a visit to my camp during this time; and it was curious how right through my trip, even though I had donkeys with me, a notoriously tempting bait for lions, they never raided my camp.

Mafoota was not so lucky, however, for when he came to this same camp with his little herd of cattle a few days after I had left, he struck trouble right away—a lion seizing and carrying off a calf the first night. The following night the rascal came again, carrying off one of his boys, and it was only on Mafoota—roused by the barking of the dogs and yells of his niggers—running out and firing some shots over him, that he dropped the boy and made off. The boy was not very badly bitten, having only been seized by the shoulder. Thinking my old camp was getting too hot, Mafoota retreated next day with his herd to his own headquarters.

But the same lion, evidently running up the tracks of the cattle, followed him right home during the night and, breaking in through his stockade of poles, seized and killed two of the donkeys I had brought over from German South-West. Again disturbed and fired at, the lion made off once more, but returned yet again the following night, when he was shot by a volley fired by a Dutchman and several natives, who were all perched in trees on the lookout for him. This particularly bold lion was still in his prime and very fat, unusual in these cases.

My three little *piccaninnies* stuck to me faithfully and nursed me, little savages though they were, all through my sickness.

It was about August 20 that a native came to my camp with letters from the Native Commissioner, Mr. Venning, from Sesheke. In the letters was the terrible news of the outbreak of war at home. Never shall I forget reading the opening lines of his letter:

> You will no doubt be surprised to learn that Germany and Austria are fighting nearly every other European nation, including England.

The shock was tremendous, and I fretted at lying there crippled, alone in a tent away beyond the Quandoo, when all my relatives and fellow-countrymen would be taking their part in the gigantic struggle. Of course it made me more anxious than ever to get well quickly, for I felt that my knowledge of those parts of German S.W., which but few other Englishmen could have been through, might be of use. I began to look forward anxiously to the time when I should be strong enough to travel, for after being laid up a little over two months, my hand and arm had almost completely healed, and I had gained enough strength to sit my old mule once more, though the fingers and wrist of my right hand were still quite useless (the wrist was stiff and the fingers had lost their use), and the arm was somewhat crooked at the elbow.

It took me about twelve days getting across to Schuckmansberg, the former German Residence. There I found a party of Rhodesian Police, white and black, in occupation, the Germans having surrendered the place without opposition. I met with the greatest kindness from the Rhodesian officers, and was fortunate in getting the professional services of the doctor attached to the troops, who found it necessary to do a small operation on the wounded hand. When I had recovered from this, I was able to make my last stage on the return to Livingstone and civilisation.

PART 2. WAR: A SCOUTS' PATROL

CHAPTER 1

Unemployed

On the news of the outbreak of war, I was at once anxious to persuade the authorities of the South African Union to attack German South-West by the road I had entered. No other Englishman, as far as I was aware, knew anything of the country between Rhodesia and German South-West, and I felt sure that even a small expedition of the right kind would be of assistance to the main work of the Union forces in the south.

When I first discussed the proposal with Major O'Sullivan, the Commandant at Schuckmansberg—a fine soldier, who later on proved his worth, and the trust his black police put in him during the repeated German attacks on his camp at Sasai—he at once saw my point, and agreed that such a move might be decidedly useful.

My next duty was to interview Colonel Edwards, the Rhodesian Commandant-General at Salisbury; and, armed with letters from him to General Botha, I then journeyed to Pretoria. Unfortunately General Botha was away, but his chief intelligence officer, Colonel Wyndham, seemed glad to meet someone with fresh information concerning that part of German South-West which was known to me, and the German colony generally, and he appeared more than favourable to making the proposed move by that route. He carried me off straight away to see the Minister of Defence, General Smuts,[1] in the hope of obtaining permission for a small expedition.

My mission now came to an abrupt and inglorious end. General Smuts would not hear of anything being done—indeed he never listened to the proposal.

It is only a hunter's idea, and all hunters are mad. Look at you,

---

1. *With Botha and Smuts* in Africa by W. Whittall is also published by Leonaur.

for instance, you have only just had your arm broken by a lion and yet you don't seem to mind.

Finally the general remarked that either the members of the expedition would be captured and shot by the Germans, or, alternatively, that the *natives would murder everybody*. Now, considering that I had been the greater part of a year hunting amongst these tribes, myself the only white man, this latter statement struck me as somewhat remarkable. As a matter of fact, I knew that, far from a small expedition having anything to fear from the native peoples, it would have been most necessary for a white man whom they knew—as they knew me—to keep a few days ahead of any armed force, in order to prepare the inhabitants for what was coming, and so, by allaying their natural anxiety, induce them to sell grain, milk, etc., to the troops. Otherwise whole *kraals* would have bolted away ahead of us into the bush or reeds.

Anyhow, that interview settled all chance of a move *via* Rhodesia. In Cape Town I saw the Portuguese Consul-General, and through him wrote to the Governor of Angola, advising him of the likelihood of the Portuguese having troubles with the Germans along their boundaries, and mentioning that later on, on the Okavango River in particular, they might expect considerable worry. I offered them the help of a small party of mounted men from Rhodesia, if permission from the Union Authorities was also obtained.

To this the governor replied that he was not authorised to accept any outside volunteers. I also had a couple of interviews with Sir Lewis Mitchell of the Chartered Co., who, hearing I was in Cape Town, was naturally anxious to possess any information which might be used to forestall a possible raid into Rhodesia by Germans or Dutch rebels from German South-West. He told me he was sending to Dr. Jameson the written reports I had given him.

There was nothing left for me now but to return home to Australia to see if it were possible to get the injured hand fixed up by an operation. I felt as miserable as a bandicoot at being a cripple when all one's countrymen and relatives were hurrying to take part in the big struggle.

No sooner had we reached Sydney than I called on Sir Herbert Maitland, one of the best-known surgeons in Australia. After a quick examination, "It is quite useless," he said; "nothing can be done for that," and he smiled when I said, "Oh, that won't do, doctor; I want to get away to the war." Examinations by other doctors followed, only to convince me that nothing could be hoped for, at any rate, for the time, from an operation. To recover some use of the hand by massage was all that could be done, and then perhaps later an operation might be effective. The hand and wrist were still sore and inflamed, and pieces of bone, splintered by those big teeth, kept working out.

In Brisbane I found a cable awaiting me from a private and reliable source, with the information that the powers that be were after all considering the advisability of making the move that I had urged. Should it come off, I knew there would be a chance for me to get employment as a guide, and this chance was too good to lose. The crippled hand made impossible any pretence of passing the medical examination for ordinary service.

Mr. Lewis, a young friend on the look-out for adventure, joined me, and we started by the first available boat for Cape Town, taking three Queensland-bred horses with us.

On arrival at Cape Town I had interviews with the Imperial Secretary, and with the governor-general, who was good enough to send for me. From the latter I heard that my proposal had been discussed, but, rightly or wrongly, so he said, had been turned down. This was certainly a disappointment, but Lord Buxton's courtesy at our interview removed at least the sore feeling aroused by my previous treatment. In the belief that, as I had written in my report, the Okavango district would be invaded by some German force later on, we then went to Salisbury, and to our great delight were at once accepted as Intelligence Scouts. The work given to us, and to four others (residents, and all known to me personally), was the watching of the Rhodesian, Angola, and German South-West borders. We were signed on as special service troopers in the B.S.A. Police.

CHAPTER 2

Intelligence Scout

Our horses and mules duly procured, we started away from Livingstone, crossing the Zambezi at Sesheke, and picking up there the eight Marosi ("Barotse") who were detailed to me as government runners for sending reports. It was glorious to be in the bush again and to feel that, after all, one was of some use.

Before reaching the Quandoo I had my first shot at a buck since the encounter with the lion. I found that now I had to pull the trigger with the second finger, and in spite of this I managed to kill a sable at the first attempt. It was a simple pot shot, but it pleased me hugely, besides giving me confidence.

In nine days from Sesheke we reached the Quandoo, crossing late in the evening and camping on the bank of the river. That night we had a great welcome from the lions; five of them, at least, roared almost continually till daybreak. Probably, when coming to water, they had struck our track along the river and followed up the scent of our horses and mules. Neither before nor since have I heard quite so much of their lordly noise.

Next morning I paid a visit to my old friend Mafoota, who was startled at the sight of a mounted man in uniform riding up. He said that at first he thought it was the "Square Heads," concerning whom at that time he lived in considerable anxiety. He had no reason, of course, to expect to see me; he was not even aware that I had returned to Africa, and the last he had seen of me was a rather sorry spectacle bandaged up and making for civilisation on an old mule.

To get boys and fix things up generally, we had to spend several days at Sepango, and this allowed plenty of time for some good yarns with Mafoota. On one occasion we were discussing the lion that had visited him (mentioned on earlier pages), and the old man reckoned that this particular lion exploded a number of theories. For instance, it is said that white clothes frighten a lion, but this fellow brushed one white towel away himself with his paw when breaking into the donkey's *kraal*. Then, too, the only donkey in the *kraal* with a bell was the first to be seized and killed by this lion—so much for bells as lion-scarers. The old man told me also that his boy, whom the lion had seized and bitten, had, when quite young, been seized by and escaped from a crocodile. "I told his mother," said Mafoota, "that he must be God's child all right."

On the second day, whilst sitting yarning together, seven natives appeared, and Mafoota, who was acting as a sort of forwarding and intermediate agent for the Scouts and their runners, began to interrogate them. Of the Scouts, West and Johnson were close to Libebe watching that corner, and Sinclair and Van Rensberg were about 150 miles farther up, on the Quito. These natives brought a letter for Rensberg, which the old man opened and started to read. Then came an exclamation, "By God, Sinclair's been killed by a lion!" It had been a horrible accident, as the letter related, and later on we learnt all the details.

What happened was this: Sinclair and Rensberg were at the time about nine miles from the Quito; the former, according to his custom, walking ahead on foot, and Rensberg behind with the cart. Sinclair had three or four boys with him, all wild Mombakush, and quite untrustworthy at a pinch. They came suddenly on a big pack of lions, perhaps half a dozen or more, who had just killed a roan right on the track. Sinclair, who had only with him his service Lee-Metford, fired, shooting one, a lioness, through the body; thereupon the lions all bolted, the wounded lioness, evidently very hard hit, retiring slowly by herself.

Sinclair, having an excellent heavy rifle, a .470 (his favourite elephant gun in fact), on the wagon, now sent a boy back for this, as he knew well the danger of a charge at close quarters with only a .303 in his hand. Unfortunately, through some mistake, he had on his own belt the key of the wooden locker in the cart in which this spare heavy rifle was kept, and the boy, returning without the gun, tried to explain that the weapon could not be procured unless the locker in the cart was opened. Angered, it seems, at the delay, Sinclair decided to see where the wounded beast had got to, and, with no weapon but the small-bore service rifle, started to follow the spoor.

The lioness had not gone far before she lay down—we saw the place a few weeks afterwards ourselves, and, of course, also heard the

Death of Sinclair

full account from Rensberg. She was lying in a small clump of bushes, flat as a hide on the ground in the way they do, and watching the approach of her enemy. When Sinclair was within about eighty yards, out she came like lightning, clearing any small bushes in the way in great, low bounds. She was on him in a twinkling, and for some reason he never fired at her; his rifle was afterwards found lying loaded with the cartridge in it. When dying, the poor fellow told Rensberg that he never knew why he had not fired, but thought that the side protectors on the foresight had worried him. It was certainly not lack of nerve, for Sinclair was wonderfully cool, an excellent shot, and only the previous year he had stopped and killed two elephants which were charging from different quarters.

The lioness seized his left arm and threw him to the ground, where he was horribly bitten and mauled. In spite of this, with the greatest presence of mind and pluck, he managed to draw his hunting-knife, and a terrible struggle took place between man and beast. The lioness herself was mortally wounded and failing, for, in spite of the terrible wounds he was receiving, Sinclair, by repeated stabs, actually killed her in the struggle. When found by Rensberg—who came up some time afterwards—the lioness was lying dead by Sinclair's side, her great forepaws stretched across his legs. The dying man recovered consciousness, but his injuries were terrible, and nothing could be done for him except to relieve his pain as much as possible and let him lie where he was found till death came.

That night the lions returned, looking, no doubt, for both the meat of their prey, of which they had been robbed, and for their missing companion. It was necessary to build a big *scherm* and good fires for the protection of the camp and the oxen, and all night beyond the fires the roar of the great cats was heard. Poor Sinclair died during the night, his Dutch comrade doing all he could for him. Amidst all the tremendous slaughter of the world war, not many died a lonelier death than Sinclair's, or in a wilder spot.

It was only a few months before that I had last seen him. He and Mafoota were then sitting yarning with me in my camp, at a time when I was myself suffering from my encounter with the lion. Sinclair had had pretty fair luck in his first year's elephant hunting in those parts, and, quite alone, had himself killed over a dozen elephants in one season. I remember him saying, when we discussed the comparative danger of various animals, that as far as an elephant was concerned, he would walk up and shoot him as he would a great pig, and think no more about it, but that for a lion he had very great respect. This remark shows the confidence he had acquired, for it is well known that an elephant can be extremely dangerous. Two days we waited for Rensberg, who was coming in with the dead man's belongings, and each night we heard the lions, some of them even continuing roaring well after sunrise.

The involved alterations in our plans. West and Johnson, capital fellows both, were out near Libebe watching the lower part of the river; we had met at Schuckmansberg in October when they first went out. Lewis and myself were to have worked right ahead of Sinclair in order to find out what was going on around Kuringkuru, the headquarters of such German force as was on the river. Now, the Quito end and the more advanced part that required watching in case either Germans or rebels tried to get across into Rhodesia had been left open by Sinclair's death and Rensberg's return, and it was necessary for us to hurry there and fill the gap in the screen of scouts.

We needed a few carriers, and when these were obtained, Lewis and I hurried off to Libebe to look for Johnson and West. The previous wet season had been the driest the people in these parts had ever known, and, consequently, the grain crop had been very poor, while the water between the Quandoo and Okavango, already beginning to get scarce, was confined to a few main pans and sandpits.

On the third day of our journey we passed my old camp, where in March I had been lying ill with fever, and only after a hard struggle had pulled round. Four months later, when I had quite recovered and was on that last lion hunt, I had passed this camp for the second time, and, stopping, had said a short mental prayer of gratitude to Providence for having pulled through and for being as fit as ever. Then three weeks later I had been carried back by six savages on an abominably hard stretcher, with a wrist and arm broken, and generally pretty sore from a mauling. I remember quite well that as I passed the old place I turned my head on the stretcher to have a look at it, wondering sourly at the same time, since my last stage seemed to be worse than the first, whether I had not been perhaps a little premature in my previous thanksgiving.

Now, however, I was not so badly off after all. Although the wrist was quite stiff, I had got back at least a good half of the use of my thumb and first three fingers, and, in addition, I was in the greatest spirits at the knowledge that, in spite of previous discouragement, I had been able to fit into some sort of service in the big struggle.

CHAPTER 3

My Fellow Scouts

Rensberg caught us up on the fourth day, and the old chap proved a great addition—a first-class bushman who could live on as little as anyone I ever met, and, like most of his countrymen, a first-class shot and a great hand at keeping the camp in meat. The old chap's only failing was that common weakness of so many Dutchmen—a lust of slaughter. It seemed impossible sometimes for him to resist shooting, even if we already possessed more meat than we could carry. (At the end we had almost a coolness over this.) However, a better mate in the bush I never expect to meet.

Unlike the Boer as generally depicted, Rensberg was a little man of rather delicate appearance; in spite of a hard life in later years spent almost entirely amongst savages, he retained the instincts of a gentleman. Some of Rensberg's remarks amused us immensely. He told us once, and as naively as a child (after all, in many ways he was little else), that "he did hope the war would last a long time so that he could earn plenty of money." Another time, whilst discussing various bucks with him, we mentioned how fine a great bull *koodoo* looked when standing alert. "He looks so beautiful," said the old man, "that you could not help *shooting him.*"

Sassaby, that very wary buck, Rensberg described as "having eyes stronger than what looking-glasses (field-glasses) are."

When, scouting together later on, it became necessary for one of us to ride forward on the approach of a party of doubtful appearance, Rensberg, who went under the name of "the old general," would dismount and take up what he called a "petition," and an exceedingly good man he was with his long Lee-Enfield to have at one's back. Once when we were scouting, he asked me, "Have you got a white flag ready in case we find we have got a bad petition? Because if we put that up and they shoot at it, *then we will know there is danger."* And he asked us quite seriously one day whether we thought a German could be killed with a "hard" bullet—the point of a .303 bullet, if not a soft nose, wants blunting to kill buck with certainty. On my assuring him that a German *could* certainly be killed with an untampered bullet, Rensberg replied that in that case he thought it necessary that the unfortunate Teuton should at least be given a "head shot."

I had the bad luck about here to lose the little Irish terrier I had brought from Salisbury; the little fellow somehow managed to stay behind at our camp one morning trek. A government messenger from Sesheke, who caught me with a special despatch from the C.G., said in answer to our inquiries that he had seen no dog, but only two lions eating something on the track. What the something was he could not say, but I am afraid that meal was the end of Bingo, for he never turned up again.

Three days from Johnson's camp we struck the *kraal* of Maruta, a particularly fat and unprepossessing Mombakush chief who bears a bad character in connection with the stealing and selling of female Maquengo children, a traffic which still goes on in these parts. I had him called before me after putting on, to be duly impressive, my B.S.A. uniform—the first uniform of any nationality seen in that district, I should think—and solemnly warned him that the English had a long, long arm, that already a black mark was against him, and that a continuation of his evil practices would bring sudden retribution and extinction upon him one of these days. I think he really got quite a bad fright, especially as Johnson, unknown to me at that time, had given him a similar warning, punctuated, I heard afterwards, by the discharge of his Browning alongside the old ruffian's ear.

During our time out there we looked into this slave trading. The Portuguese had never had the slightest authority themselves in these parts, and the practice has been for the petty chiefs to get hold of the girl children from the little Maquengo villages, and sell them, when old enough, to traders from the coast for cattle. It is particularly hard to get any accurate information, the bushmen being terribly shy and frightened of the Mombakush, and to strike at the root of the evil it is absolutely necessary to talk with the bush people in their own language. A bushman named Kavetto, who was with me on this trip, told me, and I believe he was speaking the truth, that his girl child had been stolen from him three years back, and was now in the hands of old Mokoya, the principal chief on the Luiyanna, and a notorious old ruffian.

To test Kavetto, I told him that doubtless he had himself sold the child to Mokoya; but this he most indignantly and, I am convinced, quite sincerely denied. We assured Kavetto that when the Germans were "finished "we would return that way and then his child should be restored to him. The next morning, however, the little man disappeared; either he had been frightened in the night by some Mombakush, or was fearful lest he should eventually bring retribution on himself from old Mokoya. It wants but one example to be made to stop this traffic. Let one of the implicated Indunas, Mokoya or Maruta for instance, be seized by police some fine morning and taken off in handcuffs, *not to return*, the effect would be such that it would be talked about in that country for the next 300 years, and no bush child would in future ever be touched, nor would its parents be murdered while protecting their children. Perhaps something may yet be done to eradicate from this far-off and poor corner the accursed evil of the slave trade.

Two of our horses died at Maruta's of horse sickness, and at the same time, as we afterwards learnt, one of the two left at Sepango in Mafoota's charge, died also. All the remainder, however, both horses and mules, appeared salted, and we still had sufficient mounts for the three of us besides a spare mule, old "Jenny," for the pack. As we had expected, West and Johnson were away when we reached the little vley which they made their headquarters (if they could be said to have such a thing as headquarters), but our bushmen messengers soon found them. Africa is a big country, but the wilder the country, as long as there are native inhabitants, the easier it is to get into touch with anyone's whereabouts.

Within three days West and Johnson returned, though they were thirty miles away at another pan when the bushmen found them. While we were waiting I picked up a Maquengo youth of very pleasing countenance, named Boombo: Boombo seems as common in Maquengo as "Jack" or "Tom" in England. He was persuaded to accompany us, but I did not recognise him the next morning, and neither did Lewis. This nice-looking Maquengo in the camp had quite a bright yellowish-red colour, while Boombo of the previous day was dark.

The mystery was cleared up by my head boy, who said that "he had taken him down and washed him, as he was to be the master's boy." This I am sure was the first and the last wash that Boombo every enjoyed; as a matter of fact, these people simply never do wash, literally *never*.

The same afternoon with our new acquisition I went a-seeking meat. About a mile out from the camp I noticed the boy look at something hard, then, after turning to me with a peculiar smile, he looked again and pointed. Through the broken bush I could see what I took to be three zebras, one apparently a mare with a big foal alongside. Now, though I hate and detest shooting a zebra, we wanted meat so badly that half unwillingly, and therefore carelessly, without taking trouble to stalk them properly, I walked round a patch of bush to get closer, undecided after all whether I would shoot or not.

On turning the corner the reason of the boy's peculiar smile became apparent—they were lions and not zebras; a lioness, a lion, and a young three-parts grown lioness. The lioness was quite near, and looked a very big animal; she was near enough for me to see the long sweep of the great shoulder as she slowly walked along. Naturally I made a mess of it, and tried to get into a clump of small trees, thinking I could there get a still closer and safer shot than in the open. The bushman himself stood quite still, but the lions spotted us and bolted immediately, and I only got a running shot at each of the two lionesses, in neither case registering a hit.

The bushman ran on at once to the *spoor*, without the least apparent fear or hesitation, to see if there was any blood; but, of course, there was not. That evening I presented the astonished Boombo with a new blanket, but the following morning, after I had asked him if the blanket kept him warm, and had been told in reply that "they were very nice things," he quietly disappeared into the bush with his newly won reward. Evidently having so easily acquired a fortune, he considered it unnecessary to consider the question of further work.

Johnson and West had much to tell me. These two men had been out since October watching the whole of that corner entirely alone, and for a time they had found things fairly rough, especially when they ran out of all supplies and were obliged to live on wildebeeste meat and Maboola rings, none too dainty rations. Moreover, a small German force arrived in December and drove the Portuguese completely off the river, destroying all their five forts. At Cuangar the Portuguese garrison was entirely wiped out, and a Portuguese trader called "Kajimba," well known both to Rensberg and myself, was killed there with his native wife and children.

By all accounts an Ovambo chief at Kuringkuru, named "Howango," was directly concerned with the Germans in this business. At the other forts the Portuguese had either surrendered or run away without fighting. This naturally had created amongst the natives a feeling of great respect for the detestable Germans. "Look here," the Germans had said; "you see what we have done to the Portuguese because they are friends of the English, and you can see how the English have not been able to help them."

A good deal of tact and courage was required in those days for two Britishers to hold their own out there, and make the natives believe that plenty of Englishmen would come later on if they were wanted. Johnson was a particularly experienced man with native peoples, especially with these particular savages. A splendid shot, a straight and honourable man, never wanting to bustle or hurry a native, yet possessing a pair of blue eyes that looked "no nonsense "when occasion demanded. He was an ideal intelligence scout for a job like this, and West was just such another. From first to last we had the truest comradeship from both men, and our little patrol of three out on the advanced post at the Quito always felt that we could rely on those two men behind us, even though seven days away, as though they were a dozen.

Johnson and West came as far as the river with us, and there together we sent for and interviewed old Libebe, the paramount chief of all the Mombakush. I had met the old man on a former journey through that region, and our recognition was mutual. Old Libebe wore a worried look those days, for, as Johnson said, he was between the devil and the deep blue sea. With his own eyes he had seen the destruction of the Portuguese fort alongside his *kraal*, and no doubt had heard, from the missionaries near him, the German version or forecast of what was to happen in the future. On the other hand, he had been warned by Johnson and West, in several serious talks, as to what would happen if he failed to send them every news of German movements by his fastest runner.

One of Libebe's sons, named Sisho, and his old prime minister (shall we call him?) spent some time with me on my previous hunting trip, and when they left, had been promised that on our return home a suit of clothes should be sent to each of them by the missionaries. Since then the war had broken out and upset everything. Luckily, I had not forgotten this old promise, and so had brought with me the expected clothes, and sure enough the first question they asked (for both were present at the *indaba*) was whether I had remembered the promise. When the separate parcel for each was produced, they expressed the highest delight. Even a small thing like this makes a big impression on native people, for they realise that the white man's word is as good as his bond, and can be relied upon.

Next morning we separated, our route taking us up the river, whilst Johnson and West turned downstream to investigate the report of a wagon and some white men in that direction. The Portuguese fort had been completely levelled; all the buildings had been burnt and heavy rain had flattened everything out afterwards. Thinking this sight might be a discouraging start for my carriers and Marosie runners, and knowing that the great thing with a nigger, if you do not want him to get scared, is to appear never to be hiding anything, I asked them, while they were staring at the ruins, if they did not see what the Germans would do to them if they caught us. For a second or two they looked serious, then, seeing me trying to hide a smile at their long faces, their spokesman said, "What does that matter? We are all men, aren't we, and can fight them if we meet them?"

The country was greatly changed along the Okavango since I had previously travelled it. Then it had been newly burnt; now the grass was very high and rank everywhere, and I could hardly recognise my old camps. The difference was as great as between a fat and a poor horse, or as the contrast between a lean and a well-fed beast.

A couple of days later we turned off the river and cut across through the sand *veldt*, watering at sand-pits till we hit the Quito about thirty miles from the junction. It was too open a country to travel right along the frontage without knowing how things were, and whether any band of the enemy was in the neighbourhood. Our plan was to look for some suitable, but well-hidden, camp near the Quito, and there to watch any movement or force whether coming down the river from Cuangar past Diriko, or trying to cross the Quito higher up and cut across by the Luiyanna into Rhodesia. Rensberg, who before the war had journeyed in these parts elephant hunting, was now an invaluable help.

CHAPTER 4

"Bush-Rangers' Rest"

After a little trouble we luckily picked on a camp with all the qualifications required: well hidden in the bush, but close to the river, with good grazing close by. As there were no native kraals for a good many miles on any side of us, we found game, which was absolutely essential, quite plentiful. Though never staying in one camp very long, for we always kept moving lest we should be caught or trapped, we came to look upon this as, at least, our head camp and meeting-place, and it got to be known amongst all the scouts as "The Bushrangers' Rest."

I certainly had no wish to fall into the hands of any German patrol, for I feared there might have been some little difficulty in explaining my previous trip through their colony, since, of course, I should have been recognised. Old Rensberg, too, reckoned that if they got in, "being a Dutchman "would have been ground enough for putting him out of the world.

Our first work was to see the principal Induna on the river, one Siccumberro, a rather pleasant-looking and decent native. He had behaved well to the Portuguese soldiers who had fled to his kraal for food and shelter from Diriko when the Germans destroyed their fort, and had helped them finally to get away to some of their people in the interior. With him, just as with Libebe and as with every Induna big or small on the river, who were all visited either then or later, we arranged that information and warning of any movement on the part of the Germans should be sent to us immediately.

It was here that we first learnt of parties of white men camping and hunting on the Okavango River higher up, and we at once decided they must be Dutch rebels from Maritz's former commandos, with possibly Maritz himself among them. Rensberg and I went to investigate, and found the report true—there were five of these Dutch rebels, with several wagons, a little below Bunja. Assured of this, and not wishing to attract attention, we worked back across about thirty miles of dry country to the Quito, and reswimming the river, made home again to the good Bush-rangers' Rest. Lewis had been suffering from a very severe and painful abscess on his leg, caused by one of those beastly poisonous ticks, and we found the camp almost out of meat—a serious thing for us in those parts, for it meant going heavier on our scanty supplies of flour, and using up the supply of grain for the boys.

As the previous season had been exceedingly dry on the Quito, there was very little grain to be bought from the native inhabitants, not enough, in fact, to spare for any of our horses. Native boys at a pinch can live for weeks on absolutely nothing but meat, but we always tried to give ours at least a small ration of grain daily in addition. Even a tiny cupful, with plenty of meat, makes all the difference. We never allowed ourselves to run short of salt, a little salt being tremendously appreciated by the boys, and helping besides to keep them healthy. By this time we had to depend entirely upon native grain, stamped up into flour by the women at their kraals, for our own bread and porridge. Rensberg was as usual the man to procure the necessary meat, and shot, the first evening, two beautiful sable from a big mob that came on to the flat below us.

This handsome buck can be a very determined fighter when bailed up, and a dangerous enemy to dogs: the large curved horns are sharp as daggers, and as he strikes out, the long side-way sweep throws them right back over his shoulder with a deadly swish. Even the lion, the great buck-killer himself, has to be very careful, for, as old Rensberg says, "If he (the sable) sticks his behind into a durn bush, he (the lion) can't do noddings to him."

We needed a lot of meat those days for ourselves and for our boys and to keep the camp going generally, and I rather encouraged the wandering savages who visited us in the hope of gaining a piece of meat; for by this means we were kept well informed of all the news and all the rumours, both up and down the rivers. Then, too, we were anxious to shoot enough game to give us a good supply of reserved biltong always on hand. For this reason I was particularly pleased to come upon a fine herd of forty or fifty eland, three of which I managed to kill with my little sporting Lee-Enfield—all dead shots. Of course they were really very easy shots, as the big buck were flurried and did not know which way to run.

Still, as I am but a moderate shot, and as I only used four cartridges, there was justification for boasting at the result, especially as my two comrades in the camp, who heard the four rapid shots, were sceptical when I told them what the bag was. Unfortunately, one of the three was a cow; it is always hateful to kill the female, particularly of the eland species.

Now that we had plenty of meat for some time ahead, Rensberg and I took a five days' patrol up the river beyond a place called Boopa, where there was a waterfall quite pretty, though not very high. The beautiful clear water of the Quito (a fine stream about eighty yards across at this point) falls over a cascade of some forty feet, and the noise is heard for miles around.

A small village of raw but most friendly savages was near-by. The headman, a jovial customer, brought me a little grain for my boys, and I, thinking both to repay this little courtesy and also replenish our own meat supply, made inquiries as to the chance of getting buck anywhere handy. Across the river from the *kraal* was a beautiful big plain which looked a likely place, for the green picking seemed to be coming on well. The headman told us, in answer to our inquiries, that the place would be full of game in the morning, and for further encouragement informed me that there was so much that I would be "*tired out simply firing at it.*" "I suppose," I said, "you get too much meat already"—though, of course, I knew really that they had no means of killing these buck.

"Meat!" they cried out; "why, we never even *see* it."

"But you do *like* meat?" I queried.

"Like it! "they yelled, bounding in the air—"do we like it? Just give us a chance, you will see we shall be on it like hyenas."

As a matter of fact there was plenty of game in the early morning on the big flat, and, to the great delight of the occupants of the little *kraal*, I shot a couple of *sassaby*, one of which went to the "hyenas." That night we made our camp at a beautiful spot by the waterfall. The weather all this time was glorious—bright warm days and cold nights; it brought the feeling that it was good to be alive, and I pitied anyone condemned to spend his life in an office in town. "You might as well sit in the *tronk*," [1] said my old companion.

On getting back to our main camp, we found Lewis nearly well again, and that our first mail and papers had arrived. At that time we had with us a youngster named Mayindoo, whom we had got when

---

1. *Tronk*, South African prison.

we first came to the Quito. He was very black and very ugly, but a smart little boy, who had worked for poor Kajimbo, the murdered Portuguese trader of Cuangar. As Mayindoo was wonderfully quick at understanding us, he became the chief interpreter to the camp, where, with so many different native languages, his services were in demand. As to the native speech: first, there was Sikololo, the Barotze tongue; then Mombakush, and the Quito river natives' language, which again varies a good deal from the latter. Rensberg spoke Sikololo well, but not much Mombakush.

We had to take great care of our horses and mules, now that we had no grain for them, our *piccaninnies* cutting large supplies of grass every evening. The grass we always cut is called locally *harangarura*— i.e. the grass of the tortoise. It is a beautiful, short, cane grass, resembling the Mitchell grass of Queensland, and, like it, possesses the quality of an excellent feed full of nourishment, even when quite dry and white. This *harangarura* was the mainstay for our mounts the whole of the time out there.

One afternoon, ugly little Mayindoo, who had been out cutting grass, came back with the report that an animal had passed him in the long grass, and the only description that he could give of it was that it had "a big head and long tail." He said he had thereupon climbed a tree, and, after waiting there a bit, he had returned to report. Two of us promptly went out to see what it might be, and observed three leopards who had just caught and killed a redbuck. Unfortunately they saw us and bolted across the bush, only giving us a few long, running shots.

Chapter 5

Lion Stories

We were continually shifting our camps and making patrols in different quarters where investigations were needed. Johnson turned up one evening on a visit, and we had a great talk that night. He told us he had recently seen the tracks where a couple of lions had killed and eaten a zebra. The old stallion had made a great fight for life, the lions apparently not having got a good grip at the start. Mad with pain and fear, the wretched animal had smashed and banged into trees and thorn bushes, plunging and bucking, anything to be rid of those clinging, tearing horrors. Once he actually seemed to have torn free for a few yards, only to be caught and seized again before he could get quite clear; and, in spite of this desperate fight for his life, they got him down in the end.

Johnson also told us a good story of a very big lion he had killed some years ago. (We had rather to coax the yarn out of him, but a good lion story is always worth hearing.) Johnson, it seems, had been shooting high up in Rhodesia, and one afternoon, after he had shot a reedbuck in some long river grass close to his camp, returned and sent his boys after it. Presently his boys came back saying that the buck was not to be found or had disappeared. After having a drink of tea, and cursing them for their stupidity, he took his boys down to show them where the dead buck was lying; but, true enough, when he reached there, the buck had disappeared, and had evidently been dragged off by a lion. They followed the spoor, made in the grass by the buck being dragged along, for about forty yards, and then came right on to a big lion at fairly close quarters.

Johnson fired straight at him, but the lion bounded off into the reeds apparently unhurt. On looking closer, however, at the place where he had disappeared, a few small drops of blood were visible,

Turning with a savage snarl

which showed that the lion had, at least, been touched. Johnson decided to go back to his camp and get his heavy rifle, a .500 black powder gun with a solid lead bullet. (We had one ourselves in the camp, and a very hard hitting old rifle it was.) Then, picking up all his boys, about eight or ten, he went down to see if he could get another shot at the rascal who had tried to steal his meat. To his surprise, however, even in the short time that he had been away, the lion had come back and had dragged the reedbuck farther out of sight.

Cautiously following up the track, Johnson, for the second time, came right on to the lion, now feeding and tearing hungrily at the meat. The lion was just in the act of turning with a savage snarl and bristling mane when Johnson fired, the big soft bullet smacking in close behind the shoulder and knocking the lion in a sprawling heap. In spite of this, his vitality was so great that he regained his feet and made off through the grass. The *spoor* showed he was desperately hurt, blood and pieces of lung being coughed up along the track, so Johnson said to his boys, "What shall we do now; shall we go after him still or will you run away?"

"No," said they, all showing their spears, "we won't run away, master, we will stick to you."

This showed pluck on their part, but they were a good class of African, and trusted Johnson as they would have trusted no ordinary white man. Eighty yards off the lion had lain down to die in a clump of bush, but when Johnson and his boys got up to about thirty yards from this, out he came for a last charge, game to the end, growling horribly and striking out with his great forepaws. It was a wasted effort. He could only stagger for half a dozen yards and then collapse, completely finished. This lion stood just under four feet at the shoulder and weighed 440 lb. The first shot had touched his upper lip, cutting it for about two inches; just enough to put him in a bad temper.

We were discussing what an uncertain beast the lion is, and how impossible it is to count on the behaviour of any individual, when Rensberg told us how a friend of his, John Horne, had been killed near the Zambezi. John Horne was an experienced old hand, a transport rider and hunter, a splendid shot, and a man who himself in his time had killed not a few lions. Horne was travelling with his wagons at the time this happened, and had just done a morning *trek* when he saw a herd of *hartebeeste* close to the road. Telling his boys to outspan the cattle, he started to walk down towards the buck, two of which he presently killed, the boys hearing the shots quite plainly from the

LIKE A GREAT SHADOW STALKED HIM, SIEZING HIM FROM BEHIND

wagon. After shooting these two buck, and when only perhaps a few hundred yards from the wagon, he began to walk back towards them, at the same time calling out for the boys to be quick and come for the meat. The boys, having let loose the last of the oxen, then hurried down towards where they had heard his shouting. To their horror, however, they almost ran into a big lion dragging the body of their master towards a bit of bush, stopping at times to lap up some of his blood. They pluckily drove the lion off with yells and sticks, and carried the body back to the wagon, but Horne was quite dead.

What had evidently happened, judging from the wounds, was that the great brute, lying hidden and coolly watching while he shot the *hartebeeste*, had, as Home walked back, deliberately and silently, like a great shadow, stalked him, seizing him from behind with one paw across the chest and the other higher up, and thus had killed him instantly with a single bite through the back of the neck. This particular lion was evidently an unusually daring man-eater, for about this time the same beast was responsible for the deaths of several native women in the neighbouring *kraals*, who were taken whilst working in their mealie-fields. I believe his career was finally cut short some few months afterwards.

CHAPTER 6

A Capture

The natives knew us, of course, only by the names they themselves gave us, and these names mainly represented personal characteristics. We once called up Mayindoo for an explanation of what our names all meant. Johnson was "*Kapitulo*," the man who wears shorts like a policeman; West was "*Saccarima*," which I think really means one who walks rather heavily, ploughing along. Mayindoo said it meant, "*Badeko moosha kaienda*" ("not walk well"). "*Santantorra*" was Lewis's name, and this meant, according to our interpreter, "*Moosha maboie*" ("good to the boys")—*i.e.* does not swear at or get angry with them. "*Masitaterro*" was Rensberg's, being very similar to Lewis's, and really meaning "the quiet man." My name was "*Surumatow*," or, as Mayindoo explained, "*Neemai kaienda*" ("the lion came")—more accurately, "the man whom the lion bit." The one and only *Mafoota* means, of course, "fat," and poor Sinclair, always a great and tireless walker, had been known as "*Inzea*" ("the locust").

Johnson, after a day's spell, now went back towards his own end, Lewis and Rensberg going down with him as far as the junction at Kirrico.

Our next move was down the river some miles to a place which we called Buffalo Camp, because a herd of buffalo, and later on some zebra, rushed amongst our horses and mules which were grazing and stampeded them for several miles. (Talking of zebras, I wonder whether there is much in the theory of protective colouring; the zebra himself, with the striking marks given by nature, being a great contrast to the tame and artificially bred mule, the latter, of drab colour, with the dark bands down the shoulders and along the back, is peculiarly well protected as far as appearance goes.)

Old Siccumberro, with a considerable retinue, called in one afternoon on his way up the Quito. He had heard news that a nephew had suddenly died whilst high up on the river on a hunting trip, and suspected, as these people always do, foul play by poison. Siccumberro announced that he intended, if he found out that there had been foul play, to bring the culprit down to me for trial. Of course I agreed, though the jurisdiction of the court might be considered somewhat irregular. The trip was to take him thirty days up the river, "unless hunger drove him back," and as a help towards preventing this latter catastrophe, we gave the old boy some spare meat and bones when he left.

After a time our camp was moved back again to the head of a quiet little *moromby* (a reed gully), running four or five miles back from the river. At that particular camp Lewis followed up and shot a very large bull eland one morning, a tremendous beast, and enormously fat. This excellent meat, so different from the ordinary buck meat of which we were apt to get very tired, was particularly acceptable just then, as we had for some time been out of all supplies except tea and salt, and could only get flour from the native grains. Sugar was the thing that personally I really missed, and as it is comparatively heavy, unfortunately we often ran short of it.

On coming back from a four days' trip up the river again to Boopa, where I went this time alone to save horse-flesh, and where I had justified a warm welcome from the expectant "hyenas" by managing to shoot a further couple of buck, I learnt that a runner had brought in the news that the German South-West force had surrendered to General Botha, and that our orders now were to join Johnson and West and see if we could find out the whereabouts of Maritz himself.

No sooner had our two comrades turned up from Libebe, than the joint patrol, now five strong, crossed the Quito and cut across the bush to the Okavango. Hitting the old Portuguese wagon track that runs up and down the river, we cut the spoor of some small two-wheeled cart or wagon that had just recently gone down. Both Rensberg and myself thought that this might be the little cart formerly used by Kajimbo, which must have fallen into the hands of the Germans at Cuangar. In that case, it was more than likely that the wagon would have some Dutch rebels with it. Our boys reported that they heard oxen lowing, and therefore the wagon could not be far ahead.

At daybreak next morning we had found the camp and surrounded the wagon. There was, however, only one white man, but he was one of those we wanted, proving to be W.-S. of Kemp's officers. As we surmised, it was Kajimbo's cart right enough. We also made a couple of fine fat mules, a welcome addition to our riding stock; out in that country anything in the shape of a salted riding animal, horse or mule, being worth its weight in gold regardless of looks. Just as it was said of Klondyke in the early days, "*As 'twas in Eden 'tis in Dawson City, where ANY girl looks pretty,*" so it could be said of any four-legged mount on the Okavango. With W.-S. we also collared a mob of mixed cattle which the German police at Kuringkuru were sending down to the German missionaries to be kept on the quiet. Rensberg recognised several of the cattle as formerly the property of Kajimbo and the Portuguese, the whole mob being evidently a "crook" lot, looted by the Germans in their raid on the Portuguese posts in December.

No sooner had we returned to our camp with the prisoner, than a fresh excitement occurred, some of the boys whom we left in the camp reporting that while we were after the wagon four mounted white men, riding hard, and evidently not noticing our camp, had passed down on the German and opposite side of the river. These, we thought, might probably be a patrol of Botha's troops which had come up by Kuringkuru; but as this was a matter we had to clear up, Johnson and I, mounted on the two newly acquired beasts, decided to follow them up at once. On the second day we got a good crossing in the Okavango without swimming, and followed the tracks of the four horsemen right down to the Yangana mission station. It was vastly puzzling to make out what the four horsemen were doing, for they seemed to be travelling very fast, as though frightened, neither did they seem to have any supply of provisions nor anything except just what they might have on their horses.

When we got to the mission station, we came right into a crowd of German soldiers, who seemed more astonished than even we were, and every nigger around the mission, plainly expecting that things were going to be lively, made an immediate rush for shelter. There was nothing to be done, of course, except tie up our mules; and then, putting a bold face on it, we asked them what they were doing there, and whether they were not aware that the Colony had surrendered. They got very excited for a few moments, but soon calmed down, and we began to see how the land lay.

It appeared they were runaways from down below, eight with camels, and the rest horsemen. The camel men had come straight through the dry country from Tsumeb, and did a lot of blowing and boasting as to what they were going to do. They said they were going to get

Maritz on the right, Kemp on the left, and another Rebel leader

Major R. Gordon, D.S.O., and Intelligence Scouts.

ANGOLA INTELLIGENCE SCOUTS

'THE BOYS OF THE OLD BRIGADE.'
My *askaris* and porters when the armistice came.

right to German East, fighting their way through. They swore they would never surrender: "We will die rather than give up our rifles. Let the English take us if they can," and that sort of talk. As it happened that both Johnson and I could speak German, we told them not to be fools, and advised them to go back and surrender with the main forces while they had the chance, warning them at the same time, though, of course, without giving them any idea as to what our numbers were, that if they attempted to cross the river they would immediately be fired on. At night we had quite a friendly chat with them and swapped experiences. We could have got away easily enough with their horses, but the camels, the one thing that we thought might give us trouble, were away back in the bush and too well guarded for us to catch sight of them.

The Germans all disappeared during the night, and early next morning Johnson left for Libebe to send word to our authorities. After making sure from the tracks that the Germans had retreated to the sand *veldt*, and had not yet made any attempt to cross the river, I pushed on to rejoin the other scouts higher up. On the way I down, one posing as an officer, but doing it none too well. When asked their business, they explained that they were going in from a back post higher up to Grootfontein to surrender there in accordance with their orders. This, of course, from what we had just seen at Yangana, I knew to be a lie, but it seemed safer to let them think one was fooled. These three Germans and their bogus officer had paid our camp a visit, I heard on my return, and had told the same story. The yarn itself was possible enough, but we all put down the sham officer as probably a Dutch rebel. He seemed to know his way about the bush too well to be a German.

Being anxious that none of these runaways should get between us and our Rhodesian border (not that we ever considered that they could really do much actual damage anywhere, but rather for fear that they might create an alarm and cause our authorities a lot of unnecessary worry and expense), we shifted as quickly as possible across the Quito once more. We knew then that, whichever way they came, we should be in a position to head them off. I sent in two runners straight away to Sepango to report what had happened, but mentioned particularly that there need be no alarm, and that I felt sure the five of us could easily handle any party that came up, though it might mean having to shoot their camels and horses first; that in any case I was certain the whole thing would fizzle out ingloriously.

It was a question what we were to do with W.-S. As we could neither watch him ourselves nor, of course, put him in the charge of a native, we gave him his parole and left him with his rifles in charge of the camp at Bush-rangers' Rest, with orders to make as much biltong as he could for us. In point of fact, he could hardly run away, and would have been very foolish to have attempted it. As it turned out, he kept his parole very loyally, and was of great assistance later on when shifting camp, etc. Like most of his people, he was a fine hand with a wagon or oxen, a first-class shot, and an excellent all-round man in the bush. Tall and straight in appearance, he was a manly chap too, and altogether it was a pity to see a man like that mixed up with the rebel crowd.

Chapter 7

The End of the Trail

Before the whole trip was over, and before we had parted at Bulawayo, we were on quite friendly terms, and I often had a quiet chat with W.-S. concerning the rebellion. He gave me a very interesting account of how Kemp's commandos got through from the Transvaal to join the Germans and Maritz, and he always maintained that the latter was a fine fellow. When he saw me smile, he said, "Of course, I don't expect you to think so." He told me that at first the Germans had made much of them, especially of Maritz, Kemp, and the other rebel leaders. For himself, he had a very poor opinion of the German troops, and of their officers he spoke with great dislike. To a smart Dutchman like W.-S., bred and born in the *veldt*, I can quite imagine how very useless the heavy, stolid German troops must have appeared in such a country as German South-West. The German is generally a poor bushman, and as likely as not gets lost a few hundred yards from his camp if he has no nigger with him.

For Major Franke, W.-S. had no more enthusiasm than had the German soldiers. Franke, he said, was always telling them that at such and such a place he would make a big stand; and "then we will see the vultures," said the German *commandant*. But some reason would make him decide to choose instead another position further back. That would be prepared, and again "we will see the vultures" would be the boast, but again the same thing was still repeated, and a still farther retreat without a fight to yet another position, preparatory, I suppose, "to seeing the vultures."

Leaving W.-S. in charge of our camp, we now pushed down the Quito as rapidly as possible, keeping a good look-out in case the "expedition for German East" might be coming up. We did not care how many of the "Square Heads" might come poking up, so long as we could locate them first, and ascertain their position before they saw us. At the junction we picked up Johnson again, and finding that one of the Germans, the man we knew as the bogus officer, had split from the others and made down the river towards Libebe, Johnson and West went after him, and old Rensberg and I crossed the Quito and Okavango to find out where the main body of these fellows had got to. We found they were all about thirty miles back from the river, camped at some waterholes.

From the bushmen we heard that "the tame *ingiraffes* "(*i.e.* camels) were dying, either from weakness or, we thought, perhaps from poison. I made old Yangana come across to see me, and warned the old chap that if any of his natives assisted these Germans with food or in any other way, I would have "his head for it." But the Germans, retreating like this into the bush, seemed to have earned the contempt of the natives generally, old Yangana saying, "We can all see now that the Germans are frightened of the English." The old chief, however, though I discouraged it, also spoke most contemptuously of the Portuguese, who really must have appeared in a rather invidious light to the natives. Hunted out of all their little forts, leaving four of them without even firing a shot, they had never since put in an appearance on the river, and had apparently left a few Englishmen to do all the work. Johnson and West caught our friend the bogus officer about three days down the river and returned with their prisoner. As we thought, he turned out to be a Dutch rebel, another of Maritz's men, who now went under the assumed name of W.-Z.

Then, before the scouts could join up on a little raid for the camels and horses of the main German party, we heard of the arrival of a Major Gordon, D.S.O., who had come, with two orderlies, direct from Sesheke on a special mission for the capture of Maritz. Johnson and West went off with their prisoner to meet the major at Bush-rangers' Rest, picking up Lewis on the way. Rensberg and I, who were camped near Yangana, went straight up the Okavango towards Sambiu, where we had orders to await the major and the main party.

On the road we got a few shots one morning at a lioness, and I believe my first shot with a hard bullet went right through her, for she made a great fuss and jumped into some reeds and lay down. However, she presently came out and slowly got away into the bush.

The weather had now taken the first really warm turn, and we saw a lot of crocodiles lying on the sand-banks. This river is particularly infested with them, and one brute was so enormous that even old Rensberg said he had never seen such a whopper, even in the Zambezi. At quite close quarters he appeared to be almost thirty feet, though I suppose fourteen feet would be nearer the mark. "My God!" said the old Dutchman, after a good look, "is he not an awfully beggar?" and he certainly was! The old man gave him "a good shot," and after thrashing about for a few seconds, the monster dragged himself off into deep water. Rensberg reckoned that even an elephant, if this croc, had got hold of him, "would have to pull good to get free, or else he wouldn't *make* it."

A little beyond Sambiu we awaited the arrival of our officer, who, curiously enough, was also a Queenslander by birth, whom I had known personally before. A great man was Major Gordon, without the slightest bit of side, and as manly and gallant a leader as one could wish for. The country and people were a little strange to him, but he was awfully keen on capturing Maritz, the arch-rebel. We scouts gravely doubted whether there was much chance of getting Maritz: for one thing, our crowd had become too big to be handy.

As it happened, we heard almost at once of a party of white men with wagons, said to be near Bunja on the German side of the river, and these men proved to be a detachment of S.A.M.R.—a splendid lot of fellows, who had come up to the river, *via* Kuringkuru, from Grootfontein. They brought the official news that Maritz had been arrested by the Portuguese, and that meant the end of the major's mission and our return down the river.

The scouts were a little disappointed at being unable to pay a visit to Hawonga, the Ovambo chief at Kuringkuru, a visit we five had originally planned together; the disappointment was the greater, as some time previously we had sent Hawonga a message promising to come shortly to see if he had really been concerned in the murder of Kajimbo and his family, and promising further, in the event of our finding him guilty, to hang him. On the return journey the three of the old Dutch Patrol, Rensberg, Lewis, and myself, kept to the Portuguese side, while the others followed the German track.

Four days later, just at dark, word reached us that a party of Germans, with camels and horses, had slipped through and made up the Quito. We at once sent a messenger back to inform the major, who was a day farther back, and the three of us started at daybreak in pursuit, leaving behind everything not absolutely necessary in order to travel as lightly as possible. With old Rensberg leading, we cut across the bush between the two rivers, hit the Quito again that evening, and soon saw, from there being both camel and horse spoor about four days old going upstream, that the natives had reported correctly.

That evening, whilst camp was being made, I went half a mile ahead to keep a look-out and watched two big *koodoo* bulls come down to water together. It was a fine sight to see them stalking to the river, occasionally stopping to look round and listen or to butt at each other playfully with their long graceful horns. At nightfall several lions started roaring quite close to the camp, and they kept me in some anxiety; our fires were not very big, and a stampede or accident with our horses and mules, at any rate before we had caught the runaways ahead of us, we did not want.

Lying awake, it was curious to notice how indifferent our mounts were to this unpleasantly loud noise; even "Major," my own pony, a most nervous and highly strung little fellow, took no interest in the lions, then making their presence known to all the world, though, of course, he never got their wind.

The pursuit of the Germans took us about eight days. As each day brought us nearer, the spoor of the "tame *ingiraffe*" becoming fresher and fresher, our boys began to get rather scared and to give trouble, so we had to kick the two ringleaders out of the camp, *pour encourager les autres*. After this we had no further trouble. Tucker ran a bit short, for though game was plentiful, we were anxious, as we got near the party ahead, not to shoot, lest we should alarm the Germans and so give them warning of our approach. We knew we should have them right enough, so long as they did not see or hear us first: forewarned, they might have turned the tables on us. The seventh day of the chase we came up quite close to them, and that very night a messenger arrived in camp from Major Gordon, who, with four men, was not far behind.

Both the Germans and ourselves had then crossed the river. That same night we surrounded the Germans' camp, only to find that they had made a further short trek ahead of us. In the morning Major Gordon arrived, after a quick thirty-mile ride, and the whole party followed the spoor straight on. Two Germans were taken in a canoe on the river, and the remainder were surrounded and surprised in their camp. After some demur, they came out and surrendered, though one very sulky individual tried to change his mind and picked up a rifle; it only needed a prod in the stomach with the muzzle of a Lee-Enfield to convince him that the game was up. Thanks to the major, the duties of guarding our prisoners on the 700-mile journey before us was not a very onerous one. They were simply allowed to keep together with their own camp and camels, and told to travel along a few miles either ahead or behind our party. Without arms, they were quite helpless, and could neither run away nor attempt any tricks. All we had to do was to set a watch on our own camp at night. Game was plentiful enough along the river, and we easily kept the camp in meat on the way back.

It was on this journey that, early one morning, we saw a most interesting and exciting coursing match: a leopard pursuing some young reedbuck. I was surprised that the leopard could continue the chase for so long: it must have been for at least several hundred yards. When we lost sight of the hunt he was still close up to the last buck, hoping, each bound, to seize it with his front claws. We also saw the biggest eland I have yet seen: a huge bull with a small herd of cows with him. Unfortunately, just as Lewis, who was ahead, stalking him, was about to fire, one of those ill-natured *sassaby*, "whose eyes are stronger than what looking-glasses are," gave the alarm and frightened the eland away.

It took us some ten days to work back to the Bush-rangers' Rest, and there Johnson left the party, West having previously returned home from the Okavango before the last chase had started. After a day's spell to fix things up, we started again on the road for Livingstone with the prisoners. W.-S. drove the little wagon (originally Kajimbo's), and the major, wisely, took a dozen spare oxen out of the mob we had captured on the Okavango, to kill for beef on the way, thus saving any delay to hunt game. The balance of the captured cattle were left in Siccumberro's charge.

Owing to the scarceness of water it was necessary to cut straight across on to the Lumuno, a branch of the Luiyanna, and then run the latter down again to the Quandoo. We had easy but unexciting times. Our commanding officer was more a big brother to the party than anything else, and literally shared his last biscuit amongst his men.

Being the interpreter, I often had a quiet chat with the prisoners. They told me that their first idea had been to break straight across Rhodesia to German East, but on finding themselves watched by British Scouts directly they hit the Okavango, they became disheartened, and a good many of them had returned to surrender to the Union forces farther south. Of course, the Scouts were pleased that these odd rebels and little parties of Germans had tried to come through, because we felt that it justified our existence out there.

Personally, too, I felt gratified that the warning I had written in the previous December had proved well grounded.

For two months we were travelling before we reached Livingstone, and handed over our nine prisoners. W.-Z. had been delivered to the S.A.M.R. at the Okavango, and thus, the border being now quite clear, the Scouts' duties were over. Having finished our job, we found we were free to get our discharges and seek further service elsewhere.

PART 3. WAR: CAMPAIGNING IN EAST AFRICA

CHAPTER 1
With the E.A.M.R.

It was in the hope of getting to Mesopotamia that Lewis and I left Cape Town for Bombay, thence to headquarters at Delhi. But at Delhi we were told that there was little doing in Mesopotamia, and that only men able to navigate river-boats and motor-launches were wanted. We were offered employment in East Africa instead, and knowing that B.E.A. would probably mean a speedy death for our horses, it was with regret that we gave up the thought of the Euphrates Valley.

Bearing in mind the old stoic teaching, "If you can't get what you like, like what you get," in a short time we duly found ourselves landing at Mombassa. From Mombassa we were immediately railed up to Kagiado, and from there we had three days' ride to join our unit, the East African Mounted Rifles, at Longido. For three whole days we rode through beautiful cattle country—a country clothed with fine-looking blue grasses: a heavy stocking country too. But beautiful though it appeared, there was "death in the pot," for horse sickness was prevalent. Game of all kinds abounded and lions were plentiful, for all that country had been previously a game reserve.

On this trip we caught our first view of Kilimanjaro, a wonderfully beautiful mountain, and one of the most glorious sights of Africa—a sight that never stales. At Longido, which was just across the border of the German territory, we found our unit, the E.A.M.R., a regiment composed of East African settlers who, on the outbreak of war, had immediately come in from all directions from their various farms, armed, in many cases, only with sporting rifles, and bringing with them their own mules and boys. Now these volunteers were a first-class lot of men, and if they had been kept in something like their original state, they would have been invaluable in the early stages of a campaign as irregular mounted infantry, for the Germans had no similar troops to oppose them. The mistake was in trying to turn them into regular troops.

To such an absurdity had this been carried, that I was told lances had actually been issued to some of them. They were not wanting in first-class officers, the right men for leading raiding parties: such a man, for instance, as Major Clifford Hill, an ideal leader of mounted irregulars. In spite of this mistake, the E.A.M.R. did valuable work during the early part of the campaign, when the British strength in East Africa was far from having the predominance in men and armaments it obtained later on. Personally, I liked the E.A.M.R. men immensely, and am proud to have been enrolled with them; but it is certain that for the reason stated, they were never made use of as they should have been.

Two companies of the 17th Indian Cavalry were also in camp; good men and splendidly trained soldiers, but the shocking thing was that every night, no matter where they camped, they made a hideous noise, which could be heard for miles, hammering in their iron picket pegs. They all had Australian horses, mostly Queenslanders, and I noticed many old friends amongst their brands. From this camp on the side of the Longido mountain we had a splendid view of Kilimanjaro, and in the morning especially, clad in *"the roseate hues of early dawn,"* it looked magnificent.

The usual rumours of great variety pervaded the camp. On one day alone the following, amongst others, provoked discussion:

No. 1. 20,000 Australians have landed at Mombassa.

No. 2. The E.A.M.R. owe Nazarus (Indian storekeeper) 40,000 *rupees*.

The great South African Expeditionary Force, which had taken some months to organise and train, was now declared ready for action, and General Smuts having arrived at the front, the big advance from B.E.A. began. Our Longido division, in itself a very formidable one, with many guns, took but a minor part in the advance on Moshi, the terminus of the Tanga line, and the first objective of the forward movement. The main fighting fell upon the division under General Smuts himself, who was working on the other and eastern side of Kilimanjaro and along the McTou line. The Germans put up a hard day's fighting along a line of low hills of which Latima and Riata were the principal heights, but finally they had to abandon their positions and fall back, no doubt according to a long-prepared plan, to a position near Kahe.

The chief part taken by the E.A.M.R. in these operations was a trip through the bush to cut the railway line south of Moshi. This was done successfully enough, but as it was at least twenty-four hours after the last German train had passed, it was hardly a very valuable performance. (Personally, I remember the work, because a couple of swarms of bees put up a very severe offensive against us, inflicting much discomfort on men and horses.) Our division now joined up with General Smuts' forces, and the troops moved on to attack Von Lettow's position at Kahe, where he was coolly waiting for us. The evening before the fighting at Kahe itself the Germans attempted a night attack on our (General Sheppard's) brigade. About seventy or eighty crept quite close up to the camp, and from about 8 p.m. till 1 o'clock in the morning fired into it at close range. Apparently, a considerably bigger force also came out to the attack, but either were purposely kept back to await the result of the smaller party's effort, or else got bushed in the dark amongst the scrub and palm trees between the two forces; anyhow, they seemed to spend most of the night blowing bugles in the distance.

Afterwards, when I was a prisoner, the Germans told me that the idea was to try and stampede the Indian troops by that night attack. As it turned out, the Indian troops were quite steady, and the heavy maxim fire of some of the Indian regiments must have destroyed most of that small party of Germans, for many of their *askaris* were lying dead in front of the camp in the morning. A German officer, who it was evident had bravely led the attack, was found dead in the morning within a few yards of one of our maxim pits. Our brigade had but few losses that night, the enemy firing consistently too high.

Next day came the fight at Kahe, and our regiment saw but little of the fighting, for we had only three or four casualties. During the morning, I was sent on with another trooper with a message, and, coming back, we stood watching the fusiliers pass by on their way up to reinforce the firing line. These were originally recruited from the Legion of Frontiersmen, volunteers who always had a full share of any fighting that was going. Certainly, when it came to fighting, there was never any doubt about the good old "Boosiliers," as they were nicknamed. The fusiliers halted as they came opposite us, and an officer, a man with a greyish beard and felt hat, carrying a sporting rifle, stepped out under a shady tree. Speaking to his men, he said, "Fall out, boys, and come under the shade out of the sun; we may perhaps be here for some little time." He was easy to recognise, that officer—had not I read and loved every one of his books?—F. C. Selous.

That day I also had to go across to a King's African Rifles battalion, which was with our brigade. Great fellows were those original K.A. Rifles. Alas! there were not many of them or their white officers alive by the end of the campaign. Another incident that day remains in my memory. The Germans were firing with one of the 4.1 guns off the *Königsberg* more or less all day, and their shells made a lot of noise but did mighty little damage. When one burst somewhere in the vicinity, not really too close, at the noise of the explosion a native, who was leading two mules with water-tanks alongside us, got such a fright that he fell flat beneath one of his mules. He looked so comical that I could not help laughing at him; whereupon the nigger, catching my eye and seeing my expression, immediately broke into a grin himself and jumped up, ready to enjoy the joke also. The negro is not overburdened with nerves, and hence, when trained, makes a first-class soldier.

After a hard fight all day (during which General V. Deventer, attempting with a large force of horsemen to get round the German position by a flanking movement, had been held off by the enemy), the German leader at nightfall, with considerable skill, withdrew his companies intact and unbeaten. He had, however, to abandon to our troops the big 4.1 naval gun, which, being fixed on a semi-permanent cement foundation, could not be moved quickly enough.

On joining the E.A.M.R. we had been attached to a small party of twelve scouts taken from the whole of the regiment, and in those days I remember our greatest joy was to take a message in or up to General Sheppard. It was a real pleasure to observe how coolly he always handled his brigade in action, and to find, no matter how occupied, how courteously he always spoke to any messenger. To see the General so perfectly cool under fire was a lesson. Later on General Sheppard became Chief of the General Staff in East Africa, a position he held right till the end, and no one, I suppose, carried a bigger share of the worry and responsibility of that trying campaign. Some of his admirers, however, would like to have seen him a little less tolerant of the vast horde of "*base wallahs*" that seemed to collect in East Africa towards the end of the campaign.

After Kahe came a hurried trip to Arusha, through which General V. Deventer's troops soon followed, on the way to Condoa Irangi, surrounding, on the march, a German company at Loi Kissale. This force, comprising about seventeen whites and ninety *askaris*, had to surrender after putting up a fight for some days on the mountain. The success, insignificant though it seems, was acceptable enough in those days. The wet season was now setting in, and great numbers of horses and mules began to die daily from horse sickness. Out of the twenty-two scouts, no less than eighteen died, and the only animals that seemed to survive were the little Somali mules; but even they were not absolutely immune.

From Arusha we went by road back to Kagiado, and thence right round by rail to a big camp at Mbuni. There the E.A.M.R. found their camp once more alongside our old friends of the 17th Indian Cavalry, whose Australian horses seemed to have suffered less than most. "Your regiment and ours are one," said an Indian trooper in his pleasure at seeing us again.

Chapter 2

Intelligence Department

At the end of the wet season things began to stir again, and another big move south was predicted in the near future. It was at this time that Lewis and myself joined the Intelligence Department, four other of the E.A.M.R. scouts leaving to join the I.D. with us. We had to thank Colonel O'Grady, then Chief of the Staff to General Hoskins, always a good friend to us, for getting us transferred into this new work and unit, for then began the happiest and most interesting part of our war service in East Africa. From the first minute of joining the I.D., all our time and work was a source of joy and delight. We had till the finish of the campaign the best of chiefs to work under, and were always splendidly treated, and, I think I might say, trusted. Probably we may often have deserved censure, but never during the whole time in the I.D. did we receive anything akin to a reprimand.

My first job as an I.D. was a nine days' trip with one white companion, S. Williams, and three *askaris* to Same Gap in the Impare Hills. We had to cross a very dry bit of country, and it was necessary to pack a mule with water-tanks for some way and then send it back, leaving a little supply of water in a hole lined with my oil-sheet. We had about twenty miles' walk during the night before reaching the gap, and we spent the following day in a patch of wild sisal on a little hill overlooking the German pickets. At dark next night we started on the return journey, arriving soon after daylight the following morning at the place where we had planted the water.

There we had an unpleasant surprise, for a wretched hyena had in the meantime found our plant, and, pulling away the sticks covering it, had dragged out my oil-sheet, in which he had eaten several large holes. The water, of course, was gone. The question was, could I declare a ground-sheet eaten by a hyena as one "lost in action," and so claim a new one? A second question arose: Did the hyena indulge in one of his good laughs on the completion of his little practical joke? As we found water in a little pool some miles farther on, not much harm was done.

Both Williams and I were then very fit, and I think we must have walked a clear thirty miles straight off on the return journey. On this little trip we twice saw elephants very close, and on one occasion we stopped and had a good look at a large bull standing quite near to us in the thorn bush. The big columns were already in motion on the southern advance on our return; our division, the 1st, under General Hoskins, moving down the Pangani, whilst the main German force fell back with little fighting along the railway line. Near a German bridge, on the Pangani, there was a half-hearted attempt by a few companies to hold up our column, another of the *Königsberg's* naval guns, this time fired from a truck on the railway, shelling our transport during the afternoon. In the evening someone told me, using his own peculiar classification, that the total casualties amongst the transport had only been "a horse, a mule, an ox, a nigger, and a *South African.*"

Next day we went into the Buiko, passing a smashed-up engine and train of the enemy's on the railway. We were never quite sure to whom the credit of this lucky shot was due. Was it the result of a bomb from an aeroplane or of a shell from a little Indian mountain battery, one of the best trained and disciplined units in our force? At any rate, the wrecked train and graves alongside were a satisfactory sight from our point of view—a "pretty" sight in the sense of the old man who said that he always thought "a murder and suicide made *very pretty reading*"

From Buiko, where the column halted, Lewis and I, with a third Intelligence agent, "Buster" Brown, were sent towards Handeni, our duty being to work round through the dry bush country on the right of the column. The first night we met and, after some palaver, made friends with a party of Kwafi, who are really a kind of Bastard Masai. They always looked exactly like the ordinary Masai to us; at the same time, there must be some considerable tribal difference, for the Kwafi always impressed on us "*Sisi habana Masai*" ("We are not Masai"). These Masai tribes have at last solved the problem, confessedly difficult for most of us, how to have your cake and eat it, for they live mostly on milk and blood, the latter being obtained by daily bleeding certain of their cattle, who are, of course, none the worse for this treatment.

The Masai have always had rather a formidable name, but I think as fighting men they have been much overrated, and, personally, I regard them as great cowards. Small parties of German *askaris*, not more than six or eight, would commandeer and remove their cattle wholesale, without the Masai making any serious attempt to check them, and it is well known that the one sore point with all native peoples is, the interference with either their live stock or women, particularly the former.

That night we had a long talk with the Kwafi, who agreed to supply us with guides for our trip. Our camp was about 400 yards from the village in the thick bush, and in the middle of the night some lions cut a big calf out of the Masai cattle *kraal*, or else found it outside, and began to drive the wretched animal, as mischance would have it, in our direction. It seemed that there were one or more cubs trying their hand at killing, for they were nearly an hour playing with and mauling the poor beast, and the unhappy calf kept up a great bellowing all the time. Finally they dispatched it only a short distance away from our camp. All this kept us awake, for the lions were so occupied with their sport that there was the chance that they might come slap upon us.

On the way to Handeni we passed a camp in the bush made by Captain LaFontaine, one of our Intelligence men, who some time previously had made a venturesome trip to a German tramway running to Handeni. The third day out, by sheer bad luck, we nearly walked right into a small party of German *askaris* in some thick country, and both sides cleared into the bush and lost sight of each other. After this we decided that Lewis, with one of our Kwafi and the mules, should be sent back to a camp to await us at a spot arranged between our guides, whilst Brown and I should go on a couple of days farther to Handeni. After we had picked up Lewis on the return journey, we struck the column that had first started moving south in time to see the little fight at Makalamo bridge, where a few German companies again held us up in a very awkward position adjoining the Pangani. This was really their last effort on the Tanga railway, which then fell into our hands.

From Makalamo, the same three of us, with four *askaris* and the two Kwafi guides of our previous trip, started out on the right, our objective this time being to find out what was going on in the Kiberaschi district, where there was supposed to be one German company. For some days we had very bad water, and a day's march from Kiberaschi Lewis fell sick with fever, and we had to leave him planted in some thick bush near a little water-hole. Brown and I proposed to take three out of the four *askaris* with us; but the first man we picked said he was sick, the second man complained of feeling ill, the third man said his feet were sore, while the fourth, on being told he was to come with us, thinking apparently that the supply of excuses was exhausted, immediately threw down his rifle and bolted off through the thorn bush. By that time I felt pretty mad, and so I knelt down to have a steady shot at the flying figure. But Brown, who always had the coolest head of us three, said, "Don't shoot," and sent the two guides after him.

The Kwafi, of course, soon ran him down and brought him back, and I remember that a lengthy and heated argument followed. I insisted that the man was a useless coward, that we were better off without him, and that on no account would I agree to take him. Brown was equally emphatic, maintaining that if this man were allowed to remain, all the other *askaris* would naturally play the same game. The argument was at its height when we struck on a happy conclusion. We decided the *askari* should be made to come, but his rifle and bandolier were to be taken from him, and he was to be given the load of our things to carry and turned into a *pagasi* (porter).

All that night we walked, and at daylight next morning found ourselves on a hill overlooking a German *boma*. The enemy, however, had just evacuated it, and were camped some few miles back in the hills, where we could see their fires; two or three small parties passed close during the morning. In the evening we had a walk through their former camp, which must have held about 10 whites and 100 blacks; it still contained about 50 unfit porters, left behind in a terribly emaciated state. The local inhabitants were friendly to us, and we spent the next day in hiding by the side of the big Kiberaschi road which runs to the west.

We failed to catch anybody, and, being anxious about Lewis, walked back all that night through the bush to find him at daybreak just where we had left him. He was none too well, but able to ride, so from there we rode back to Kiberaschi again, and paid a visit to a big German rubber plantation at a place called Kwedi Boma. The fine homestead there had been left as if the owner had just gone out for a walk. We entered the house without hesitation, and inside helped ourselves to many necessaries, particularly quinine, of which we were badly in need, for we were, all three, more or less suffering from fever that day.

Not daring to stay very long, and having learnt that the German overseer, a Goanese, had been cutting trees and falling them across the Kandeni road as obstacles to any British motors, we collared him and took him along with us, the most wretched-looking prisoner you ever saw. We camped that night about a mile from Kwedi Boma, and in the middle of the night our prisoner came alongside me. I could hear him stirring about, and on my asking him what was the matter, "Please," he said, "can I go home and say my prayers?" This was about 1 a.m., so he was told rather forcibly that he could not. Two days afterwards we got Lewis, who had a bad attack of fever, sent to the hospital at Handeni, whilst Brown and I worked round, and finally joined up with our column at a place afterwards known as Shell Camp. We had been away nineteen days.

We left Shell Camp about June 24 on what proved to be the longest and last trip we three were to make together. There were practically no rations obtainable, the whole column living from hand to mouth on what was brought up daily from the rear. All we could rake up was half a bag of *posho*, eight tins of bully beef, and a couple of pounds of coffee, but we knew we should manage somehow, for if "old soldiers never die," neither do "old bushmen ever starve." Taking with us a mule each, two pack-mules, and four I.D. *askaris*, we soon got clear of the column and worked round, cutting the Handeni road, which the enemy was still using, for they had a big camp a few miles below where we crossed it; parties of their *askaris*, who had been cattle raiding from the Masai, were continually coming back. The natives were friendly, and guided us safely. We always told them we were just the eyes of the big columns of English, looking out for water and roads, and that the big Safaris would soon be coming to eat up the Germans.

The work was interesting and care was necessary. It was usually hard to get natives to take notes back to our chief, though they were willing to guide us, each taking his turn for a day or so, and then handing us over to others. They naturally disliked the job of taking our information back to the columns, for they feared to be caught carrying a note by the enemy, which meant being promptly hanged.

We next worked through another chain of German outposts running south from a round mountain called Geira. It was near there that a rather amusing incident happened. Brown, being in front, had stopped and questioned some natives at a small *kraal*, and as I rode up I noticed, when about 100 yards off, one of the natives (the *jumbe*, as it happened) speak to a youth, who immediately ran off up the slope and disappeared. On reaching Brown I asked why the deuce that nigger had been sent off in such a hurry. Brown said he had not noticed him. "Well, I did," was my answer, and told him (he was the only one who could then speak Swahili decently) to ask the headman why he had sent the boy away like that.

"Why," said the *jumbe* quite innocently, "there is a post of two white men and some *askaris* just over the hill, and I sent to tell them that you are coming to see them and are quite close." We were not long in concluding our interview and getting away into some thick bush again. In those days we still wore our old E.A.M.R. scout felt hats, so the natives on first acquaintance generally took us for Germans.

We were now working round in a south-west and southerly direction towards the German Central Railway. Tucker was not very plentiful just about then; still, we generally got something or other each day to keep us going. At one small village I well remember buying, cooking, and eating five great pumpkins, the only food procurable, for our daily meal. The little camp in the bush to which we had retired with our prey must have astonished anyone who may have seen it afterwards, with its heaps of pumpkin rind.

CHAPTER 3

A Capture

When about eighteen days out, and after having turned more east, we came close to the German line of communications between their main army at Turiani and their principal depot at Kimomba on their Central Railway. That night we camped in the bush close to the *barabara* (main road), which we crossed at daylight next morning, to lay up in some thick stuff close to the road. The *barabara* was evidently being greatly used, and a telephone ran along it. Soon after daybreak big processions of porters began to pass along the road towards the German camp, which must have been about thirty miles ahead; various mobs of pack-donkeys, with Greeks in charge, were also passing, but only an odd *askari*.

All this we watched from the bush, and then decided to go round and cut the road a bit higher up and try our luck at some bush-ranging. Accordingly, about a mile up we left two *askaris* and our mules in the bush, and then crept close to the road, where bush and long grass ran right up to the track. We struck this point on the temporary halt of a great number of porters, who were all singing and clapping their hands.

Stepping into the road, we walked up towards them. As usual, with our felt hats (I always wore a beard too), we were mistaken for Germans. An askari guard, jumping up from the side of the road, saluted me with "*Jambo Bwana.*"

"*Jambo Askari,*" I replied, and then in execrable Swahili, "Why do you not clean your rifle?" taking it at the same time from the astonished-looking man. He was at once put in charge of one of our two *askaris*, and with the other I started after the long line of porters, who were now swinging away up the road with their loads. Shouting and cursing at them in German, I got these puzzled fellows to turn back with their loads, while Lewis and Brown, stopping the porters as they came back, made a big fire and kept throwing the loads on to it as they arrived. As fast as the porters were relieved of their loads, they were made to collect more and more wood for the bonfire. There were loads of various things: clothing from Europe, cases of schnapps and vinegar, bags of rice, beans, flour, and other native foods, also about twenty loads of sugar.

After going up about a mile, I found there was a break in the line of porters, but by shouting I got some of those who were still in front to turn back with their loads. Then came another break, and by that time, being over a mile up the road away from Brown and Lewis, I got frightened, and returned, hurrying up the rear porters. Of course, when the porters reached my two comrades and saw their loads thrown on to the bonfire, they realised what had happened. *Ingreza!* We had cut the telephone wire. The last load of all was a bag of sausages, a great prize indeed to hungry men; keeping this and the prisoner, we then cleared.

The porters we left gaping on the road, and, checking the tendency of some of them to follow us, we generously, on behalf of their real masters, gave them all permission to disperse to their own homes and districts. As a matter of fact they all went back in a great mob to their depot, where, I have no doubt, they told their German masters a wonderful account of their adventure. We had burned, I fancy, a good 200 loads, and, as we hoped, "*stirred the possum*" at the German Headquarters when they learned there of the attack on their communications. We also hoped a little raid like this might force them in future to detail more *askaris* from the front to guard their convoys.

CHAPTER 4

The Hunter Hunted

The job being completed, we wasted no time ourselves in getting back through the bush, picking up our mules and clearing out in an easterly direction. We travelled fast all that afternoon and struck water late at night, cooking some food and then going on another hour in the moonlight before camping. We intended, of course, to stick to the bush, thick bush if possible, but next day, after travelling hard till one o'clock, we were still without water, and had not seen any natives. We were forced, therefore, during the afternoon to swing back towards the Vami River, which we reached before evening.

We by no means liked doing this, for the villages were thick all along the river; still, we had to get water. We camped and cooked food close to the river, and we saw various natives, from whom we tried to get both guides for ourselves and messengers to go back to the column. They made us promises they would supply these early next morning. We did not, however, remain camped that night in the same spot, but after the natives had all gone we moved off and camped about three-quarters of a mile off. We should have gone farther on.

That night I felt very anxious and hardly slept. There was bright moonlight, and about four in the morning, lying awake in my blanket, I heard whistling some way off. It appeared to me as if someone was trying to locate our camp and expecting to get an answer from it. Jumping up immediately, I shook and woke Brown and Lewis. "Look out," I said, "there seem to be natives trying to locate us; it may be the natives promised for guides and messengers, but it seems too early, and I don't like it. Better get ready to get out of this quick." Grabbing my rifle and *bandolier*, I went out towards where one could hear at intervals the whistling in the distance, to see what could be made of it. I worked around, and the whistling began to get nearer.

To cut a long story short, I found myself in a short time between two small parties of German *askaris*; we started to shoot at each other at close range, but in moonlight. I soon got the worst of it, receiving a bullet through my *bandolier* and a wound near the hip, and cleared out, to discover that I was on the bank of the river; I had not realised I was so close. To save myself from being surrounded, in I had to go; the water was quite warm, and, after partly wading and partly swimming for a couple of hundred yards or so (besides having to rescue my old felt hat, which started floating off on its own), I got out on the same side again and started to work back toward where I imagined the camp to have been.

For some reason the Germans had not followed me up or it would have been all over with me, for it was very bright moonlight, and, in addition, almost daybreak. My head would have been a fine substitute for a ginger-beer bottle for some target practice in the water. Later, at Morogoro, when a small mob of Germans came round me to inspect the notorious prisoner, an officer amongst them asked me where I had hidden myself. "Did you stick yourself away in the grass," he said.

"No," I said, "I jumped into the river. But how was it" (asking him something in his turn) "that your men did not come and finish me off when in the water?"

Looking a bit sheepish before the other Germans, he replied, "We did not have our old *veldt askaris* with us."

In the meantime Brown and Lewis, with three out of the four *askaris* and most of the old boys, just got out of camp in time, abandoning everything except their rifles and *bandoliers*. As they left, another party of the enemy began firing into the camp, probably at the mules, which were still tied up. Lewis and Brown and the *askaris* wasted no time, but wisely made off straight away, and after six thin days in the bush—days when they had several narrow escapes from running into parties of the enemy on the look-out for them—they managed to work right back through the German pickets into our own column, which was still camped at Shell Camp, where we had left it a month before.

After getting out of the river I picked up one of our own *askaris*, a young Wakamba rejoicing in the name of Jambo, and we two lay up that day not far from the camp of the night before in some scrub. Till about midday the enemy were poking about in the neighbourhood, and we could hear them talking. That night we too cleared out with the intention of working round to try and get back to the column. As a matter of fact, we really followed very much the same direction and track that Lewis and Brown had taken (not that we knew it at the time), and were always a day or so behind them. The greater part of one day we waited lying up in the bush close to the big German road that runs direct from Kidete to Morogoro, a road which the enemy were then using infrequently. The wound in the hip, though but a slight one, became very sore from the continual walking and rubbing in the tall and long grass, and I hoped we might have found a rider of some sort—perhaps carrying a message—on a mule or donkey, which I could have ridden, and thereby obtained relief from the continual irritation. As it was, the *askari* and myself travelled mostly by night, getting green mealies, then luckily in season, from the native *shambas* (cultivation patches), and in the daytime lying up and sleeping in the grass or bush.

On the fifth evening we arrived, tired and very hungry, at a native *kraal*, and we knew we must be somewhere near both the English and German main camps. From the headman of the little *kraal* we got some eggs and native *posho*[1] and a promise that at daylight he would lead us round next day to the English camp, which we should reach, he said, in the afternoon. In the meantime, however, our friend (unnoticed by us, though we were not unsuspicious) had managed to send out a messenger to the German main camp, which was perhaps less than six or seven miles away.

Next morning at daylight we set off with our supposed friendly guide, and after travelling about an hour or more on a small native track, we almost ran into a German patrol of two whites and a number of blacks. We only just saw them in time, and before they saw us we bolted into the bush; evidently they were on the look-out for us. In making my escape, I lost sight of poor Jambo, who, as I afterwards heard that evening, made across to another native track which led him right into a German picket, who shot him. I was more lucky, and that day made a big round through the bush, picking up in the afternoon two more natives. Under their guidance I hoped to reach a village that night which they said so far neither Germans nor English had visited. However, these two fellows apparently knew all about us, and had their orders from the Germans.

It was very tiring, and the wound had become very sore during the afternoon, and I was tempted, foolishly indeed, to follow once more those natives along a small and unused native track. The relief from walking through the long grass was too great a temptation to be resisted.

---

1. *Posho*—ration allowance.

Chapter 5

A Prisoner

About five o'clock I found I had been led, quite unsuspectingly, into a party of the enemy waiting for me in ambush right on the track. I only remember yells of "Hands up" and two men in particular pressing their rifles into my ribs. Too flabbergasted to do anything, I stared at them in a hopeless and stupid sort of manner, while they continued pressing their rifles up against me. It never went into my head, so surprised was I, to drop the rifle which was slung over my right shoulder.

Presently it dawned on me that the two men, whom alone I seemed really to notice, were not Germans at all, but evidently Dutchmen. "Good God!" I said, "you don't want to shoot your own men, do you? I am not a German."

At this they started laughing, and one of them asked me, speaking in English, "Don't you think we are Germans then?"

"Of course you are not," I said; "you are Dutch. What are you, Brits' men or who?"

This seemed to tickle them more than ever, and then a big man on my right spoke to me, calling my attention to the round German rosette, or whatever it is, on his big felt hat. I realised right enough then that the two men on my right, though Dutch, were enemies; they were two of the Dutch settlers of Arusha. In all there were ten German whites in the party that surrounded me, including a doctor. They were quite decent, and several of them complimented me on our trip. ("*Sie haben eine shone Patrouille gemacht*") "You have made a fine patrol, but you made a mistake in attacking our convoy. That was your downfall," they said. They had a snack of brown bread and dripping and cold sausage in which I shared, without being pressed, and we then set out for the main German camp. The place where I was captured was apparently about midway between our camp and the German. "Don't try and run away," said one of the Dutchmen.

The German main camp, the headquarters of Von Lettow himself, was a very big affair. Fires stretched as far as the eye could see, and much noise and singing by enormous numbers of porters greeted the ear. I was taken to the doctor, and had the wound in the hip dressed; there was no sign of gangrene or anything. "*Sie haben gluck gehabt,*" said the German doctor; a fraction nearer would have smashed the hip-bone. Then to tea with the two Dutchmen, an odd German being present on and off during the meal also. Surely I had a great feed! Fresh meat, rice, sweet potatoes, and coffee.

During this Von Lettow himself came across. The two Dutchmen jumped up and spoke to him, and then he had me called over. I heard Van R. say to the German general before he called me up, "We have got Wienholt" the general's reply, "*Das ist famos, das ist famos, das Kommt nicht wieder,*" meaning presumably the raiding of his convoys. Von Lettow spoke to me—in German, of course—for a few minutes, asking me what nationality I was. "I am an Australian, sir."

"But your name is German."

"Yes, the family is of German extraction, though not for the last three centuries."

"But the name is German."

"Yes, certainly, sir; originally, I believe, from near Bremen."

Again he asked me, "Have you had fever?"

"No, sir, I have no fever."

"Oh, it is wounded then that you are?"

"Yes, just slightly."

"Ah," said he, "we have known all about you." Then he asked me if I was the leader of the scouts, and I told him I was the oldest.

The German general impressed me favourably. Roughly dressed, wearing slacks, heavy ammunition boots, and a coat not unlike a British warm; his manner not at all overbearing; his face the face of a strong man. He called some young officer over to him and led him off by the arm, evidently giving some instructions.

A bad night is a man's first night as a prisoner, resembling the new boy's first night at a big, strange school. It is then in the quiet that the iron enters one's soul. Next morning, however, we were off down to the central line with two companies then being sent, I gathered, to help in the Muansa district, at that time hard pressed by the Belgians. Just as we left camp one of our aeroplanes came over, dropping small bombs. The *askaris* made me step off the road with them, but otherwise took little notice, and continued to roll their cigarettes: so much for the yarns of the native terror of our "*indegi*" (bird).

On the fourth day we reached the German Central Railway at Kimomba, and the two German N.C.O.'s in whose charge I had been travelling, and who had treated me civilly and well, handed me over at the railway station. Whilst waiting in the station building, two petty officers of the *Königsberg*, doing railway duty, entertained me with the German view of things: "In four months in Europe it is all over." "France is finished." "This I must say, the Englishman is no soldier." It is vain to argue with the Master of Forty Legions, and my only retort was to ask innocently for the latest news about Verdun, and if it had yet been taken.

That evening we went by train to Morogoro, where quite a little crowd of Germans had collected to see the captured bush-ranger. It is only fair to mention that from Von Lettow downwards no one ever appeared to have any idea of attempting to ask for information. The prisoner slept that night in a little detached room close to the railway station, perhaps formerly a lamp and oil store. In the night came further excitement, for several boxes of old ammunition stored in my room were remembered, and these had to be taken outside lest, I suppose, the desperate character within should attempt to blow his way out of prison.

The journey was resumed next day, and we arrived at Dar-es-Salaam about 9 p.m., to find the inhabitants of that town, in true colonial custom, assembled to meet the train. My destiny was the gaol, where the warder, who, not really a bad sort, welcomed me with the following information: "*Frankreich ist caput*" (France is done for), "*England hat kein geld mehr*" (England has no more money), "*und Russland ist auch caput*" (Russia is also done for).

Early next morning we were marched down the coast, in charge of another stout little German and seven *askaris*. My guardian, in private life the skipper of a small coasting boat, was again a good sort. He told me as a great joke that an English hydroplane from our warships had lately flown over Dar-es-Salaam dropping bombs, but the only casualties were four Goanese tailors—"your own subjects," said he, with a chuckle. As a prisoner, I now believe firmly in having *fat* men as guardians.

We reached the Rufigi River after some days, crossing it not far from Mohoro. Though it is a fine stream, flowing strongly and fully

400 yards across, I felt no great enthusiasm for it, realising that it was another considerable obstacle between me and our columns. "Here will come the big fight," says my German guardian, and later on he tells me in confidence, "Here the English will have the bush war." That night we camped near the river bank at the German post, and the German in charge informed us that there were two bad man-eaters about, and that he had lost several porters lately from these lions.

As a prisoner I take accordingly an unusual interest in the strength of the walls of the little outside hut I am put into for the night, and console myself with the thought that should anything happen during the night, the *askaris* on guard will doubtless be taken first.

Kilwa was our next stop, and in the meanwhile I had been transferred to the charge of a wretched little creature of a German N.C.O., who I noticed, with misgiving, was *very thin*. His heart was bad, and so he rode the whole of the next twelve days to Liwale in a *machela* (hammock or chair fixed on poles and carried by natives). To me it seemed a long twelve days' walk, for on the journey I began to get weak with fever and dysentery. Liwale, formerly an ordinary police station, was then used as a prison for English officers, of whom about fifteen were there, in company with two Portuguese and two Belgian officers.

I, as the only English non-officer prisoner in the place, was kept in a cell in the actual *boma* building, outside of which was a barbed-wire fence. The English officers were not allowed to speak to me, but I found I had fellow-prisoners in the shape of two Portuguese infantrymen. They, however, were not so strictly guarded as I was, for they were allowed to go outside the *boma*, and to speak to their officers. I tried hard to persuade my companions to teach me their language, but they were evidently not inclined to do this. Through the freedom allowed to the Portuguese, I managed to answer, of course, in secret, a series of questions from the British officers, who, naturally, were hungry for news:

1. Is it true Kitchener is dead?
2. Which ships did each side lose in the Jutland fight?
3. Has the Canal been taken by the Turks?
4. Where are our troops now in G.E.A.?
5. How long do you think it may be before we are relieved?

A young *Königsberg* sailor was in charge of our food and domestic arrangements: quite a nice lad, who was anxious to learn English, and looked forward to going to Australia "when the war was over." But instead of going to Australia, he died later of blackwater. Our food was at first both good and plentiful, but I own I hardly found my two companions congenial. It was hard to kill time in those days. Then in November some fifteen batches of South Africans, captured near Kissaki, were brought in, special *bandas* having been built for them outside the *boma*, and I was lodged with them. At once the chance of escape became practical.

All this time the wound in my hip, though very slight, had kept running and would not heal. It was getting sore, and needed attention. An old German doctor, Herr Anning, formerly, I believe, a member of the Reichstag, now came to the post, and he, most courteous of men to us prisoners—officers and men alike—cured and healed the wound for me. Just before the South African prisoners came in, a *safari* of twenty chained porters, carrying loads of English potatoes, left the *boma* in the direction of Kilwa. Five days later they returned with their loads intact. Also, about this time, I seemed to notice something of a change in the attitude of the German *askaris*. "Did you get a sniff of anything today?" said the big German—a very decent fellow, in private life manager of the Liwale Rubber Plantation—who took us out walking every afternoon. The fact was that our troops had recently landed at Kilwa and Lindi.

The next thing was a general move of the whole of the prisoners' camp right back to the Luwego river, a fourteen days' trip, where a camp was formed in the bush close to the river at a place called Mangangira. New buildings were quickly erected and the camp routine established. Food had now become very scarce, and henceforward the prisoners were badly and insufficiently fed; often we were really very hungry. For breakfast all we had was a plate of *matama* porridge; lunch was a plate of rice and a small ladleful of beans; for tea, a plate of *matama* again and some rice. When any of the Germans shot a buck or, better still, a pig, we had meat in addition to the above rations, and that day fared well: otherwise we went to bed hungry. At the same time, continual attacks of dysentery brought me very low. Heavy storms, too, fell nearly every evening, for we were now in December.

Against these discomforts was the knowledge that the chance of escape had become much more hopeful. We were in a wild spot, and the Germans were getting careless.

At Liwale I had shown my companions how to preserve their meat by making "biltong "and "salt junk." I liked doing this, as I generally took the opportunity to cut off and fry two big steaks on some coals, one (need I say?) being for the *askari* guard. I had also volunteered for this job because it let me out through the barbed wire of the *boma*, and I hoped it might offer an opportunity for escape. However, at that time I was too well guarded.

The prisoners' greatest luxury in the matter of food came on "Rissole Day," when fresh meat had been killed. For then our native cooks, chopping up the meat fine, each with two big sharp knives, played a *rat-a-tat-tat* on the meat-board, the pleasantest of music to hungry men. Great were our expectations when the "song of the rissole" arose from the kitchen. "Fatty," as we named the stout German who mostly shot for the camp, made himself unpopular, because, as we hungry men declared, he would only shoot pigs to the neglect of all other game, such was his love for pork. Some of this pork, too, he used to smoke in an ingenious smoke-box, though, needless to say, *we* never tasted these home-made delicacies.

For Christmas Day the prisoners had been told they would each receive two pieces of lump sugar as a treat; but on that particular morning, when we woke up, something started us singing "God Save the King," and thereupon the furious commandant, Oberleutenant Papke, rushed out of his neighbouring *banda* ordering us to stop that noise, and further punishing us by cancelling the issue of sugar. Not that anyone really cared, and between Papke and most of us there was never any love lost.

One of our German guards, known as the "Bosun," was really a great character. Originally one of the *Königsberg's* crew, a gruff old sailor with a big red beard, he was rather terrifying until one got to know him a little. To be able to speak German was, of course, a tremendous advantage in many ways to a prisoner, especially with a man like old "Bosun" in the camp.

One fine day there was great excitement, for an order had come that one of us was to go over to the "Bosun" to draw elephant fat. As a speaker of German, I, as usual, went over, to find the old "Bosun" in great good humour; some friends must have sent him a bottle of *schnapps*. A great bucket of beautiful white elephant fat and a dipper were by his side.

"Good morning, Herr Bosun, how is the fever this morning?"

"Oh, still bad," and a dipperful of fat goes into my basin.

"You suffer a lot, we notice, Herr Bosun."

"Yes, it is a dreadful country"—a second dipperful of fat.

"I often wonder, Herr Bosun, how you manage to stick it out as you do"—another dipperful. "Anyone else would have had to be carried on the last *safari*; you must have great pluck and a wonderful constitution"—yet another dipperful. At last, in shame, I start to withdraw the now nearly full basin, but, "Wait, wait," says the old chap, "just one more for *backshishi*."

On my return the booty is shared out before fifteen hungry and watchful pairs of eyes, and it amounts to just a condensed milk-tin full for each man. Mine lasted four days, and I felt much the stronger for it; in fact it just made all the difference, for one had begun to crave for fat, sugar, and anything in the way of vegetables.

As to vegetables, there had been a bitter disappointment some time previously, after Zimmermann, the *Königsberg* baker, and now our quartermaster, kindled vast hopes with the news, "Today you will get cabbages from the cabbage palm; yes, and it is much better than common cabbage, and very hard even to tell the difference." He also said that in peace times this alleged succulent luxury was protected by a heavy fine, since to get the cabbage the tree must be killed. We had that vegetable for lunch; but Papke must have eaten the cabbage part, and all that we seemed to have got was some of the trunk ten feet lower. Alas! the hungriest could not eat it. For my own part, I prefer bottle tree, and I consider that heavy fine unnecessary.

In January our hunger was still keener, and it seemed a painfully long time between meals. Game was decidedly scarce anywhere near the camp, and meat was not so frequently obtained. The officers who were on parole were trying to increase their supplies by snaring partridges, but I, being in the ranks, was always guarded day and night. In those hungry days philosophy taught one that, after all, the nicest things are really the commonest and simplest. When "hungry" talk started in the *banda*, as it did each evening, it was noticeable, when anybody was choosing the food he would have if he were free, how he invariably chose something plain, like roast beef and potatoes, a good fresh herring, or, again, a fresh loaf of bread and some butter. My choice was always a big bowl of brown bread and milk with plenty of sugar.

CHAPTER 6

My Escape

With my health somewhat restored by the elephant fat, I decided the time ripe for a dash for liberty. It was now or never. One of my fellow-prisoners, a South African wireless operator and quite a boy, knew weeks before that I was going to try and escape if chance offered, and had said that he wished to go with me. He was now told "tonight's the night," and was also informed of my plans. We needed to take a little rice and *matama* flour with us in order to avoid, as far as possible for the first three or four days, all intercourse with native villages. We had to ask B., another South African prisoner, for this food, because he had charge of all our rations, then still drawn ahead from the Germans for about five days.

The Germans, to save themselves trouble, had made us draw our rations in one lot for a couple of weeks ahead, and this, as it happened, proved rather an unwise proceeding. B., when asked for the food, of course, wanted to come with us, and he also had a mate, M., who wished to be included. So in the end we agreed to take these two with us, thus making a party of four in all.

As an old bushman, and the only one speaking Swahili at all, I was to be the sole boss.

At nine in the evening we were to try and sneak out one by one to meet, if all went well, at a certain big tree a few hundred yards away. There was but little to be done in the way of preparations, for our worldly goods were not numerous; each took a small grain sack, with a little flour, rice or salt, a spoon, a sort of blanket, and one a knife and a couple of small tins for cooking purposes. I also had a compass, secretly obtained from Lieutenant Sankey of the *Goliath*, who, being in the plot, had provided us, in addition, with a box of matches.

At 8 p.m. I went quickly round to every man in the *banda*—all the prisoners as usual were at that time lying on their stick and grass beds—and told each man it was best for him to see nothing, say nothing, and do nothing. This was the first intimation that anything was going to happen, and there was no discussion.

About half-past eight a great thunderstorm came up, and we noticed with some pleasure that the *askari* known to us as "Smiler," whom we hated worst of all the guards, had come on duty. In a few minutes a dreadful storm of rain, with great flashes of vivid lightning, broke over the camp. The *askaris* had an open guard *banda* alongside ours, in which the corporal and other *askaris* stayed every night, a huge fire being built between us.

As the storm broke, our friend "Smiler" hurried across to get into the guard shed. Everything outside the fire had become pitch black except when broken by the gleams of lightning. Now was our chance. Rapidly following each other, we slipped through the side of our *banda* whilst "Smiler" was round the other side, and soon had joined up a little way off in the dark.

After following a little track for some time, and keeping touch in the blackness and rain only by holding a hand on the leading man's shoulder, it was evident we could not get far by night in that weather. It was a very big storm, and though uncomfortable to be out in, a very good friend to us. My companions were shown that to travel in that storm and in the dark would only leave us completely done up by morning, with but a few miles between us and our late prison. Therefore, after marching for not more than an hour, we camped quietly for the rest of the night, the rain completely washing out all signs of our tracks between the prison camp and where we slept. At the earliest sign of dawn we set out in dead earnest, steering a little north of east to hit the coast, as I hoped, somewhere north of Kilwa. I counted on leaving to our right the main body of the Germans opposed to our Kilwa column.

The country was just a big sea of level bush, with but little really thick thorn bush. We went fast, and though not very strong (our feet got very sore and badly cut), we travelled like madmen; for we were free, and terribly afraid of being recaptured. The fourth day we struck a party of *Shensis* (raw natives) in some quiet bush. They looked well disposed, so, putting on a bold face, we had a long talk with them. Of course they knew what we were; for it is not the custom for white men to travel unarmed and without servants—to say nothing of our generally disreputable, runaway appearance. They were promised good *backshishi* to take us through to the English, and warned that if they told the Germans and got us recaptured, they would themselves have to answer for it eventually to the British. As they knew that the English were slowly eating up the Germans throughout the whole country, the natives decided, after a long talk, to accompany us as guides.

At once we were off. It was most necessary to get away before they had time to change their minds. Our hopes of getting through were now high, for our guides were scared and taking no risks, which facts made it all the safer for us.

The enemy were scattered more or less all through the country we travelled, and occasionally we heard them shooting; but I felt sure our guides were thoroughly to be trusted. We were very careful; always camping at night in the thickest scrub we could find, and, when food had to be cooked, never stopping a minute longer than was necessary at a fire. Our guides, too, only entered a village when they knew that particular friends or relatives resided in it.

Hungry times we had, often living on wild fruit, though once indeed we managed to get a whole chicken. The rain made it rough travelling; continual heavy storms all night and almost every night, for the wet season had now set in, and we were utterly without shelter. Still it was always a warm rain, and, above all, we were once more at large and free.

On the fifteenth day after leaving Mangangira we reached a little advanced post of our K.A.R. at Nambangi, where an *askari* corporal was in charge. There we stayed a day, eating up, I fear, between us all his, and his men's, fat ration—about half a kerosene-tin full. Thence, through pouring rain and flooded creeks, we came to Chemera, the advanced post of our Kilwa force. I need not say we were well received, the more so that one of our Intelligence officers, Lieutenant Gattwood, was there. He looked after us with paternal care, while all the promised *backshishi* was duly given to our guides. It was grand to get some news again, though I was terribly sorry to hear that Frederick Selous had been killed.

After waiting a day at Chemera, orders came for me to report to my chief at the headquarters of the first division. In the camp General O'Grady came up and shook hands, and it was good to find him alive and well. We all, even then, thought him a great soldier, though he was still to make, in the Lindi area later on, that splendid reputation (amongst the men at the front at any rate) which endeared him to all who served under him. Brave as a lion personally, he was, above all other general officers on our side, a man, who, like the German leader himself, would appeal as a personality to negro troops. It was a great misfortune that he went back to India when the Germans later on broke south across the Roouma, and so was not available in the field for the campaign in Portuguese country that followed.

The general situation in G.E.A. had not, after all, changed much during the six months that I had been a prisoner. We had, it is true, taken and occupied the Central Railway and the enemy's capital, Dar-es-Salaam, and had landed at Kilwa and Lindi and occupied the country south as far as the Rufigi River; but the German Army, though much reduced in numbers, was still in the field and undefeated, with the morale of both whites and blacks probably higher than ever, and with a great stretch of country most suitable for a defensive and bush warfare still in enemy hands. Again the big South African Expeditionary Force, including its leader, had melted like butter in the sun, and another tombstone had appeared in that African graveyard of military reputations.

There was indeed one Boer general in the south well able, both by natural military skill and by experience, to command in this most awkward of campaigns, and in whom the troops, I believe, would have had great confidence. Unfortunately, his heavy responsibilities as Premier of South Africa in those troubled times made this impossible. As it was, it was a poor consolation to those left in the field to read that our late commander-in-chief had been acclaimed as the conqueror of German East, and to read, in the papers we received, that the German forces were now nothing but scattered fugitives amongst their fever swamps and jungles. Later on, just about the time of the fight at Narungombe (when we had more casualties than at Colenso), I remember being distinctly annoyed by a letter from a friend, who asked me why I stayed on in East Africa, on a "black *veldt* police patrolling job," now that the campaign was finished there.

Whilst I had been in durance vile, the excellent Nigerian and Gold Coast battalions had arrived on the scene, soon to prove themselves some of the best black troops we had in the whole campaign. I found that General Hoskins, our old chief of the first division, had now become commander-in-chief, and on taking over he must have had a very unthankful and heart-breaking task with all the straightening up and reorganising of the British forces that was required. He had quite lately driven Von Lettow's main force from its positions around Kibata in perhaps the severest engagements of the whole campaign.

Just before we escaped we had heard the guns at Kibata, at the Luwego prison camp, plainly enough, though the firing must have been well over 100 miles away.

When I had reported to my chief, I journeyed down to Kilwa, where I saw General Hoskins himself; and soon after this the dysentery, from which I had suffered more or less all the time of my captivity, took a bad turn, and this meant going into hospital. To pull through this attack proved a hard fight, and indeed recovery could not have taken place without the unceasing care of the hospital staff generally, and the special orderly who looked after me in particular. It is impossible to speak too highly of the care and attention that brought me round, and, for my own part, I rank the *pukka* R.A.M.C. man very high in the army list.

From Kilwa I was moved to Lady Colville's Convalescent Hospital in Nairobie, a place so nicely run that a few weeks seemed to work miracles in us patients. It was there we heard the bad news that General Hoskins was leaving, and I was not the only one who felt depressed about it; I am convinced that there would have been no campaign in 1918 in Portuguese East Africa had he remained in charge. The general came to say goodbye to us at the hospital.

I was nearly fit again when I paid a short visit, on convalescent leave, to my old school friend, Cole, who had a property at Gilgil, where he was running about 13,000 sheep, managing the place as far as possible on Australian lines. The sheep—quite fair-looking Merinos, cutting a good fleece—had been bred up from native stock with Australian imported rams. The herd of cattle, too, had also been bred up from native cows and imported bulls, the first cross showing really extraordinary improvements. My friend's fat wethers were fetching nineteen shillings off shears at that time, and the fat bullocks, quite decent looking beasts, going not far short of 700 lb., £7 10s.

The owner, however, was not without his troubles, for he had to contend against a good deal of disease amongst his flock, besides the worry of big herds of zebra eating his grass and drinking at his troughs—a proof that the country was still in its pioneering stage. He also had to endure raids on his stock by predatory beasts, some of them humans. My friend showed me his yearly accounts, and it was amusing to notice such an item as £3 bonus for trapping a lion, and the considerable expenditure for umbrellas for his Masai herdsmen—who dislike their *coiffures* getting wet.

On my telling Cole one morning that it was a good plan to cut the tips of bulls' horns to prevent them seriously injuring one another, he mentioned that the Masai themselves acted on rather a different plan; they *sharpened* the horns of a favourite bull to enable him to assert his superiority against his rivals for the favour of the females, and by this means get a bigger percentage of the calves.

It was a jolly and a recuperative holiday, mentally no less than physically, for my friend was a charming host, and it gave me the chance to see more of that rich and delightful country, British East Africa.

CHAPTER 7

Back to Duty

Fully recovered, I returned to the front *via* Dar-es-Salaam, which I now viewed under happier circumstances. The beautiful little natural harbour is rather small, and apparently the narrow entrance has its drawbacks.

From Dar-es-Salaam I went to report to my chief, the C.I.O., who was with the column at Matandawala. There I found my old comrade, "Buster" Brown, and had a lunch with him that was remarkable for one of his cook's masterpieces, a blancmange pudding flavoured with chopped onion.

My first duty, after getting six or seven I.D. *askaris* and half a dozen porters, was to go north and learn if there appeared any likelihood of a German force working around from the northwest to our lines of communication from Kilwa. My six porters were Kavirandos—very black and of the truest negro type. The *krooboy* is generally quoted as being the purest type of negro, but the Kavirando also appears to be a very pure species. They are fine porters—happy, cheerful fellows—and I took a great liking to them, though really I prefer the Mnyamwezi. These particular six Kavirandos I had for many months, and the reason for their leaving me was that they poisoned themselves in true negro style, by eating some awful-looking red and yellow toadstools.

None of them actually died, but at one time it looked as if they all would. I dosed them with charcoal, for I had nothing else, and I had once heard that it was a certain cure for a dog that had taken a bait. Only a week previous to their poisoning these Kavirandos were great black shiny creatures; after their recovery they were so thin and wretched that I had to pack them off to the nearest hospital—and I almost cried at losing them.

On this first trip I found all the Nambangi district and the country north of it very dry, with water extremely scarce, and the land absolutely stripped of all food, whilst most of the natives had come to us from the Chemera district or farther inland for protection and food. Our farthest outpost was then at Namatiwa, where some eighty K.A.R.'s were stationed under two white officers, very youthful both, but good soldiers, experienced and careful. Pleasant hosts they were to the old bushman who stopped the night with them, and fared sumptuously on their "*Pie à la Namatiwa*" (bully beef, onions, and beans).

During this trip we twice saw lions, but of the enemy we saw nothing, though we heard them shouting in the bush, and at the end of a fortnight we were back at Chemera. I reported that owing to the bare state of all that belt of country, it was most improbable that anything more than a very small raiding party of Germans could work round to do mischief.

Orders now came from my chief for a more definite piece of work—to discover and then destroy the enemy's little post and store at Mtundu, about forty-five miles north-west of Chemera. Two *ruga-ruga* (armed local natives) came to me as guides, and I was lucky to get them. The main guide, Abdulla, from a village called Mpotora, was a grand figure, a young man of perhaps twenty-six years; a really nice fellow too, and a born gentleman, straight, tall, and lithe as a panther, but, as his yellowish colour indicated, not a pure negro. Of all the aboriginal peoples that I have come across, this man was the smartest and bravest of the lot, and never have I liked any native African so much. Thanks to Abdulla, who, of course, knew all the inhabitants around Mtundu (his own village Mptora being in the same district), we had an easy job. A copy of my telegram to my chief will be the best and shortest way to describe the work:

At Mptora found nothing; at Mtundu caught two German whites, one *feldvebel*, one *Königsberg* deck officer, and one *askari* (Tanga company) . Found little in magazine, some few bags each rice, beans, *matama*, and dried meat; some ammunition. Place also lately used as salt-making depot. After distributing surplus food among local natives, burnt whole post and returned with prisoners to Chemera.

That expedition accomplished, orders (sanctioned at Dar-es-Salaam) came from my chief that I should raise and arm a small force of *ruga-ruga* from the natives of the neighbouring districts, and enjoy a free hand generally for bush-ranging tactics against the enemy's posts, convoys, and "magazines" (stores) in the Mlembwe, Madaba, and Liwale districts. One of our white Intelligence Agents and twenty-five more I.D. Scouts were also sent up later to join me.

This was the best part of the whole campaign to me. The Kanzus *askaris* (*ruga-ruga*) were capital fellows, working well under their own headmen, to whom I gave honorary rank of corporals and sergeants, and never giving the least trouble. Abdulla himself got hold of a single silver-coloured German lance-corporal's chevron, which he wore proudly as a badge denoting the rank of staff-sergeant-major; I always kept him with me. Bahkari, a very smart, well-mannered man, had the name of another *ruga-ruga* chief. There was also an old negro called Wazeri, a good sort and quite an old bush general. Many of these chaps before the war had been gun-bearers to white men out elephant shooting. Rifles and *bandoliers*, with a pair of shorts and a shirt each, completed the equipment of my force. The headdress was as each man fancied, and this gave scope for plenty of variety.

The German East campaign proved, at any rate, that, with training and discipline, the negro can become a first-rate soldier. In fact he really seems a born soldier, with his love of drill and parades, and my I.D. *askaris* have more than once asked me, when it has happened that we have been waiting a day or so in a big camp, "if they might drill tomorrow." Big children though they were, Von Lettow's *askaris* gave an example of bravery, discipline, and loyalty on a losing side rarely excelled. At the same time, it is doubtful whether it matters much to the negro under which white man he is enrolled; it is sufficient for him to be an *askari*.

There is a story, said to be quite true, of a K.A.R. soldier who, after apparently puzzling over the matter for some time, complained to his officer that he saw other *askaris* wearing a medal for a certain campaign and fight (of some years back), and asked why he had not got one also, as he, too, had been there. The officer made inquiries, with the result that the *askari's* tale was found to be true; he had been fighting right enough, but *against us*. Now we can understand how, under the world's supreme military genius, and for a personality only once equalled (the little Corsican), the black Numidian horsemen of Hannibal cut to pieces time and again the sturdy legions of Rome. The black soldier requires above all that his actual leader shall be a man to look up to, and in this German East campaign the enemy's General was such a man.

The first trip after recruiting the *ruga-ruga* was in a way unlucky, for while passing in the bush by a little village called Marosho, we got news that a patrol of German *askaris* had just caught two of my unarmed natives, previously sent out as spies. With our other work on hand at the time I should have preferred leaving this little post of the enemy's, but it was, of course, necessary to try and effect my men's release. So, from the long grass around, we rushed the few huts of the enemy, and all save one German *askari* bolted. This man, a huge, savage-looking *onbasha* (corporal), promptly shot and killed the guide by my side, and with a second shot chipped some wood off Bakari's rifle; thereupon he was shot dead by Abdulla and others. I took a lion's claw charm from his neck, and, whatever its potency against lions may have been, the charm had not been proof against an enemy's bullets. It had brought him at least a brave man's death.

We hurried on that evening, but next day were mixed up again with another little German patrol. On our attacking, the enemy's *askaris* bolted in time, but the white man, though I told him to drop his rifle, started firing at us, and so my men had to shoot him. Knowing that now all other enemy posts around would have had warning, and having had my new levies out on their first trip, we made back to our main camp in the bush near Mponda Creek. My white subordinate (I had been given an officer's commission after getting away from the Germans) now came up to join me, and it was a pleasant change to have a white man with me, though we were not very often together.

From that time onwards I was engaged on short trips similar to those described. Another small column, under Lieutenant Thornton (a very able I.D. officer), was working north of us not many days away, and as they were working down towards Madaba and Mlembwe, we went across and cut that road in the bush above Mlembwe, picking up a few prisoners. All the natives were very friendly, and in each village there were sure to be relatives of the *ruga-ruga* with me. At one village I noticed particularly a man with two frightful old scars on his head; it was horrible to look at them; the skull seemed to have been, at some time, cut open in two places with a chopper. He told me that a leopard had seized him when a child.

In those days the local inhabitants always gave us splendid information of the German's movements, and I think but very little of our movements were made known to the enemy. We were entirely dependent on the local people for information, and it makes all the difference to an Intelligence man when he has the native residents whole-heartedly on his side.

About this time a small party of Germans, three whites and some *askaris*, with a picked party of porters, carrying picks and shovels, tried to work back towards the Rufigi to get some buried ammunition; but all their movements were made known to us by the natives, and after Thornton's men had ambushed and scattered the party in his district, we caught them all as they drifted back in twos and threes, with the exception of one white who was taken by Thornton. Our success in this case was entirely due to the information supplied from native sources.

Later on we payed a trip to a German post at a place called Ku-ku, where on our departure, after taking a couple of small enemy convoys of native food, and catching a white man and a few *askaris*, we, as usual, burnt the post. From the way they helped us, it was obvious that the local natives were of opinion that the day of the German was nearly over. One of our guides at this time was a most interesting-looking nigger, whom we called the "Gorilla Man." He was a very big negro, with unusually prominent teeth and sloping forehead, yet a remarkably intelligent fellow.

Once more the rainy season approached, and the beautifully clear moonlit nights were almost too bright for sleep. All this time we had been working farther west and getting closer to my old prison at Liwala, and at Mlembwa we were lucky enough to make prisoners of twenty-six German whites. On sending them away, I allowed each prisoner to keep one box for his best clothes and belongings, but all their old clothes, spare blankets, cooking-pots, cutlery, etc., were legitimate booty for my *askaris*, as, in any case, there were not sufficient porters to be sent with the prisoners. This small but well-deserved loot was only the just due of my faithful though ragged *ruga-ruga*.

By November the sands of time left for German rule in the East African Colony were running low. The Belgian troops—good *askaris* they are too—from the north-west, and General Northey's columns from the south-west, had now cleared the whole of their great areas and were about to join with the main coastal columns. Von Lettow, fighting with consummate skill and frequently holding up our forces in heavy engagements, had been gradually pushed farther and farther back by our troops, and with his companies greatly reduced by losses, had come to realise that to delay any longer meant being caught between our coastal and "Norforce" columns.

Accordingly he broke quickly south, crossing the Rovuma at Ngomano into Portuguese territory. Colonel Tafel, with a somewhat smaller force, coming down from the Luwegu, was less fortunate, for, delaying too long, he was caught, short of ammunition and supplies, in a completely starved-out district, and had to surrender with about 100 whites and 1,200 *askaris*.

This was by far the best single success that we had throughout the whole campaign, and it was particularly pleasing to learn that the I.D. had behaved well in the actual capture. One of our officers, Lieutenant McGregor, with a force of about sixty I.D. *askaris* and *ruga-ruga*, had been attacked in an isolated position by superior numbers, by a part of Tafel's force that was attempting to break south. This attack took place early in the morning, and McGregor put up a fine defence, but was unfortunately killed about midday; whereupon, there being no other white man with the party, the old black sergeant-major commando (a Mnyanwezi) took charge, and towards evening had completely beaten off the enemy. The retreat of Von Lettow's force into Portuguese territory was again the subject for further and very premature congratulations in high quarters, and once more the conquest of German East was hailed in the papers.

The sale of the bear's skin had twice been concluded, though the animal himself, in the shape of Von Lettow and his little army of picked men, was very much alive, and marching south to some purpose. In his last message to the *Kaiser*, the late Governor of German South-West had mentioned, in advising his imperial master of the surrender of that colony, that owing to the condition of their animals and the dryness of the country, it had not been possible for their troops finally to break north into Angola (Portuguese West Africa) as originally intended. But, as we have seen, there was some attempt by a few diehards to carry out this plan of campaign, and work across Rhodesia for the purpose of uniting with the German East forces.

As for the campaign in the Cameroons, it had ended with the German forces, as a last resource, crossing into Spanish territory, preferring internment to capture.

There was never any doubt in most of our minds as to what Von Lettow's last move would and must be; yet in spite of all this, and in spite of the example and fate of the Portuguese force at Newala a year before, a large Portuguese force with great supplies of arms and ammunition, but totally unsupported by any British troops, was allowed to collect at Ngomano at the junction of the Rovuma and Lugenda Rivers. The German leader, as at Newala, left the rich prize to ripen till the very last moment, and then, crossing the Rovuma, scattered the

Portuguese with one sharp attack. The serious part of all this was the great number of maxims and rifles and the amount of ammunition that fell into his hands. Destroying their German weapons (for which ammunition had by that time run perilously low), the whole force was rearmed with new Portuguese .256 Mausers, with ammunition more than sufficient.

Thus rearmed, and with every available porter and local Shensi loaded with boxes of their new ammunition, the enemy moved leisurely south along the Lugenda River, a big tributary of the Rovuma, rising near Nyassa. The great raid on Portuguese East, or, as the Germans called it, the "Opera" War, against our Allies had begun.

My *ruga-ruga* had now unfortunately to be disbanded, and sent, less rifles and equipment, to their homes. I hated parting with Abdulla and the others, and afterwards missed them very considerably. They were willing to come on with me, they said, if I wanted them, but orders were to dismiss them, and perhaps they would hardly have been so useful in a strange district, amongst people whose language even was quite different from theirs, as they had been in their own areas.

CHAPTER 8

Hard Times

Following our latest instructions, Henocksberg and I, with about forty I.D. *askaris*, then went south, crossing the Rovuma at Ngomano. The water was at its lowest, and the big river, still some 1,200 yards across, and flowing majestically, was fordable chest high, and extraordinarily warm. It was delightful wading across, especially as for the last six months we had been in country mostly watered by sand-pits. It must have been owing to that crossing that I retain such a pleasant impression of "that great river, the River Rovuma."

Leaving the Lugenda to the west, we went straight on through what must be in the dry season an uninhabited and waterless belt. The first early thunderstorms having brought water here and there, we suffered no privation, but there was neither road nor track, and for some days we were continually in bamboo country. Now, to march through such country is particularly tedious and irritating, and I got to detest these bamboo forests in P.E.A., with a sort of personal hatred for the detestably noisy stuff.

Christmas we spent in the bamboo, and, after crossing the Muiriti River, twelve days from the Rovuma found us at the Portuguese *boma* of Coronge on the Msalu River. The place, only lately abandoned by its owners, was in good order, as was also another smaller and abandoned post at Nicoque farther south.

The German force, after following the Lugenda southwards, had scattered a good deal, some of the companies going west towards Nyassa, and other small raiding parties reaching to the coast. It was only the arrival by ship of the Gold Coast contingent, under Colonel Rose, at Pemba (Port Amelia) that had prevented the enemy entering and taking that port. The main enemy forces with Von Lettow occupied a stretch of country between Mweri (Medo) and Mahua, in the very centre of northern P.E.A., and to dislodge them our communications would have to be lengthy and difficult.

Our own little party, reduced by sickness and desertions to twenty-seven, had formed a camp amongst a little rocky outcrop in the bush, about five hours north of Mweri—where two companies of the enemy, under Hauptman Kohl, one of Von Lettow's best officers, were then stationed. With the heavy rains now beginning to fall almost daily, it was necessary for us to build some sort of shelter.

The Germans had found that food of every kind, except meat, was most plentiful; fowls, also fruit, rice, and other indigenous crops, were in abundance. The inhabitants, too, had everywhere welcomed them with enthusiasm, for the Portuguese rule was not of a character to command either the respect or the liking of its subjects. The Germans were hailed by the poor *Shensis* as being nothing less than heaven-sent deliverers from their cruel and cowardly oppressors. The Germans, of course, seized, looted, and burned every one of the Portuguese *bomas* they came across, the little garrisons invariably bolting on the approach of even the smallest party of the enemy. Every burned *boma* was to the native population a little Bastille going up in flames.

We English, as the friends of the Portuguese, naturally found the inhabitants against us, and, generally speaking, throughout the P.E.A. campaign we intelligence men never got the slightest voluntary help or information from any native. On the other hand, the Germans were advised immediately of any of our movements, and could always obtain guides, porters, etc., from the *Shensis* whenever needed. An enemy *askari* whom we captured told me, "Night and day the *Shensis* are coming into us with news." I knew that frequently our notes to and from the columns were taken into the German camps. The contrast with German East, where we were amongst friendly people, was most striking to us Intelligence men; but I was myself stupidly slow to realise it sufficiently, and before long I had to pay severely for this mistake.

It was indeed a Promised Land into which the war-weary and ragged German *askaris* had been led; plenty of food ("We are tired of chickens," said one captured *askari* to me), loot from the Indian stores and Portuguese *bomas*, with women in abundance. "Never," said a captured German's diary of this period, "have we fared so well during the last four years."

The enemy soon got to hear that we were in their neighbourhood, especially as we were getting in the government tax food from the various villages, to prevent it falling into the enemy's hands. However, we had our own troubles close at hand, for a few days after making our temporary camp and erecting shelters, a leopard, coming into the camp at night (we had, of course, no fires), seized and terribly mauled my white companion. The horrible beast, sneaking in, had seized his victim by the head, and, dragging him off his stretcher, had actually taken him away some fifteen yards before we were able to help him. Being asleep at the time, I was rather muddled for a few seconds when his shrieks started, and I fear was all too slow in coming to his assistance. It was not till he had cried out "*chui*" (leopard) that the situation was made plain to me, and meanwhile the man-eater was worrying him.

Calling out to Henocksberg so as to get his position (it was drizzling and pitch dark), I fired to the left of his voice, and thereupon the beast left him and made off. The poor fellow was very badly bitten about the head, the worst bites being directly around the throat and eyes. By the light of a fire, which the men hurried to make, I bathed the injuries as quickly as possible, washing the whole head, arms, and shoulders with permanganate, for the wounds were far too numerous to be dressed individually. Making doubly sure no small scratches had been missed, we made him as comfortable as possible, myself and several *askaris* lying close at hand by the side of one of the many fires we had kindled.

Hardly had we finished attending to Henocksberg, than shrieks and shots from the lower part of the camp told us that the leopard had again attacked. This time he caught an *askari*, one of the picket, a Kafirondo named "James," seizing him, as before, by the head, despite the fact that the man was in his blankets right alongside the sentry. The leopard was, however, on this occasion immediately driven off his prey, and James, not nearly so badly hurt as poor Henocksberg, escaped with a few nasty bites on the head and one above the eye. As I dressed his wound, the difference between the head of our brother Ethiopian and the head of a white man was made very plain, and the amused, sheepish smile on James's round, good-natured face made me realise why the negro fighter has always held his own in the prize ring from the days of Richmond to those of Johnson and Langford.

The attendance on James being completed, I really did hope our troubles for the night were over—but not a bit of it. Within half an hour another series of yells and howls from the porters' camp hard by revealed that the spotted devil had returned to the charge. After

THE VERY NEXT NIGHT IT KILLED A WOMAN

the *askaris* had driven off again our too persistent visitor, this time with shots sufficient to represent creditably a small battle, they brought along a sorry-looking spectacle in the shape of my *neapara* (head porter), who had been snatched from his blankets and dragged off several yards. He, too, was badly bitten about the head and around the eyes. All this must surely have been most trying for poor H., horribly mauled and in great pain himself, but like the plucky chap he was, he only remarked that I seemed *to be running a casualty clearing station*.

There was no more sleep for anyone that night; my men, all crouching around the fires, discussed this new business that had befallen us. "That's no leopard," I said; "that must be an old lion," and though they agreed with me, I could see they did not believe it was so; and indeed it was proved to be a leopard when daylight came. A lion, too, would certainly have killed all three men if he had seized them in such a manner by the head, and, in the first instance, he would no doubt have taken his prey clean away into the bush. More dangerous than the lion in cunning and daring fierceness, the leopard luckily has not the terrible punishing powers and strength of the bigger cat.

I could hear one of my men, formerly an old German *askari*, telling the others that "that was no leopard; that is a *Shensi* who has got some medicine." These people implicitly believe that the man-eating lion or leopard is a native in disguise, who has turned into the African equivalent of our werewolf. They say that the ordinary bush lion is a lion right enough, but that the man-eater is a man temporarily transformed. Often afterwards I discussed this with my Makua boy, Moosa, and others, and they seemed most interested when I suggested to them the melting down of some *rupees* to make silver bullets as the only sort to prove effective against these Walk-o'-Nights.

Next morning at daylight Henocksberg was sent back on a rough stretcher with eight porters and some *askaris*, whose orders were to impress as extra bearers every Shensi they could catch, and to hasten by forced marches north to Muiriti *boma*, about five days away. At that place a large Portuguese camp had been made, and a doctor might be found there. I heard months later, with great delight, that Henocksberg made a wonderful recovery.

As for that cursed leopard, the very next night it killed a woman in the nearest village only six miles away. From the local people I learnt a good deal of the history of this particular beast—the most daring man-eater I have ever heard of. It began killing people on the Msalu River before the war, and in latter years had made its headquarters in

BRINGING IN THE SPOILS

AN AFRICAN BEAUTY

the Nicoque district, where the big granite hills, covered with boulders and scrub, made a series of impenetrable retreats. Its victims must be estimated during these years as running well into three figures, mostly women and children. No wonder the natives were afraid to stir out of their huts at night, or even to go anywhere alone in the daytime. To travel after nightfall through the Nicoque district was indeed in those days to walk through "*the valley of the shadow of death*"—Death, spotted and whiskered, stalking its victims on those silent pads of velvet, with glaring eyes and swishing tail.

Trouble, as usual, was not to come singly; in the morning, two days after my injured companion had been sent away, the enemy rushed our camp, the local natives having led a party of the 11th and 17th Companies, with two maxims, through the bush from Mweri, guiding them through our three pickets. We were nearly caught, but just escaped in time, thanks to getting a few seconds' warning; for the enemy, for some reason, began the attack in a rather spectacular manner by blowing bugles and opening fire from the two machine guns. We put up a very poor show, and lost all our camp and belongings—everything, in fact, except our rifles and *bandoliers*. Luckily, all my *askaris* got away, and the enemy captured only one old, sick porter.

In the scramble and confusion in the bush we managed to take a prisoner, one of the 17th Company *askaris*, and a very useful capture he proved from an intelligence point of view. This affair is a good example of the "ups and downs" of a scout's life. At 7 a.m., monarch of all one surveys in one's own little camp; at 7.15 a.m. tearing through the bush like a fugitive from justice, and wondering if one will be lucky enough to get some *ugare* (native porridge) by evening.

The principal native against us was a certain Jumbe Nabom, who, from his village about twenty miles away, had personally led the enemy into our camp. We "reorganised" back in the bush for a few days, *i.e.* got together some loads of rice and other native food, and I started housekeeping afresh with an earthenware pot, two native grass mats, and a calabash of honey. Then, after sending half a dozen sick or sorry *askaris* back to Muiriti with the prisoner, we set off south again through the bush, with an unwilling but well-watched *Shensi* guide, to see if we could not return our friend Nabom's visit, and with the full inclination of hanging him in his own village if he was at home. Finding signs of a German picket there, however, and my men being still a bit scared over the last business, I thought it better to postpone the visit for a more suitable occasion.

We then worked round the enemy's district, and found the natives decidedly unfriendly. It rained heavily, and in nine days' time, not far from the coast, we joined up with Colonel Rose's column which had lately left Pemba. There, to my pleasure, I met Lewis, who had just returned from a trip to Australia on sick leave, and I revelled in comfort after the fortnight or more of nigger food and no stores. At such times we undoubtedly learn to appreciate the common, homely things—soap, a towel, a spoon, and a blanket, for instance—and to enjoy to the full the luxury of a looking-glass, nail-scissors, and a toothbrush.

From Ankuabi I had to go straight away down to Pemba (called by the Portuguese Port Amelia), to report to the commander-in-chief and General Sheppard, who were there at that time on an auxiliary cruiser. I by no means underestimated what was likely to be before us in this new campaign in Portuguese E.A., for I told the chief of the staff that though it might appear a very small German force that had come across the Rovuma, yet I felt sure it would prove a very strong one and very troublesome.

CHAPTER 9

A Fresh Start

After getting some new equipment for my *askaris* and porters and trying to get some sort of fresh kit (precious little could I get) to replace all I had lately lost, we marched back again to Ankuabi, where the column was still halted—for the rains now made all transport from Pemba very difficult—waiting to push on to Meja, another Portuguese *boma* previously taken and burnt by the Germans, whose advanced post was now quartered there. I started a day and a half ahead of the column with my party of I.D. *askaris*, and my orders were to go round through the bush and cut the main road west, behind Meja, and leading back to the main German force facing the Pemba Column, then known as "Pamforce." We hoped to pick up something if the enemy retired that way from our main force. Lewis went with the advance guard of the main column, which was mostly comprised of the Gold Coast Regiment. On the fourth morning we reached the road behind Meja, and on that day the Gold Coast troops, if all had gone well, should have been close at hand hunting out of Meja what enemy force remained there.

We took up a position by the side of the road, but it was hard to find a really satisfactory spot for an ambush—it is always advisable to have a reasonable chance of escape in these entertainments in case something rather bigger than is expected comes along. We did no good that day. During the afternoon one solitary German *askari* came striding along the road fearing no evil, and coming quite close up to me. Hoping, of course, to take him prisoner for information, and whispering to the twelve *askaris* with me not to shoot, I spoke to him suddenly when he was nearly opposite me. The man stopped dead, hearing the voice, but still not locating me. Again I said, "*Emanie tupa bunduki*" ("Hands up, drop your rifle"), and then, like a buck, he vanished, tearing off into the bush.

Of course, we all shot at him, and of course all missed, for he got clean away. Whether he was just an odd man, or the advance scout of a little party following, I do not know. Anyway, I had made a mess of things, and all that remained was to curse long and heartily. Not but that the plucky fellow well deserved his escape.

Of course, all this noise had queered our pitch as far as the road was concerned, and the only thing to be done was to start back through the bush towards Meja and get a decent, quiet camp, away off the road, where we could cook our day's food. When we picked up our little mob of porters, whom we had placed in some thick bush a few hundred yards off, I found that two of them had bolted on hearing the firing; the very fact of hearing shots had been quite sufficient for them to imagine the worst, and they evidently were taking no chances.

Next day we reached Meja, where the column had just arrived, the advance guard having had a little opposition here and there along the road from some four whites and forty *askaris* with a couple of machine guns. We had a spell of some days with the column at Meja, during which time my two runaways found their way back to camp. As I always disliked very much the flogging of my own natives, especially porters, for anything except stealing (an offence, by the way, which they never committed), it was a case of how to make the punishment fit the crime. Eventually I ordered the two delinquents to stand on boxes in a prominent position for half an hour, each with a large pumpkin on his head; a performance which naturally entailed no small amount of ridicule.

At this time the main force of the enemy confronting our "Pamforce" column was six companies under Kohl, that fine soldier, each company having two maxims. Of these companies, four were in and around Mweri *boma* some forty-five miles away. (This place was wrongly called Medo by us, Medo being the name of the whole of that large district.) The other two companies were probably split up into advanced posts towards Meja, and into flanking pickets and patrols. Von Lettow himself with the greater part of his force was about Nanungu, some ninety miles from Meja, with outposts still farther west, towards Mahua. The enemy were thus spread over a considerable area, with the native population in general entirely favourable to them.

On March 10 Lewis and I left the column at Meja, taking with us forty I.D. *askaris*, twenty-five of whom, at least, were new men and unknown to us. Our plans were to work round between Mweri and the Msalu River, and to cut the two *barabaras* from Maria to the Lujenda and from Maria to Nanungu—well behind Mweri. We hoped to capture some messengers or enemy *askaris* on these roads, to do some raiding if possible, and generally to find out all we could of what was happening behind Mweri, and what was going on between Kohl's and Von Lettow's forces. They were just the orders to delight the heart of an Intelligence man. The main difficulty before us was that, in our passage through old Nabom's district, we should probably find the natives, as proved by their behaviour in January, to be entirely favourable to the Germans. It was almost impossible to pass by these villages without the news being at once taken to the enemy. As a Dutch Intelligence man put it "As soon as you come to a village, then *someone is running.*"

We decided that the best plan would be to make a surprise visit to Nabom himself. If we caught him, then he should be made an example of for that January business, for the encouragement of all other native spies.

On the fifth evening out we surrounded Jumbe Nabom's house, or rather huts, at dusk; but the bird, having no doubt had warning, was flown. Pushing on from there, we burned a small supply store of the enemy's outside Mweri. We knew, of course, that the enemy would by now have certainly got wind of us.

Hearing of a German post away to our right near the Msalu, we waited a few hours on the road to Mweri, and picked up a couple of their notes. One of the messengers we caught had, curiously enough, in his skin bag my bunch of keys, lost in my camp when it was taken by the Germans in January. I greatly rejoiced at recovering them, for they fitted some spare trunks and boxes left at Mombassa. However, the enemy got them once more a few days later, and no second prisoner's bag ever disgorged them again. We had great difficulty in obtaining guides; the two men of old Kisimo's, one a *jumbe*, who had followed me round to our column in January, became too frightened to go any farther with us, and were therefore useless.

Ten days out from Meja, on the morning of the 22nd, we had to go back a short way on our own track to try and find another way round; it was rough country, and we ran into a party of the enemy whom the natives had brought and were guiding along our tracks. The country was pretty thick with patches of bamboo, and both sides could hear their opponents farther than they could see them. I could hear quite distinctly the German whites talking rapidly together. When the firing started, a large number of our *askaris* at once slipped away to the rear; in fact they bolted, and, seeing them run, all our thirty porters, of course, threw down their loads and also ran into the bush. Thirteen *askaris*, however, stuck to Lewis and myself, and to save ourselves from being surrounded, we also were soon obliged to retreat. As we retired we had the pleasure of seeing our abandoned loads scattered here and there through the bush.

It was not exactly a bright episode, especially as I doubt if the enemy were more than a small force—perhaps three or four whites and forty *askaris*, judging by the size of the camps we saw some weeks later. The only two men who came out with flying colours were our two "personal boys": Lewis's boy "Hammond," when the porters started to clear, pounced on two who had loads of Lewis's, one a roll of blankets and the other his tin box, and actually bullied them into sticking to their loads and to following him when he too made off into the bush; and as he luckily took the right direction (northwards to the Msalu), Lewis recovered these two loads of his some days later. (As the tin box contained a precious bottle of Bovril and 5 lb. of sugar, this recovery was of no small importance.) My boy, a little Makua Shensi named "Moosa," whom I had obtained in Pemba, and who could not speak a single word of Swahili when he first came to me, also did well, running to me and giving me my rifle when the firing started and stopping with me throughout; whereas my *askari* orderly, with my spare bandolier of cartridges, disappeared at the start.

Finally, with our thirteen *askaris*, we set off northwards to the Msalu river, reaching there late in the afternoon and in the rain. We counted on finding most of the missing members of our broken *safari* along the river, and counted rightly as far as the *askaris* and eight porters, including Hammond, were concerned. But the main body of porters on bolting had gone to the left and southwards, and, minus two (whom the local natives tomahawked, killing one, and taking the other to the Germans), eventually reached our column, where, of course, in true negro fashion, they gave a highly imaginative account of the whole affair. All they had heard was some shooting, and all they had seen was some *askaris* running past them, but they were able, nevertheless, to give to the column Intelligence officer the following account, and perhaps by that time had come to believe it themselves:

We heard tremendous firing. There were great numbers of

Germani; we *saw* them ourselves! The two Bwanas were completely surrounded and fighting when we left; they *must* both have been killed or captured. The Germani chased me for miles, when I finally just had to drop my load and escape.

As we worked down the Msalu River we began to pick up stragglers, but we could not find any villages or get any food on our side of the river. There were villages on the other side, but the river, being in high flood, we could not get over. Lewis, Moosa, and Abdulla, the I.D. corporal, swam to a *shamba* on the second day, and, having made a raft, piled it with green mealies and pumpkins. But the current was too strong when they tried to get back, and the raft, laden with these good things, gradually beat them, to be swept hopelessly away, accompanied by many groans of disappointment from our side, groans that came straight from our hungry stomachs. The current was really so strong that I was glad to see Lewis and the men get back safely, even without the raft. We had no food whatever for the first two days, and consequently were hungry.

At noon on the third day we struck two *mongopla* trees with heaps of fruit on them. These trees were new to me, and I never saw any others, though Moosa said they were fairly common on the high stony ridges in that country. The fruit was something like a fig, but it dyed one's fingers a mulberry colour. In the afternoon of that third day we discovered a native track, and, following it up, arrived later at a village, and there we all had a great feed of green mealies. Next morning we crossed the Msalu in native bark canoes and then took stock of our position. The main part of the village was on our side of the river, and here enough good food could be obtained for all my party.

I used to think that the nigger ate more than the white man, but now I am convinced that the former really eats, and needs, considerably less as a daily business; though when very hungry no doubt he can get through a larger amount of food—especially meat. Probably he would consider this to be getting even with his "back rations." The pleasures of the table are regarded differently by white and black. The white man finds satisfaction and enjoyment in the actual eating, whilst his black brother appears to eat rather for the sake of that feeling of fullness and contentment that follows a meal.

In taking stock of our position we found we had now collected thirty-eight out of the original forty *askaris*; the two unaccounted for, we afterwards heard, returned safely to the main column, and altogether it had been a bloodless battle.

With nothing but a blanket each, and rifles and *bandoliers* (Lewis also had about forty *rupees* in Portuguese notes, not very acceptable payment in that part of the country), we decided to follow up the river along the north bank for some days, and then recrossing, to go south, as originally intended, to the enemy's communications between Mweri and Nanungu. We thought it likely that after dispersing us in that fashion, and annexing all our baggage—not that we had much of value, our cooking-pots being the worst loss—the enemy would take it for granted that we had gone straight back to our column. This idea and the flooded river should give us a better chance than ever, it seemed, of arriving at our planned destination without the enemy being warned of our movements. Of course, this plan involved a long spell of native food in native style, but we could not starve, and I had for companions men no daintier than myself.

No sooner, however, had we started up the river in a south-west direction, that is, back towards the enemy zone, than a fresh trouble overtook us. Our *askaris* began to desert us daily, mostly from the rear-guard, and in twos and threes. In the course of a week no less than fourteen had left us, and it was impossible either to prevent these desertions or retake any of the deserters, even had they been worth the delay. Moosa's home was not far off up the river, and, luckily, he knew something of the district, for the guides, as usual, bolted if left for a second unguarded.

For several days we went through a district devoid of inhabitants, though we were close to the river and the land was fairly fertile. We passed by an old deserted Portuguese fort at Dmpati, apparently abandoned seven or eight years ago. We saw the remains also of old villages and the charred stakes of high poles that once formed small stockades. According to Moosa, all this district was formerly well populated (the Portuguese seldom build a *boma* unless the neighbourhood is populous), but had been forsaken of late years simply through fear of the lions. These daring beasts had taken such a toll from the villages that the natives had abandoned the district *en masse*.

After following the river for a week, and being then about a day from Quigeia, we came upon a village where the Portuguese had a post (Msolu *boma*) before the Germans arrived on the scene. Finding there a couple of small bark canoes, we decided to recross the river and go south, but it was necessary to wait a few days first while Corporal Abdulla went to some villages higher up to procure a supply of native flour for the trip. While we were waiting, one of our *askaris*, a man with a most villainous squint, who afterwards deserted, managed to shoot a big water-buck. How he did it I cannot imagine; perhaps it was because of his squint, the bullet hitting the mark when his cross-eyed sight aimed elsewhere. Squint or no squint, the meat was mighty acceptable.

It was during that halt that a most magnificent young savage, a Yao, came into the camp and was introduced by Moosa, now close at home. This Yao was not less than six feet three or four, and was remarkably strong, powerfully built, and perfectly proportioned. I tried hard, through Moosa, to get him to come with me for a trip, hoping to make a sort of personal porter of him, and thereby have someone to carry me over the innumerable little creeks and wet gullies, but he was too shy. Moosa now heard that his father had recently been killed by a lion: I cannot say I noticed any decrease in his usual high spirits after receipt of the news. Abdulla having returned with some bags of *uraisi*, a reddish-coloured native flour, we started next morning to re-cross the Msalu, which, though lower, was still in flood. It was not an encouraging start, for six more *askaris*, evidently not liking the idea of re-entering the enemy's country, deserted, disappearing together in a mealie patch. Lewis, too, had begun to develop fever, which was not improved by crossing the river in the hot sun.

After some trouble we obtained two guides, and in the afternoon set out southwards through the bush. At the first halt my little lance-corporal, Kufakwenda, a most reliable little Mnyanwesi, who had been with me all the time from German East, came running up from the rear to report still more desertions: the rear-guard of three *askaris* had again deserted and disappeared.

It turned out that these three, joining up with the six who had bolted that morning, actually went back overland to Dar-es-Salaam, where they sneaked into the I.D. Depot camp, hoping to be lost amongst the other *askaris*, who, of course, would not have given them away. Unfortunately for them, however, Lewis himself happened to be at the depot, on his way back to the front from hospital, and, recognising them, had them arrested. Subsequently they were court-martialled and convicted at Pemba.

We were now reduced to fifteen *askaris*, practically the same men who had stuck to us at Mtupwa Hill, when the Germans previously attacked us. Luckily the goats had now finished drafting themselves from the sheep, and the fifteen remaining men were a decent lot; all of whom, less those who were lost through sickness and other accidents, I retained from then onwards till the final windup in P.E.A. Lewis's fever being no better, I had to leave him with Kufakwenda and a few *askaris* to camp in the bush, while I took a short trip farther south on the Maria-Lugenda road. No signs of an enemy movement northwards could be detected, and on return I found Lewis worse. As all our medical stores had been lost at Mtupwa, and we had nothing for the sick man except native food and the one treasured bottle of Bovril, I decided to begin moving back in the direction of our column. Lewis was now so weak that it was necessary to make a rough hammock and get him carried.

During our return journey, though we avoided all villages as far as possible, we went through one ruled by a *jumbe bibi* (a woman headman). I am no believer in women's franchise, but I must own that the village was far tidier and the huts much neater than usual. The *bibi*, decidedly handsome, was lighter in colour than most of the inhabitants in that region—owing no doubt to some strain of Arab blood. She was, too, most friendly to us, the first Englishmen, probably, that she had ever seen, and showed us the way herself for one long day's march. I wished, when she left us next day, there had been some little trinket that I could have given her for a present.

As we began to work round Mweri again on our way home, it became more necessary than ever to be careful, especially with one of us sick and being carried. It happened, and we could tell from the guns that there was fighting, that we were very close to Mweri on the day our Pemba column drove the enemy from his position there. Kohl's six companies, with the advantage of being in good positions, put up a good fight all the morning, but eventually began to get rather a rough handling and had to fall back towards Maria. Our little party, catching a German *askari* of the 17th Company, learnt from our prisoner what German pickets in front of us were to be avoided, and thus we got through without any trouble. Three more days later (after a third unsuccessful attempt on the old fox Nabom) saw us at Manumbiri, which was then well behind the column. Not knowing the result of the fighting at Mweri, we were frightened to cut in too high for fear the column might have had a check.

It was just five weeks since we had started from Meja, and the expedition with its hardships had proved disappointing and unsatisfactory. Not that such reflections prevented us thoroughly enjoying a meal of tea, jam, and biscuits after the long spell on nigger tucker.

The doctor at the field hospital collared the expostulating Lewis, who, despite his assertions to the contrary, was really in a high fever. Next morning I went up alone to Mweri by car, where I found, to my disgust, that owing to the alarmist reports of our returned porters, and our delayed return, we had both been officially posted as "missing" some weeks earlier. Lewis was soon sent down to the Pemba hospital, and from that time till the end I worked always by myself.

At Mweri I was just in time to report to the C.I.O., "Pamforce," and to see General Edwards, who took me on the staff, which was hurrying to catch up the troops then pushing ahead towards Maria. "Pamforce" now consisted of two columns, one under Colonel Rose and the second under Colonel Gifford; General Edwards, whom I got to like very much, and whom I always found most considerate, being in charge of the whole force. That evening we were in time to join up with Colonel Rose's column, which had been held up most of the day by Kohl's rear-guard companies in a very wicked little position amongst thick bamboos, across the Maria road, the fighting lasting till some hours after sundown. Thence into Maria, where Maria himself, the *sultani* of all the Medo district natives, came to see us.

No doubt Maria previously had done everything possible to help the Germans, but it was a good sign now to see him turning his coat, and I thought it might make our intelligence work a little easier. The former Maria and rightful *sultani* had been imprisoned by the Portuguese and interned on Ibo Island some years previously for killing a Portuguese *askari*: and from what I saw of the Portuguese *askaris*, I should say the deceased well deserved his fate, if only on general grounds.

At this time, being very destitute, I managed luckily to get a couple of blankets, a few clothes, and, above all, a saucepan and frying-pan from the sale of kit of a recently killed officer; while Moosa was rewarded with a shirt, a pair of shorts, and one of the blankets.

At Maria I had instructions from the general to go across and get into touch with an advanced "Norforce" column, supposed to be then near the Msalu, slightly north-west of Nanungu. It is unnecessary to describe in detail all the subsequent trips, for they much resembled one another. It is sufficient to state that in eight days we reached this Chisona column under a Major Fraser, with whom on the night of arrival I had an hour's talk, telling him all I knew of the position of things on our side, and getting from him direct his intentions and return messages (I never carried papers or anything of value in the way of information of use against our forces). In the Chisona camp, to my great pleasure, I found an old Queensland friend, now a Rhodesian, Captain Mills, and he and I yarned far into the night.

Leaving at daylight, enriched by a basin and two plates from my good friend Mills, we recrossed the river, and, not knowing where we should find the "Pamforce" column, made a shot at it by first cutting the Maria-Nanungu road about twelve miles from Nanungu. However, we only observed German porter traffic on the road, and, finding an enemy post not far off, we had to work round through the bush for a couple of days, keeping above the road, and out of the way of any enemy rear-guard. At Coronga we found the column hung up for rations, and fully thirty miles farther back than we had at first hoped. Of course, if the native people had been friendly, we could have kept in touch much better; but I had learnt that it was generally better to avoid villages as much as possible, and to be careful the natives did not bolt when they saw us approach the village.

We had now entered a very curious and striking country, a land that would greatly rejoice the heart of a geologist. Stern and mighty granite peaks of various sizes, with smooth domes that apparently consisted of one huge slippery rock and rose high and clear from the lower block of the mountain, were scattered freely about. To what height some of these awful rocks rise I cannot tell, but it must be many thousand feet, and most of them appear quite inaccessible to any climber. One of the biggest and grandest of them all is the great peak of Mcopa, near Mahua: this we saw for three days before we reached it. Sometimes, when camping below these mountains, I have wondered how far back in time one would have to go before the slightest change in that cold-looking mass would be noticeable. If one could but ask the great peaks, "Were you just as this in the days of Cephren 6,000 years ago?" the answer could only be, "In the days of Cephren? Why, that's *now!*"

From Coronga we went off south, below Nanungu to Mahua, the base of another "Norforce "column which had just left to move in towards Corewa and Nanungu. On the way back "the woods were full of Indians," and we had to be careful, but I did not know till I reached the column near Nanungu that Von Lettow's whole force, after a stiff fight near Corewa, had broken southwest. He had evidently crossed just about a day behind us on our return journey, for we had marked no big enemy track.

After a day's spell we were off again, this time on the enemy's left, to watch for any sign of the enemy working out or sending detachments from that side. My boy Moosa had to be left in hospital with a sore leg: like all native-born Africans, he had picked up Swahili wonderfully quickly, and I now used him as my main interpreter, the local people in this part speaking only Makua, their own language.

Troubles never come singly, and my cook-porter, an amazing coward, now asked me to let him go into the Carrier Corps, having evidently had quite enough of being with a *"Bwana-ya-Scoutie"* (Intelligence Officer). Luckily, there were several recently captured German *askaris* in the camp at that time, and I secured one, a youth of about fifteen. He informed me that his name was Tomaas (Thomas), and that he was a Christ o (Christian): a very good, quiet boy he turned out to be—though he was never as bright and quick as Moosa—and I kept him with me right to the finish. Tomaas, the Christo, and Moosa, the Makuan heathen, would have been a dangerous combination if both of them had not been very honest youngsters; but, as a matter of fact, I have always found native Africans honest except when spoilt by town civilisation.

Moosa eventually caught me up a couple of weeks later. He had done well in following me so speedily on his own, though, of course, as a Makua, he was travelling amongst his own people the whole way. My little Mnyamwezi corporal, Kufakwenda ("Go-to-kill"), whom I had to leave behind with toothache, never rejoined me, and his absence was a great loss. One of the worst features about our work was that the leaving behind of a good *askari* whom one may have had for a considerable time, usually meant his non-return; probably he would be drafted into someone else's party. "One man, one boss," is a good rule, especially with the men of these African tribes.

Chapter 10

The Last Phase

The German force had now broken south-west towards Malema, crossing the Luiyanna and the bigger Luli, and at first travelling fairly well together. It was followed by Colonel Gifford's column (K.A.R. 2nd Col.). My little party crossed some miles lower than the enemy, and we could get neither guides nor information from the ill-conditioned inhabitants.

Four days after crossing the River Luli we were in wild and broken country apparently unpopulated. There must have been a fair amount of game in certain parts, though on account of the long grass we seldom saw it. One morning, about an hour before dawn, two or more lions came down to drink at the little creek by the side of which we had camped, perhaps eighty yards away. An uneasy stirring and rustling in the camp, made by the sleepers half-waking and turning in their blankets preparatory for a final snooze, generally betokens the approach of daybreak.

Suddenly, with the roar of the lions, I could feel the whole camp instinctively stiffen silently, and I remembered the remark of an old Dutch hunter:

"When the lion roars, every beast in the *veldt* must stand still and the natives too must hold their breath."

These lions continued roaring close by till the first sign of the coming light. I tried the old joke, "Moosa, fetch me some water." No answer. "Moosa, fetch me some water from the creek." (The *askaris* and porters now begin to titter.) "Do you not hear, Moosa?" At last a small answer, "*Bwana ngopa samba*" (Master, I fear the lions).

Not far from the camp we passed the lions' kill, a young wild sow, the head of which—and that was mostly death grin—alone remained amongst the trampled and stained grass. Alas! poor piggy, she must have made just some little slip in her watchfulness, perhaps rooting just a trifle too greedily, and then in a flash the great cats had her. I doubt, however, if even a couple of lions, much less a single one, are keen on tackling a real old man boar, whose long sharp tusks (you can see the shining ivories sometimes 100 yards off) make him particularly dangerous to such soft-skinned enemies. Besides, when bailed up, no braver fellow walks the bush than "Billy the Boar."

Near the main Malema-Mozambique road we came into K.A.R. 2nd Column, and thence onwards I was working under Colonel Gifford, a splendid chief. This column of his can well be said to have been the one bright feature of the Portuguese campaign on our side. It certainly bore the brunt of the fighting, it always gave a good account of itself, and it never suffered any kind of a reverse: no mean record for troops measured against Von Lettow's four-year-old veterans. The column at first consisted of the 1st and 2nd Battalions of the 2nd K.A.R. Regiment, and later the 3rd Battalion of the same regiment also.

Quite young, tall, strong, and straight, with a handsome and taking personality, Colonel Gifford himself, an efficient and tireless soldier, expected his officers and men to be the same. Cool and collected in any engagement, he was, as I have said, with his column, our one redeeming feature in this 1918 campaign in P.E.A. This campaign can hardly be considered either fortunate or creditable, but without Colonel Gifford and the K.A.R. 2nd Col. it might easily have been almost disastrous. The Colonel, whilst I served under him, payed me the best of all compliments—he worked me hard.

The German force, still going south ahead of us, was now spreading its companies more widely and over a bigger area. Müller, another fine soldier, who appeared to be generally in the advance with our old friend Kohl, had, as usual, the rather unthankful job of holding off our forces with little rear-guard actions. The Portuguese *bomas* of Moloque, Ille, Majema, Lugerra, and many other places fell before them like ninepins, in most cases being abandoned well beforehand by the Portuguese. If not abandoned, a few shots and the Germans quickly had them. Some of these *bomas*, and this was the serious part for us, yielded considerable quantities of food, cloth, and other useful booty. And this was the "Opera War," this campaign of 1918!

After joining Colonel Gifford, for the first few weeks I was out between K.A.R. 2nd Col. and the nearest "Norforce" column; afterwards we were generally out some way from the column on one side or the other, seeing our troops only occasionally and at intervals, sometimes of several weeks. Great prudence marked our methods. My porters and *askaris* had now been trained to walk through the bush in silence, and to keep a strict quiet in our camps at night—no small trial, for the jolly sociable negro dearly loves noise and talk. However, by this time, having had a few good frights, he had begun to see the wisdom of this camping and travelling quietly.

Moving at the first sign of light, we were generally camped during four or five hours of the day, if possible, in some fairly thick bush, leaving a little picket of two or three *askaris* watching some way back on our *spoor*. During this halt all our cooking and eating for the day would be done, and, moving off again in the afternoon, we would camp just at dark in some quiet spot in the bush away from any track or road. Of course we had no fires at night, and only on rare occasions, such as when holding prisoners, did I ever have a guard at night, thus saving my few *askaris*. I never allowed a *Shensi* who had come into my camp to leave it till we ourselves were on the move. If any natives happened to be with us when we made camp for the night, they had to stay with us and could only return to their village next morning.

Some time previously one of the "Norforce" Intelligence officers had been killed by the inhabitants of this Malema district. The natives guided a party of the enemy and surprised him in his camp; though severely wounded, he managed with a couple of his *askaris*, also wounded, to escape from the Germans into the bush; but the local natives, following up his spoor, speared him and his two men to death.

My kit and worldly goods did not in those days amount to very much—not more than four loads—and I had no tent or stretcher. My boys always cut a bundle of grass for my bed each night. Food we were never really short of, and we could generally buy it with the cloth (*Americani*) issued to us for this purpose. We could, too, nearly always obtain *mohogo* in the villages, even though the owners had been frightened away from the place. This *mohogo* is a kind of arrowroot, and, if nicely baked, or, better still, fried in fat, closely resembles our English potatoes. The quality varies a good deal according to the soil in which it is grown, the best being got in light, but good red loam. Towards the end I became quite an expert in cooking this food.

The German force went as far south as Namacurra, about fifty miles only from Quelimane and within a few days' march of the Zambezi. There, after scattering and taking two guns from a considerable Portuguese force, they attacked and badly cut up an advanced part of one of our K.A.R. battalions. It may be of interest to mention that the fighting at Namacurra was the best part of 1,000 miles away from Dar-es-Salaam, the headquarters of our commander-in-chief. In this district the Germans obtained a great quantity of European supplies from the Portuguese, and much loot in the way of cloth, etc., from the local stores. I believe the German whites had a tremendous spree with the captured Portuguese wine and other liquors, while their *askaris* collected a considerable number of *"bibis"* (women), the very essence and cream of all booty for black soldiers. Nor were these women altogether such a handicap to their force as might be imagined, for all, acting as extra porters, carried loads of loot and food for their masters, besides cooking their food.

From Namacurra the enemy next turned sharply east or rather north-east, a threat to our communications on the Mozambique side. Again he hit us hard at Namirrue, where he had apparently surprised and surrounded, on a little rocky hill just above the Portuguese *boma*, a small force of ours that included some Gold Coast M.I. I doubt if in the whole campaign the German general showed anywhere to better advantage than in this region. This little band of ours on the hill, though without any water except such as it had carried up, put up a brave and determined defence. It meant heavy losses, which the Germans could not afford, to attempt to storm the place without artillery, and a column of two battalions of K.A.R. under Colonel Fitzgerald was advancing down the Namirrue River towards the *boma* from the north, while Colonel Gifford was only a couple of days off attacking from the west.

Von Lettow as usual acted coolly and promptly. He left just enough companies to hold up and delay Colonel Gifford's force with a series of rearguard actions in suitable positions, and while still keeping his grip around the force on the hill, attacked with his main force the column under Colonel Fitzgerald, then only a few miles away. The advanced battalion of K.A.R. was driven off, with the loss of some of their Stokes guns and maxims, and numerous casualties, and in spite of the efforts of the second battalion the column had to retire.

Returning and using the unexpected weapon of the newly captured Stokes gun against the little force on the hill, the Germans captured that position also. Then after burning the *boma* buildings according to custom, the enemy retired farther east before Colonel Gifford's troops, and halted at Chaluwe, a large Portuguese post. As the enemy forces probably needed a good rest, they rested in the calmest fashion for some ten days, apparently taking but little notice of the movements of our columns in the neighbourhood. Their *askaris* undoubtedly were in great spirits over their recent run of successes.

With a few *askaris* I had gone from Namarve towards the *boma* at Salapa, between K.A.R. 2nd Col., who were keeping somewhat north, and the German force; and when near the *boma* at Salapa I heard from some natives, who, mistaking me for a German, were most friendly, that the *boma* had been hurriedly abandoned by the Portuguese, but that as yet no Germans had been there to loot and burn it. *Eureka*! I thought at last we have found what we always dreamt of, a *boma*, abandoned by the Portuguese, but missed by the Germans. Visions of a fine set of cooking-pots, perhaps some chest of drawers full of clothes, or something good in the tucker line from the pantry, were conjured up; perhaps a well-stocked vegetable garden. My *askaris* and porters, as well as myself, were pretty ragged just then, for I had only a little time before again lost half of such belongings as I had at Namirrue, where we had got into a little trouble the day before K.A.R. 2nd Col. came up. A crowd of willing natives soon collected to guide me to Salapa, no doubt hoping to indulge in the joy of seeing their hated Bastille go up in flames.

Selecting two as guides and driving the others away, we went as far as the usual clearing around the *boma*, reaching this just at dark. We decided to camp quietly in the bush for the night, and at dawn work round to where the bush came nearest to the buildings, and then it all was clear to go in and see what was to be found. At dawn next morning, full of hope as to what we might find in our ally's abandoned post, we approached the edge of the bush surrounding it, when, to our utter disgust, we suddenly noticed little tongues of flame leaping simultaneously from every corner of the various buildings. The *askaris* and myself regarded each other with blank faces, "*Madachi!*" (Germans). We had been beaten on the post; four whites and about thirty or forty *askaris* of the enemy, evidently encamped, like ourselves, somewhere close to the *boma*, had entered it in the early morning.

After sending back two of my *askaris* with a note to the column, which I guessed was only about a day away to the north, and thinking this might prove to be just the advance party of the whole of the enemy's force, there was nothing else to be done but to retire a little way into the bush and await further developments. I quote an entry in my notebook for that day:

10 a.m.: Germans burning *my boma*.
Supplies: One tin of bully beef and mohogo; no fat; no letters for three months, and shirt as usual under strong suspicions.

The Germans, as I have mentioned, had made their headquarters at Chaluwe, taking scant notice of the column moving around them; but I have no doubt they had plenty of natives watching and reporting on all our movements. The people about there were particularly enthusiastic towards the enemy forces, providing them with abundance of food, for which the Germans paid in captured Portuguese cloth.

After our columns had moved eastwards, it being apparently taken for granted that Von Lettow's next move would be either towards Mozambique and our main communications, or towards Barapata (Antonio Annes) on the coast, the German leader quickly marched straight back in a north-westerly direction without meeting any opposition. Continuing in the same direction, he repassed near the big *boma* of Ille, sacked and destroyed by his men on the trip down, and still pushing on, attacked and drove our troops out of their position at Nammeroe.

A peculiar and unlucky similarity of names marks the three places where we had these reverses. On receipt of the news that the enemy had broken back, Colonel Gifford acted promptly, marching his force by long stages to Alto Moloque, and keeping a line north of the enemy's route. I had again picked up the column, and now had instructions to work across, keeping more to the south of the column. This would enable me to cut, farther on, all the different valleys running north towards the Inagu Mountains and the Upper Luli, and up any one of these valleys the Germans might perhaps turn.

In some ways this was the pleasantest, if the least eventful, trip that I had. The country was very high, the creeks being mostly the heads of the Malema River, and the climate delightful, with really cold nights. As we had only one blanket each, we were all only too glad to try and find, when possible, long grass to camp in at night. The country was mostly red volcanic soil, very fertile and full of villages; the twinkling fires of these villages at night, and their smoke in the day, could be seen all around on the steep hillsides. I imagine that Europeans, as far as the climate is concerned, could live and thrive quite well in this particular district. Great peaks arose everywhere, some of them, especially the huge granite mass of Namuli, on whose slopes we camped one night, being most awe-inspiring. The inhabitants too in these parts were quite friendly, and it would seem that just around that part they had been less harried by the Portuguese and their hateful police *askaris*, who, great hands indeed at rape, pillage, and murder amongst the poor *Shensis*, proved completely useless and cowardly when it came to anything in the way of fighting. This district had not been in any way touched by the enemy up to this time.

After the affair at Nammeroe, the enemy moved up one of the valleys towards a place called Lioma, travelling now nearly due north, and there Colonel Gifford's column, which had continued travelling fast through Inagu, arrived and attacked. It was only his own skill and the disciplined courage of his veteran troops that saved the German general from complete disaster, for several "Norforce" battalions also reinforced the attackers. I doubt if Von Lettow was ever in a tighter corner. As it was, he lost about twenty of his irreplaceable whites, killed and wounded in the fight, and probably not far short of 200 *askaris*; he also had to abandon a good deal of his baggage, and, best of all (for us), a good many loads of his ammunition. Our losses, too, were considerable, but we had at last scored a distinct success.

Breaking north again, the Germans crossed the Luli once more, Colonel Gifford still closely following, and a force of those fine N.R.P. troops close at hand. A day north of the big river the Germans, this time themselves taking the offensive, turned and attacked our column. The country was all open forest, and along the creek, where the main fighting took place, there were patches of bamboo. Accordingly, a somewhat confused fight took place during a greater part of the day.

The 2nd/2nd (second battalion of the second regiment) were the first attacked and had the lion's share of the fighting. Lucky in having as O.C. an able and cool soldier in Colonel Greig, who is never more at home than when in action, the battalion fought steadily and well, the enemy getting precious little change out of them. Meanwhile Colonel Gifford himself, with the other battalions of the column, began to come to their assistance. Finally, the Germans had to draw off in the afternoon, Von Lettow being too good a soldier not to realise that he was up against rather more than he bargained for. He had to leave behind his hospital with wounded, which fell into our hands. I am inclined to think that for once his information was badly out when he made this attack; possibly he thought it was a different column of perhaps less steady and experienced troops. As it was he had gained nothing by the day's fighting, whilst again having casualties amongst both his whites and blacks that he could ill afford.

Thus the tireless care and energy and soldierly qualities of K.A.R. 2nd Col.'s leader had twice borne good fruit. An I.D. man has no regiment, and therefore should not be considered prejudiced in believing that the colonel, young as he was, showed himself head and shoulders above all other column commanders of ours in the P.E.A. campaign. It is rumoured that the intention is to reduce the K.A.R. to eight battalions of picked men, and that Colonel Gifford may perhaps be the future head of this force. It is to be hoped so, for, if true, there will eventually be no finer regiments in Africa.

This was the last fighting in P.E.A., for after their unsuccessful attack, the Germans continued to march rapidly northwards, crossing the Lugenda River, and later the Rovuma again, to the southwest of Songea—thus passing through the extreme south-west of their old colony of German East, and out of that again into Rhodesian territory. There the Armistice, following the complete collapse of Germany and her allies, found them, and one of the clauses of the Armistice necessitated their surrender. It is only fair to acknowledge that the end of the war found Von Lettow himself and his little force still unconquered.

The lion hunt was at an end.

At the camp on the Luli a telegram was received from my chief, saying that there were now at Pemba, under arrest, seventeen of the twenty-three I.D. *askaris* who had deserted in such a cowardly manner from Lewis and myself on the Msala River in March. These men were waiting to be court-martialled, and it was necessary that I should come across at once with all other witnesses for the trial. We reached Barama on the "Pamforce" line in nine days, and there got some equipment for my very ragged *askaris* and porters. Also I got some badly needed shirts and trousers for myself.

Owing to the enemy having gone straight towards German East, many K.A.R. battalions were on the move for Pemba for transhipment to Dar-es-Salaam. Two were in Barama the night we reached there, and the noise of great *ngomas* (songs) was heard right up to midnight. The words of some of these songs were rather to the point, and after hearing them sung in continual repetition for many hours, I am not sure that I did not begin to recognise some tune in them. Such songs, however, are not conducive to sleep, especially as the musical accompaniment consists of the thumping of innumerable kerosene tins. These are the words of three of their songs, as far as I can roughly interpret the meaning.

Song 1

The K.A.R. askaris
Are fierce in fight;
But go carefully,
There are lions [1] in the bush.

Song 2

The big Bwanas [2]
Stop away behind.
We others have fighting and hunger—
What kind of business is this?

Song 3

The Portuguese are no good,
When they hear a shot they run;
Nor will they stop
Till they reach the sea.

Leaving the main road to our north to avoid the bustle, dust, and nuisance of other troops going down, and travelling by native tracks, we arrived at Pemba in another nine days. One had heard at Mologue a month or more earlier, and also at Barama, that we were doing very well in Europe, that the news everywhere was very good, and that we had recently taken a lot of German guns and prisoners. But beyond the ordinary feeling of satisfaction, I paid little more attention to this news now than I had frequently done during the war, when things happened to be looking up for us. That the *big thing* was rapidly nearing to its close I never even suspected.

Still on this final trip, somehow, we all travelled with light hearts. Far from any enemy, I found myself gaily whistling as we marched, or talking to and asking questions on subjects of native interest from my boy Moosa, who, as always, followed next behind me, carrying my rifle. At night the men made as many big fires as they wished, and my Mnyamwezi porters were in great spirits. The twelve of them who had been with me for so long a time were mostly originally German porters, and either had been captured or had deserted to us. Splendid porters—with never the slightest grumble, however long the day or heavy their load—these twelve never seemed to get sick or sorry and never gave the slightest trouble.

---

1. Germans.
2. Higher rank *base wallahs.*

I was most particular not to allow an *askari* in any way to order or bully my porters, or to have the slightest thing to do with them regarding their loads; for an *askari*, if not watched, is inclined to consider himself superior to a common porter, and to try and impose on him. My *askaris* were often told that I might manage without *them*, but never without my porters.

Truly the Mnyamwezi porter is a wonderful animal; there is no other living thing that can carry proportionately as big a load so far and so continuously. I have never altered my opinion that from the earliest days we should have thoroughly organised our unlimited man power of porters, and that if we had put a tenth part of the cost of those expensive, useless, dying live stock, and a tenth part of the cost of those ruinous, column-delaying motors, into providing extra food, clothing, and shelter for porters, more porters, and still more porters, the East African campaign could never have dragged on as it did.

Old Rensberg used to say, "*A nigger is a nigger, and he dies a nigger,*" and I believe he spoke truly. Still, I found much to like, and frequently much of the gentleman, in the raw, untutored native African.

A relative of mine told me that when quite a young nurse in a Western Queensland hospital she had as a patient for some time a great big negro, then dying of consumption, whom they all came to like for his nice and gentlemanly ways; it was Peter Jackson. Certainly I had become exceedingly attached to these poor loyal *pagasi*, who had been through so many ups and downs with me.

On the trip down we passed through certain villages where a couple of man-eaters were apparently starting their evil practices, a man having been caught the previous night by lions and carried off a little way into the bush, where he had been eaten, head and hands alone remaining. Still farther on we passed a fresh grave, which the *Shensis* said was that of another victim.

According to local custom, over the little mound of hard-plastered soil forming the grave, a little grass roof was erected, whilst on the grave itself were cloth and new earthenware bowls, the latter, I believe, for beer. I would like to have asked Moosa what was the purpose of these offerings, but I knew he would think I was making fun of him. This was indeed far from my intention, for the white man is on dangerous ground here. I have heard of someone who, noticing a Chinaman putting a bowl of rice on a grave, and asking him, "John, when do you think he will come up to eat that?" got for reply, "Plaps same time your friend come up to smellem flowers."

HEAD AND HANDS ALONE REMAINING

On the ninth day we reached Pemba, crossing over its big landlocked harbour. At ten o'clock that night the sergeant-major came to the tent with the official news, "Bulgaria has surrendered unconditionally." That night I felt almost afraid to think what this might, probably would, now mean to us all. Then followed in those short intervals the collapse of Turkey, Austria, and Germany!

ALSO FROM LEONAUR
AVAILABLE IN SOFTCOVER OR HARDCOVER WITH DUST JACKET

AT THEM WITH THE BAYONET by *Donald F. Featherstone*—The first Anglo-Sikh War 1845-1846.

STEPHEN CRANE'S BATTLES by *Stephen Crane*—Nine Decisive Battles Recounted by the Author of 'The Red Badge of Courage'.

THE GURKHA WAR by *H. T. Prinsep*—The Anglo-Nepalese Conflict in North East India 1814-1816.

FIRE & BLOOD by *G. R. Gleig*—The burning of Washington & the battle of New Orleans, 1814, through the eyes of a young British soldier.

SOUND ADVANCE! by *Joseph Anderson*—Experiences of an officer of HM 50th regiment in Australia, Burma & the Gwalior war.

THE CAMPAIGN OF THE INDUS by *Thomas Holdsworth*—Experiences of a British Officer of the 2nd (Queen's Royal) Regiment in the Campaign to Place Shah Shuja on the Throne of Afghanistan 1838 - 1840.

WITH THE MADRAS EUROPEAN REGIMENT IN BURMA by *John Butler*—The Experiences of an Officer of the Honourable East India Company's Army During the First Anglo-Burmese War 1824 - 1826.

IN ZULULAND WITH THE BRITISH ARMY by *Charles L. Norris-Newman*—The Anglo-Zulu war of 1879 through the first-hand experiences of a special correspondent.

BESIEGED IN LUCKNOW by *Martin Richard Gubbins*—The first Anglo-Sikh War 1845-1846.

A TIGER ON HORSEBACK by *L. March Phillips*—The Experiences of a Trooper & Officer of Rimington's Guides - The Tigers - during the Anglo-Boer war 1899 - 1902.

SEPOYS, SIEGE & STORM by *Charles John Griffiths*—The Experiences of a young officer of H.M.'s 61st Regiment at Ferozepore, Delhi ridge and at the fall of Delhi during the Indian mutiny 1857.

CAMPAIGNING IN ZULULAND by *W. E. Montague*—Experiences on campaign during the Zulu war of 1879 with the 94th Regiment.

THE STORY OF THE GUIDES by *G.J. Younghusband*—The Exploits of the Soldiers of the famous Indian Army Regiment from the northwest frontier 1847 - 1900.

AVAILABLE ONLINE AT **www.leonaur.com**
AND FROM ALL GOOD BOOK STORES

www.ingramcontent.com/pod-product-compliance
Lightning Source LLC
Chambersburg PA
CBHW031618160426
43196CB00006B/177